A CHRONICLE OF THE

A Chronicle of the Peacocks

Stories of Partition, Exile and Lost Memories

by

INTIZAR HUSAIN

Translated from Urdu by
ALOK BHALLA
VISHWAMITTER ADIL

OXFORD
UNIVERSITY PRESS

OXFORD
UNIVERSITY PRESS

YMCA Library Building, Jai Singh Road, New Delhi 110 001

Oxford University Press is a department of the University of Oxford. It furthers the
University's objective of excellence in research, scholarship, and education
by publishing worldwide in

Oxford   New York

Auckland   Cape Town   Dar es Salaam   Hong Kong   Karachi   Kuala Lumpur
Madrid   Melbourne   Mexico City   Nairobi   New Delhi   Shanghai   Taipei   Toronto

With offices in

Argentina   Austria   Brazil   Chile   Czech Republic   France   Greece   Guatemala
Hungary   Italy   Japan   Poland   Portugal   Singapore   South Korea   Switzerland
Thailand   Turkey   Ukraine   Vietnam

Oxford is a registered trademark of Oxford University Press
in the UK and in certain other countries

Published in India by Oxford University Press, New Delhi

MR. Omayal Achi MR. Arunachalam Trust was set up in 1976 to further education
and health care particularly in rural areas. The MR. AR. Educational Society was
later established by the Trust. One of the Society's activities is to sponsor Indian
literature. This translation is entirely funded by the MR. AR. Educational Society
as part of its aims.

ISBN-13: 978-0-19-567174-2
ISBN-10: 019-567174-0

Typeset in Minon 11/13
by Excellent Laser Typesetters, Pitampura, Delhi 110 034
Printed in India by Roopak Printers, New Delhi 110 032
Published by Manzar Khan, Oxford University Press
YMCA Library Building, Jai Singh Road, New Delhi 110 001

Contents

Acknowledgements

I t is sad that Vishwamitter Adil passed away before this book could go to press. He would have been delighted to see these translations in print. He had worked hard and long on them. Without his continuous and enthusiastic involvement this book could never have been completed. He belonged to a generation of writers for whom the primary function of language was to make the world a more elegant place instead of making it a more politically acceptable one. In spirit he was, thus, closer to Intizar Husain's world where a story is primarily an imaginative act and not an ideological statement.

I had the good fortune of meeting Intizar Husain a few times. We first met in Lahore when I was working on a book of stories about the Partition of India. We got together again in Hyderabad and Berlin and continued the conversation about our understanding of the civilization of the Indian subcontinent. Unfortunately, we haven't talked to each other for a few years now because the world of pluralities and tolerance we long for seems to be crumbling, and hate seems to be drawing borders between people once again.

I should like to take this opportunity to express my genuine thanks to the editors at Oxford University Press, for their work on these translations.

There are others too without whose help and support this book would have never been possible: Sukrita Paul Kumar, who took the trouble to comment on the translations and point out avoidable errors; Amanullah Khan, who always found the time to help me with the Urdu texts; Muhammad Umar Memon, of Wisconsin University, whose own translations of Intizar Husain first introduced me to his wonderful fictional world; Mubarak Ali and Masud Ashar, who were my gracious literary guides in Lahore; Asif Aslam Farrukhi, in Karachi, who shared my enthusiasm for Intizar Sahib's stories and always helped when I needed it; and Peter Bumke, of the Goethe Institute, who arranged for my trips, first to Pakistan and then to Germany so that I could meet Intizar Husain.

Finally, I should, once again like to thank my wife, Vasundara, who put aside her own work to hammer poorly translated texts into more readable versions. If there are still problems with these translations they have to do with my own cussedness.

The stories in this volume have been arranged chronologically so as to convey a sense of Intizar Husain's development as a fiction writer and a thinker. Different versions of these translations were published earlier in various places.

ALOK BHALLA
HYDERABAD, INDIA

Introduction

'Every people has its tolerant path, its religion and its temple.'
—*Nizamuddin Auliya*

Before I met Intizar Husain in Lahore, I was told that he was a simple man of gentle wit and great learning who was always willing to travel miles to pay homage to an old banyan tree or an ancient village well. Since I was familiar with his stories, I recognized that his search for a well resonating with the uncanny or for a many-rooted banyan tree was not a strange eccentricity. In his stories, the well with a parapet wall or a banyan tree with its spreading shade were sites of a soul-saving pilgrimage his wanderers felt compelled to make to places of continuous replenishment and generous shelter. The well, in his fictional mythos, was connate with the sacred foundations of a human settlement, and the banyan was a privileged village-centre under whose shade all claims about the innate differences between the sage, the beast, the parrot and the jinn were inadmissible and unsustainable. The well and the banyan were, for him, the abiding and the organizing symbols of an older cultural faith of the subcontinent which assumed that it was always possible for different communities to create a life of 'complex and pluralistic wholeness' (the phrase is Charles Taylor's)—a faith which had been lost in the melodramas of grievance and revenge enacted during the Partition and the religious enthusiasm of mobs for God's paradise and martyrs.

I was, therefore, not surprised when Intizar Husain, at the very beginning of our conversation about the Partition and the subsequent problems of migration, Islamic nationalism, religious selfhood and the sources of culture-making in the Indian subcontinent, said, 'I have no idea what a purely Islamic culture is.' The Hindus and the Muslims of India, he said, were not two strangers fated to move along different paths, but shared the same spaces and made their human way together through the same history. As if responding to the criticism often voiced against his work by conservative Pakistani critics, he assured me that he was not striking one of the many notes of nostalgia one hears so often in Pakistan, and believed that the formation of the nation-state of which he was a citizen was an irreversible part of the geopolitical reality of the region. He was, however, convinced that the analysis of the formation of Pakistan as 'historically inevitable', was fatally flawed because it failed to take into account the civilizational interactions between the Hindus and the Muslims over centuries. For the politicians, the question of religious identity was merely a useful instrumental and rhetorical device for attaining power. It was not a mode of moral discourse about how we should live or a form of social inquiry about how we conducted out daily affairs as Hindus and Muslims in non-religious or agnostic spaces. People of different faiths had, after all, managed to live decent and productive lives in India without giving their religious selfhood precedent over interpersonal or familial or village solidarities. To say, therefore, as the Muslim League had, that the Islamic identity in the Indian subcontinent had always been utterly distinct from Hinduism's notion of the identity, and had been formed in an antagonistic relationship with it, making the formation of Pakistan a political necessity and a logical outcome of cultural differences, was not only bad history but also bad metaphysics.

The best Muslim minds, Intizar Husain said, like the best minds of any community were in love with the 'good'. They realized that in a place like the Indian subcontinent, where there was a plurality of gods and a plurality of 'truths', ethicality and religiosity were not the exclusive preserves of any single community or sect. The Ramayana and the Mahabharata, the Buddha and the Jatakas, Mirabai and Tulsidas, he said were as much a part of the literary, moral and religious habitat of the Muslims as Nizamuddin Auliya and Amir Khusrau, Baba Farid and Ghalib, the *azan* and the Koran were of the Hindus. And, then, characteristically mixing personal memories, political history and metaphysics, he confessed, 'I am a Muslim, but I always feel that there is a Hindu sitting inside me.' Later, as an explanatory gloss, lest his statement be misunderstood by the Muslim zealots in Pakistan and misappropriated by the Hindutva enthusiasts in India, he added that the Hindu was not a figure who beckoned him back to India, but was a fellow pilgrim and a perpetual questioner who helped him sharpen his own religious convictions, and urged him to understand the multiplicity of religious influences that had gone into the making of his Muslim and Pakistani selfhood.

Speaking about his own life, he refused to assert that he had 'migrated' to Pakistan; that as a Muslim, he had consciously chosen Pakistan as a place where alone his religious and cultural identity could flourish and be safeguarded. Only later had it occurred to him that the caravans of people moving across the border could, perhaps, be equated with the *hijrat* (exodus) of the Prophet and his followers to Madina; that the analogy with their exile, which was one of the foundational moments of Islam, could give to the suffering of all those who had to migrate, a consoling significance. Initially, however, there was no teleological hope that had made him decide to move to Pakistan. The decision to go to Lahore had been taken rather casually and impulsively. Once he had got there, however, he decided to stay on, partly because Lahore was an attractive city, and partly because the riots had made it difficult for him to return. He was bitter about the violence that had accompanied the foundation of Pakistan and which had forced people like him to migrate, but he was also nostalgic about his life back in Hissar, Dibai and Meerut. He was not, he said, a man of strong religious beliefs, but the place where he had been born, the *basti* which had nurtured him in his childhood, still had its mysterious charm and pull. For him *watan* (homeland), he insisted, was not merely defined by the territory within which he now claimed his rightful citizenship, it was also the larger civilizational space from which he derived his imaginative strength. That is why, he said sadly, as if echoing the sentiments of countless migrants during the Partition, 'I still feel that I am an exile who wanders between Karbala and Ayodhya.' I should add that his Ayodhya was not a real place on some political map, but the utopian kingdom of Rama, where an examined life of truth and moral law alone can confirm God's presence; and, his Karbala was not the present city with a specific geographical location, but a richly imagined site where the traditions of the Prophet gave life a coherence, a reason and a balance.

Given Intizar Husain's understanding of the Muslim identity in the subcontinent, and the way in which it is inextricably 'knotted up' (his phrase) with the Hindu and Muslim history, it is not surprising to discover that his stories are complex, difficult, ambiguous and sometimes perplexing. He rarely writes linear narratives like the progressive writers of Urdu and Hindi in the 1930s and 40s whose stories were important in the development of his own literary career. The stories of the progressive writers bemoan the fate of the oppressed and promise a better future. In contrast, Intizar Husain insists that 'the light of hope or peace' rarely shines through his stories. While, in his tales, there is always a reference to a forgotten ethic, or a memory of someone whose life had, for a moment at least, dispelled hatred and opened the path to grace, none of his characters seem capable of understanding either. Their experiences leave them staring at the world in blank vacancy. Especially after the humiliating violence that accompanied the Partition, Intizar Husain insists that he can never presume the existence of a rationally comprehensible or a socially coherent world-view that would enable any of us to make sense of those tragic days.

Indeed, for him the Partition was the single most important event which disrupted his life and shaped his creative self. He still finds it difficult to make sense of the events that led to Partition. Those days, after August 1947, still haunt him; he sees them not only as enactments of his own fears and nightmares which intrude into stories like 'The Jungle of the Gonds', 'Barium Carbonate' and 'A Letter from India', but also as examples of how atrocious our lives can become when our social, moral and religious imagination fails. A story like 'The City of Sorrows' (*Shahre-e-Afsos*), for example, is made up of symmetrically repeated instances of brutal and degrading horror. A darkly ironic version of the pòpular Urdu genre known as *Shahr-i-ashoob* (song of praise for one's place of birth), the story is about people who are no longer ashamed of what they do. Three men, without names or faces, describe how during the war in East Pakistan, each one of them had raped and killed repeatedly. Unable to mourn, unable to repent, they become horrors to themselves; they can neither find a place in any society, nor find a spot on earth where they can bury their own corpses. One of them remembers the Buddha, who had been born in the area of their haunting. But, the recollection is fleeting, for the Buddha's moral realm is remote from their structures of experience in the present and can offer no refuge.

In his stories, Intizar Husain has set upon himself the profoundly difficult task of retrieving all that was good in pre-Partition India, while at the same time analysing the causes of evil which lie both in the soul of man and in the social circumstances in which he finds himself. He tells stories in order to understand and at the same time repudiate hatred; to turn the accuser away from seeking revenge and to win his trust once again in the ordinary and daily kindnesses which also make up our lives; to heal wounds; to find consolation in memories of lost mustard fields, trees crowded with parrots, sweets sold in forgotten streets, kites flying over familiar terraces and other emblems of innocence and joyful communities; to notice the world in its daily transactions once again with all our empathy and our imaginative resources; and, to discover a minimum ethic by which we can live. Like all serious writers, he wants to give back to us a world in which we can cultivate our sense of justice and moral goodness; but, like all fine writers, he also knows how difficult that task really is and how often we fall out of language and community and history into labyrinths of evil.

'An Unwritten Epic', for example, is a complex story which is told in two parts. The first part is a linear narrative because it describes a stable and established life of ordinary events in Qadirpur, a small town in pre-Partition India. Written with harsh irony, it tells the story of Pichwa, a wrestler and local bully who is enthusiastic about the idea of Pakistan but doesn't know where it is. He is convinced that Qadirpur, given its name, must naturally belong to Pakistan. He fights the Hindus, not because he hates them as *kafirs* or as oppressors, but because he wants to show them that he can wield the *lathi* better than they can. To be able to wrestle better is not a matter of religious pride for him, but a simpler matter of physical superiority. Besides, local folklore and customs of his community expect him to prove his jousting skills, and in turn he knows that his community will fulfill its obligation towards him if he needs help. He has a sanctioned place in the wrestling tradition which bestows upon him an heroic status. Neither society's expectations of Pichwa nor his sense of belonging to an abiding community, are derived from any notion of Islamic selfhood, but are examples of the common ways in which religious differences were negotiated and the possibility of violence was deflected. To help us understand that the interaction between the Hindus and the Muslims had a long and sustained history, Intizar Husain deliberately locates an old Peepul tree, sacred to the Hindus, next to a Muslim shrine at the outskirts of Qadirpur.

The second part tells the story of Pichwa's life after he migrates to an unnamed town in Pakistan, and is told in the form of random notes in a diary. The grand narrative about the 'historical inevitability' of the formation of Pakistan is reduced to a collage of anecdotes which record the attempts of a bewildered and sadly diminished wrestler to find ways of conducting a few meaningful tasks, in the society in which he finds himself, in order to survive. Paradoxically, Pichwa realizes that the Partition, which was supposed to have given him a more secure identity, has robbed him of it. He is reduced from being a man of uncomplicated courage to being a self-pitying and blustering fool. In the older order, there was a social consensus within which he felt that he had a continuous self. He was a wrestler, and his life had a cultural purpose, even a kind of heroism, because it was a part of an inherited compact between the Hindus and the Muslims about how to conduct their lives within shared spaces. In Pakistan, his dream of cultivating the land is an embarrassing reminder of the promise that had once been made of providing a new moral and rational base to the lives of all Muslims. The new heroes of Pakistan are the cynical manipulators of law and economics, not the common men who had hoped for so much. Pichwa becomes an emblem of lost memories and abandoned hopes, and the narrator acknowledges, in the secret of his notations, the impossibility of imagination in a society which has been ruptured from its older forms of life. Frustrated and nostalgic, Pichwa returns to Qadirpur, only to discover that it has been erased from the new map of the subcontinent and renamed Jatunagar—the city of the Jats. He is killed and his head is stuck on the peepul trees beside the mosque. The cycle of degradation is complete when the narrator, instead of writing his epic about the origins of a new nation, compromises with local bosses and gets them to allot him a flourmill abandoned by its Hindu owners. The political and civil space is corrupted by thuggery and the lot of the Muslims continues to be as vulnerable as it was in pre-Partition India. But, while the narrator gives up his expectations of finding humane and imaginative ways of living, Intizar Husain sees in the very persistence of the memories recorded in the first part, the possibilities of a different future for the communities of the subcontinent. This act of rememorialization of a communally responsible past has nothing to do with nostalgic evasion. It is, instead, an attempt to rediscover a habit of thought and a mode of living that may provide us with ideas and examples that are sufficient to resist the drummed-up enthusiasm of the crowd and its blasphemous assumption that its slogans are the words of God.

Trying to give shape to his unique understanding of the Muslim identity in the Indian subcontinent, Intizar Husain draws freely and imaginatively upon the rich and fascinating narrative traditions of the Indian subcontinent found in such diverse sources as the *Katha Sarit Sagar*, Puranic lore, Sufi legends, religious epics, Jataka tales, popular lore about talking animals and birds, *Hatamtai*, anecdotes about rishis who have the learning to challenge the gods but are yet fallible. A thoroughly modern writer, he uses them to reflect upon religious faith and identity, historical truth and moral delusions, power and the endless failure of reason. Thus, in his retelling of the Jatakas, he points out how difficult it is in the present to locate the 'good' and, on the basis of our understanding of it, perform the right action in the public realm. In the older Jatakas both these actions are unproblematic. The 'good' is unambiguously located in the Bodhisattva and is available in every generation to all living things. The Bodhisattva is reborn as a man, a woman, a king, a woodcutter, a witch, a tree or a monkey. Each incarnation of the Bodhisattva reasserts the fact that the 'good' is eternally available, and each story about him recalls for us the fact, which we tend to forget, that ordinary people, with the most limited of intellectual and material resources, can always recognize the good man and follow his example. The Bodhisattva of these tales is the ideal man whose personal inwardness is never distinct from his public actions. He is a self-governing moral agent who always acts responsibly towards the rest of creation.

In Intizar Husain's rendering of the Jatakas, one is at first enchanted by the tranquility of the forest and by the silence of the *bhikshus* who walk through them. Unlike the listeners of the old Jatakas, we are located in a world which is noisy and agitated. Intizar Husain startles us by reminding us of the fact that even though we live in cities, the realm of trees, birds, rivers, animals and the sky is in our neighbourhood, and that we are both dependent on it and responsible for it ('My relationship should also be with the pigeon and the ant,' he said to me). In the old Jatakas, such a lesson would have been enough to make people see, in the world around them, signs of the divine presence. The pilgrims of Intizar Husain, however, are like us. They are baffled exiles far from home:

They could not remember when they had left their homes or how long they had been tossed about in the midst of those thundering waters.

'Will we ever go back?'

'Where?'

'Home.'

'Home?'

They were bewildered and anxious once again. Home. The very thought of home threatened to shatter their sanity just as the storm threatens to uproot trees…

They could not remember when they had left their homes or how long they had been floating like leaves in the middle of that vast body of water.

The bhikshus in Intizar Husain's stories understand the lessons taught to them, but they do not know how to act correctly. They fail to understand that an action is 'right' only if it is based in the 'good'. A good man can, at times, make mistakes without jeopardizing his goodness, but a man who has not achieved wisdom can perform the right action and yet bring disaster upon himself and others. The bhikshus in the Jatakas, who found themselves in the presence of the Bodhisattva, never went back to their old ways of ignorant living. The bhikshus in Intizar Husain's stories are told a countless number of moral tales, but fail to recognize how the 'good' can be achieved in the world in which they live. They cannot reconcile the beauty of the world and the joy of the senses with the demands of renunciation; the demands of humanity with the fear of entrapment in the vast network of illusions. Like many of the protagonists in his Partition tales, they find themselves staring at blank spaces where identities are utterly confused. At the end they give up their quest and are stranded on the border between forests and villages, rational knowledge and uncontrolled passion, religious faith and despair. The learned man of 'Complete Knowledge' thinks that evil will always be with us and is paralysed by that knowledge; the wise seeker in 'Tortoise' stands alone at the edge of the forest, after he has failed to attain peace, unsure about which path he should take next; the good bhikshu at the end of 'Leaves' sits with yellow autumnal leaves in his hands, wondering when the next cycle of the seasons will begin or when the divine would be incarnated on earth again. There is no nostalgia in these tales, only a profound sorrow and a hopeless longing for a world different from the one we have created.

2002 ALOK BHALLA

1

An Unwritten Epic
(*Ek Bin-likhi Razmiya*)

I n Qadirpur, too, the battle was so fierce that those who heard about it covered their ears in dismay. There was panic everywhere. Life was so cheap that human beings were sold for a rupee or two. One was killed as he retreated a step or two, another lost his life as he stepped forward. One was stabbed in the back; another received a blow on his chest. Qadirpur, itself, was an insignificant village—how could it have stopped the storm that had even shaken mountains? But thanks to Pichwa's courage, Qadirpur earned a name for itself. His friends picked up their shrouds, sought their mother's blessings, committed their wives and children to the mercy of God, and marched into battle with such dignity and courage as to recall the heroes of ancient wars. The fighting was very fierce; the earth was soaked with blood and littered with corpses.

The Jats were as valiant. They had heard of Qadirpur because Pichwa's skills were famous. That was why the Jats had gathered together from all over; mounted on richly-adorned elephants, they had set out at night in a torch-lit procession to conquer Qadirpur. The Jat army was well equipped and disciplined. Their elephants were loaded with guns and ammunition, swords and spears, and they marched in a military formation.

Majid had been hiding in the branches of the banyan tree near the Idgah when he caught sight of the torchlights in the distant horizon. He rubbed his eyes a few times, watched the procession carefully, listened to the slogans, and was soon convinced that the moment they had all been waiting for had finally arrived. He began to beat his drum frantically. When the people of Qadirpur heard the drum, there was panic in every house. Naim Mian's sons, Owais and Azhar, who were sleeping on the terrace, lost their nerve when they heard the drums and the slogans. Owais was speechless with fear, and Azhar was so disoriented that he jumped from one terrace to the next till he reached the Julahonwalli Masjid beyond which there were no more terraces. Bewildered, he didn't know what to do after that. Rehmat, who was on guard in the street below, banged his *lathi* a few times and challenged, 'Who's there?' Azhar somehow managed to regain his composure and identified himself. A ripple of laughter ran across Rehmat's face, 'Mian, you have disgraced the name of Aligarh College.' Rehmat's taunt was just, because when Azhar and Owais were students at Aligarh College, they had been amongst the most enthusiastic participants in the political rallies. Their voices used to ring with unusual conviction when they shouted, '*Kat ke rahega Hindustan, ban ke rahega Pakistan*' (India will be divided, Pakistan will be created). After the Partition, however, they had begun to live in fear.

When Naim Mian woke up, he discovered that Azhar's bed was empty and that Owais was speechless with terror. He impulsively grabbed his rifle and a box of cartridges. But, the moment he heard the crowd in the village square shout, '*Allahu Akbar*,' with wild enthusiasm, the box of cartridges fell from his hands. Alerted by the drums, people began to gather in the village square with their weapons.

Jaffer straightened his turban, picked up his spear and walked towards the square smoking his hookah. Pichwa, who was following him, tightened his *tehmad* and shouted, '*Pehlwan*, this is no time to smoke a hookah.' Jaffer quickly dropped his hookah, banged his spear on the ground a few times and stepped forward to join the crowd. Deliberately, and with great confidence, Pichwa knotted his tehmad, adjusted the amulet around his neck, rolled up the sleeves of his *kurta*, spat on his palms to moisten them, and then balanced his lathi in his hands to feel its weight. As he walked towards the square, he called out, 'Abbay Mammad!' When no one replied, he shouted angrily, 'Abbay Mammad, you son of a pig, are you dead?'

Mammad, struggling to put on his vest, came running from one of the street corners, 'I'm here, *Ustad*.'

'Aren't you coming, you bastard?' When he saw Mammad, his voice softened, 'Listen, hold your position around the Julahonwalli Masjid, I'll handle things here.'

After giving instructions to Mammad, Pichwa left with his gang to examine the other positions. He first stopped at the *haveli*. Kalwa and his group were posted there. The moment he saw Pichwa, Kalwa stood at attention and shouted, 'Don't worry, Ustad, we'll send those bastards straight to hell!'

Pichwa was particularly anxious about the defence of the haveli. The matter was very delicate. The women of the *basti* had taken refuge there. There was a dark well inside the haveli, and every woman knew her duty in case of defeat. As an extra precaution, a few gibbets had also been erected inside. Pichwa had placed the most trusted members of his gang around the haveli and told them, 'If any coward runs away, I'll roast the bastard alive and eat him!' However, he had faith in Kalwa's courage, and was relieved to hear a ring of confidence in his voice. Weighing his lathi in his hand, Pichwa walked on ahead.

The drumbeats grew more frenzied and the sound of the conch-shells louder. Pichwa began to walk faster. More and more people came out of their houses. Qurban Ali hurried out carrying the side-bar of his cot. He had turned his house upside down in search of a weapon when he heard the commotion. He had not found any—not even an ordinary stick. Infuriated by Aijaz's mother's jibes, he smashed his cot and grabbed the side-bar. Saiyid Hamid Hasan had several beautiful walking sticks from Nainital and Dehra Doon, which had been presented to him, but none of them were as strong as a lathi. After a frantic search, his wife and he finally unearthed a rusty old dagger. Munshi Sanaullah had no such problems. There was a bamboo stick used for removing cobwebs lying in the corner of the courtyard, he grabbed it and rushed out. As far as Subedar Sahib was concerned, the question of looking for a lathi had not even arisen. He had a double-barrelled gun, which he always kept well oiled. Indeed, in the forest of lathis outside there were quite a few gun-barrels glittering in the torchlight. Hamid had a catapult made of polished *shisham* in his hand and a pocketful of pebbles. Standing behind him, Rasulla and Bhallan carried an entire arsenal of firecrackers, trumpets and swords. Allah Razi's group had dragged out a misshapen cannon from somewhere. Allah Razi had no idea how it worked. The cannon had actually been fired only once before. It's another matter that it had been pointed in the wrong direction. The result was that many people standing nearby had been badly hurt, and the police had arrested Allah Razi and his friends. But this time, Allah Razi was convinced that, instead of wounding his own people, the gun would blow their enemies to smithereens. Pichwa's gang normally fought with ordinary lathis, but given the times, they had taken the trouble to modify their weapons a little. They had attached small daggers to them, so that they were no longer mere lathis but spears. Pichwa's lathi, however, remained unchanged. The only difference was that he had soaked it in oil for three days so that it was well seasoned and hard. If he had attached a dagger to it, he would have transformed its essential nature. Once a dagger is attached to a lathi, it no longer remains a lathi but is metamorphosed into a spear. The lathis of Mammad, Kalwa, Rehmat and Jaffar had changed their nature and become spears. But Pichwa's lathi was still a lathi, and to modify it would have required a complete transformation of his character. His lathi was an inextricable part of his being. In fact, his lathi had surrendered its own identity and become a part of Pichwa's self. It was no longer an ordinary lathi; it was Pichwa's lathi. It would be wrong to compare it with the staff of Moses; that staff had a power of its own. One can, however, say that while Moses needed the staff, the staff didn't need Moses. But Pichwa's lathi was Pichwa's lathi. And, though it had performed many a heroic feat, its real strength lay not in itself but in Pichwa's arms. There is proof of that. Tidda and his gang had once cornered Pichwa without his lathi. They assumed that Pichwa, without his lathi, would be helpless. They said to each other, 'Let's finish him off.' Pichwa, however, was unfazed. Without hesitation, he unwrapped his turban, took a coin out of his vest pocket, tied it to one end of the cloth, and baffled them with his skill. Within five minutes, he had broken so many bones that Tidda's gang was forced to surrender their lathis. Then he thrashed them so hard with their own lathis that they took to their heels.

Tidda and his gang were, of course, small fry. Pichwa was capable of taking on an entire village. Once, it so happened that when Subedar Sahib was surrounded by the villagers of Lachmanpura, it was Pichwa who had to go to his rescue. It was Subedar Sahib's fault. He had gone to shoot duck, but frustrated at not finding any, he had shot a few peacocks. As expected, the people of Lachmanpura were enraged. The village thugs picked up their lathis and descended on Subedar Sahib. Naim Mian, who always avoided a confrontation, ran away the moment he realized there was trouble. Hamida, confused by the sudden turn of events, hid in the cornfield nearby. Allah Razi thought he could get away without a thrashing. But as bad luck would have it, he tried to escape through a field where a farmer, who was ploughing his land, grabbed him and gave him a few nasty slaps. Saiyid Hamid Hasan got into trouble because he was much too slow. He tried to talk his way out of the difficult situation, but the villagers were unimpressed. Subedar Sahib was so nonplussed that he didn't know what to do. Pichwa, however, was undaunted. Picking up his lathi, he shouted, '*Ya Ali*,' and entered the fray with such fury that he killed a few attackers, broke countless bones, and forced the rest of the men back to their village. Finally, when Subedar Sahib and Pichwa returned to Qadirpur, along with the peacocks they had slaughtered, they also triumphantly brought back a huge pile of sturdy lathis that they had captured.

It was only by chance that Pichwa and Tidda had found themselves in conflict over Billo, a tribal woman from the hills. The truth is that Pichwa was not particularly interested in women. His interests lay elsewhere. Billo was only an excuse. Tidda and he had earlier fought over Naseera, who was an acknowledged member of Tidda's wrestling gang. Pichwa could never control his tongue, particularly when he was either chewing *paan* or smoking a *bidi* at Allah Razi's paan shop. Then his speech was even more extravagant and colourful.

One day, while he was sitting at Allah Razi's shop, Naseera passed by. Pichwa couldn't resist calling to him, 'Turn, my dear, and look at us.' Naseera was very embarrassed. When Tidda Pehalwan heard about it, his blood began to boil. Had it been anyone other than Pichwa, he would have beaten him to pulp at once. But attacking Pichwa would have been like a camel charging against a mountain. Tidda, however, was so furious that he interpreted Pichwa's vulgar comments as a declaration of war. Over the next few months, they fought many times, but Tidda was humbled on each occasion. The quarrel over Naseera was only an excuse. The truth was that Pichwa and Tidda hated each other.

Tidda Pehalwan was proud of his wrestling skills, but Pichwa refused to acknowledge that he had any. Whenever anyone mentioned Tidda, he would lose his temper, 'That son of a barber is not a wrestler, he is a cowardly bastard. Mian, you know quite well that around *tazia* time his gang is always the worst.'

'But, *Khalifa*,' Ali Razi added mischievously, 'this time he is training very hard.'

Provoked, Pichwa would explode, 'What bloody training? He can only whisk his razor around. Does he know how to wield a lathi?'

Whereupon, Mammad would get excited and add, 'That son of a barber needs to be taught a lesson. One punch and the bastard will forget his heroism.'

'Mian, once I thrashed him till his brains spilled out, but the bastard has started boasting again,' Pichwa complained.

Mammad, who was not the kind to be impressed by past deeds, would add, 'Ustad, that was a long time ago, the bastard needs to be taught another lesson. I swear, Ustad, this time I'll beat him till his joints begin to rattle.'

'Abbay, even I am itching to pluck the feathers of that hero. But the bastard always manages to get away.'

Pichwa had reason to complain. Tidda was a braggart. Whenever there was the possibility of a confrontation, he always managed to avoid a final showdown.

Sensible people of Qadirpur knew that Pichwa was only a wrestler, but the superstitious ones thought that he was a sorcerer and spread strange rumours about him. Bhallan was the most insistent of the gossip-mongers. Wherever he went, he whispered, 'Mian, no matter what you say, Pichwa knows sorcery.'

Rasulla not only agreed with him, but also provided supporting evidence, 'I have seen many a wrestler, and I can tell you Pichwa isn't one. Once, I saw Pichwa fight a jinn and pin him to the ground. A wrestler may also be skilful with his lathi, but he can't defeat a jinn. I can give it to you in writing that he is a sorcerer who knows magic.'

Allah Razi suspected that the amulet around Pichwa's neck was a talisman. Hamida was even more emphatic, 'With my own eyes I saw him standing on one leg in a newly-dug grave behind the Idgah, reciting something. I am sure a fakir gave him a magic spell to make him strong and invincible.'

But Jaffar had a different story to tell, 'Mian, the truth is that when those Hindu bastards tried to demolish the Julahonwalli Masjid, Pichwa alone faced them courageously. You should have seen him wield his lathi; the bastards didn't know what hit them. And, you know, that very night, Maula Ali visited him in a dream and blessed him. Pichwa and his skills would have been worthless without Maula Ali's grace.'

No one doubted Pichwa's courage, which had been tested and proved many a time. However, they explained the source of his strength and its effects in different ways. Pichwa always found some excuse to fight so that he could practise his skills and display them. He always fought fearlessly, without worrying about the outcome. And he never allowed a selfish thought to sully his temper. He fought without reason or purpose; he fought for the sake of fighting. That is why when the storm of communal violence swept across the country, he didn't stop to ask uncomfortable questions. The riots gave him the chance to display his expertise with the lathi without any restraint. Excited and confident, he barked at his gang, 'Tighten your belts, you bastards. Maula Ali has, at last, heard our prayers. By His grace, we are about to reap a rich harvest.'

When the members of the gang heard his command, they swelled with pride. Mammad exclaimed, 'Ustad, I swear that if you don't see the flags of Qadirpur flying everywhere, you can call me a bastard.'

And Kalwa boasted, 'My lathi was being eaten by termites! Now, at last, I can season it with blood.'

Pichwa's gang had begun to make elaborate preparations for the coming fight; it was as if they were getting ready to celebrate Id. But all their efforts were wasted. They realized that the nature of the conflict had changed. There was no question now of flying Qadirpur's flag. They weren't even confident of defending their village.

Pichwa was used to picking up a fight; now, after a few hard knocks, he had to learn to defend himself. His blood froze when he heard about the creation of Pakistan. Wringing his hands in despair, he complained, 'Mian, while we were twiddling our thumbs here, they had already conquered the fort over there.' He cursed the people of Qadirpur for their lethargy, because while a new country had been carved, he had not shed a drop of blood for it. Full of bravado, he said, 'Let's forget the past and fly a Pakistani flag on the peepul tree near the Idgah.'

When the people of Qadirpur heard about his plans, they were paralysed with fear. They tried to reason with him and showed him where Pakistan was on the map. Pichwa was out of his depths. He couldn't understand how Qadirpur, where he lived, could have been left out of Pakistan. At last they persuaded him not to fly the Pakistani flag. Mammad and Kalwa, however, convinced him that, since Pakistan didn't care about its religious brothers, they too shouldn't give a damn about Pakistan. They should form their own Pakistan, and fly their own Islamic flag on the peepul tree near the Idgah. This suggestion made the people of Qadirpur even more nervous. Poor Naim Mian, who was already trembling with fear, collapsed when he heard about Pichwa's plan. He tried to explain to Pichwa that the situation was dangerous, but Pichwa told him bluntly, 'Mian, listen with your ears open; the Congress flag will never fly in Qadirpur, only Pichwa's flag will fly here.' Naim Mian felt humiliated, but was helpless against Pichwa. He no longer had any hold over him. There was a time when Pichwa had treated him respectfully, but of late he had begun to question his authority. Actually, Naim Mian had also changed. He was still regarded as one of the leaders of the Muslim League, but now he didn't want to have much to do with it. Earlier, when he had been riding a high horse, he had bristled at the very mention of the Congress, and had thought it was beneath his dignity to talk to a Hindu. But, immediately after the Partition he had changed his attitude.

The creation of Pakistan had put him in strange dilemma. He had begun to shudder at the very mention of the Muslim League and Pakistan. But he did find a way out of his confusion fairly quickly. By the end of August, he had fled to Pakistan. In Qadirpur, however, he told everyone, 'We are only going up to Delhi.' Fifteen or twenty days later, he sent a letter to Subedar Sahib from Lahore. He wrote, '*Bhai,* all the important people we met in Delhi convinced us that there was no security or future for the Muslims in India. Only Pakistan can offer them work and a home. The journey here was fraught with dangers, but with Allah's help, we have reached this country safely. Azhar Mian has found a job with the Rehabilitation Department. And, *Inshallah,* Owais Mian too will find a job soon. What is left in Qadirpur now? You should also come here. By Allah's grace, I have some influence here and should be able to help you find your feet.'

When Pichwa heard about the letter, he stood before Allah Razi's shop and let out a stream of abuses against Naim Mian. But there was no point in attacking the tail after the snake had slithered away. In any case, Pichwa was partly responsible for the speed with which Naim Mian had packed up and fled. Naim Mian had tried to persuade him not to hoist his own flag, but Pichwa had remained adamant. The Jats would have attacked in any case, but had held themselves back because they were afraid of Pichwa. His flag was a provocation they couldn't ignore. Guided by the principle that it was better to do today what could be done tomorrow, they decided to attack Qadirpur. It is another matter that in that battle, Pichwa and his gang made the Jats bite the dust. Naim Mian, however, was no fool; he knew the shape of things to come. Calamity may have been averted for a while, but defeat was only a matter of time.

Naim Mian's letter sent a shock wave through Qadirpur. Three days later, Munshi Sanaullah packed up his bags and left. A week later, on market day, there were piles of household goods for sale at the second-hand shop. The most prominent amongst them were Saiyid Ali Husain's walking sticks from Nainital, Qurban Ali's cots made of shisham wood, and Munshi Sanaullah's crockery.

3 April 1950

I started writing this story several months ago. Had I known then that it would be ruined, I would have finished it at once. But after I began writing it, I realized that Pichwa's character needed something more substantial than a short story. Only an epic could do him justice. It occurred to me that no one had yet written an epic about the riots. Since I was not a poet, I thought I would write one in prose. In any case, this is not the age of great poetry. There are no heroic figures now about whom epics can be written. In fact, I was fortunate that a character like Pichwa has fallen into my hands. Well, at that time, I couldn't have known that calamity would follow calamity, and that Pichwa would leave for Pakistan. Why did Pichwa, who had confronted the rioters so bravely, lose heart and run? What a terrible fate has befallen Qadirpur! Where did Kalwa and Mammad go? I don't know. I neither have the heart nor the strength to ask Pichwa.

What really upsets me is that the plans for my novel have been reduced to dust. Both Pichwa and I are unlucky. He is not fated to be the hero of an epic, and I am doomed to write second-rate stories about ordinary people who are more dead than alive. I suppose readers will scorn them. Pichwa may not have been a great general or a magnificent emperor, but he had dignity and courage. Besides, I wasn't planning to write another *Shahnama*. Can't one write an epic entitled *Jumhurnama*? Anyway, there is no point now in discussing that; all my plans have crumbled.

7 April 1950

I don't understand the logic of writing about those who are alive. I only write about those who are dead. After all, how can one write about people who are still alive? They have the certainty of two plus two. They have no mysterious corners, no meaningful shadows. One can write reportage about them, but not a story or a lyric. That's why I get confused when I have to confront people who are still alive.

The critic, who said that a writer must keep his window open when he writes, was a simpleton. Who says one should keep one's window open during a storm? I am surprised that people manage to write with their eyes open. I write with my eyes shut. I pick up my pen only when an idea becomes part of my inner being. I can't write if the object of my concern is before me. In Qadirpur, it never occurred to me that Pichwa could become a character in my story. After reaching Pakistan, my relationship with Qadirpur snapped, and its people and environment became a part of my fictional world. I didn't care whether Pichwa was alive or dead. As far as I was concerned, he was dead; out of sight, out of mind. But he is now before me in flesh and blood. The result is that the character I had imagined has vanished, as surely as horns have vanished from a donkey's head. I have been robbed of the hero of my novel. May life, which has snatched him from me, be damned.

12 April 1950

Should I write my novel or abandon it? The question haunts me day and night. Damn it, I should start writing. People do write about the living. In this bathhouse, everyone is shameless, and the sky won't fall if I too am shameless. But I can't get beyond making resolutions. My mind urges me on, but my heart is on satyagraha. The character I had created with so much effort lies in ruins. How the hell can I write when everything has turned to dust? Even the living model has become blurred. In Qadirpur, Pichwa had the qualities of a hero in a story, but here he has acquired so many kinks. I had always thought of Pichwa as a melancholic lover. That's why I had cast him as a character in my novel. But here, he is merely a dispirited man looking for a job. This morning, he said, 'Mian, find me a job. In this damned city, I can't find a place to rest my feet. *Babu*, if you can't find me a job, at least get a house allotted in my name.'

I was shocked by his plea for help. In Qadirpur, he had been unconcerned about food or shelter. But here, he begs for food and looks for a roof over his head. How can I get him a job or a house? I can only make him the hero of my novel. Originally, I had thought of him as a sort of twentieth-century Tipu Sultan. Now I can't. Since his arrival in Pakistan, all he seeks is food for his stomach and a place to rest his head. All his arrogance and pride have crumbled into dust.

17 April 1950

Pichwa goes from place to place in search of work. Today, he went to see Naim Mian about it. But Naim Mian is no longer the same Naim Mian of old. Now he doesn't condescend to talk to people who are dark-skinned! He scolded Pichwa, 'Damn it, everyone gets up and heads straight for Pakistan, as if his father's treasure were buried here. Can't you see there is no room here?'

Pichwa complains that Naim Mian has grown arrogant after coming to Pakistan. But why should he complain? Naim Mian is now an important man, and if he can't lord it over people, who can? Of course, in Qadirpur, Pichwa would never have swallowed this bitter truth; but, in Qadirpur, Naim Mian would never have dared to look down on Pichwa. There, Naim Mian was scared shitless of him. But an ant is a tiger in his own home. It's obvious that Pakistan is Naim Mian's home, not Pichwa's.

20 April 1950

The thread of my epic story may have completely unravelled, but a few knots still remain. Pichwa may have lost his prestige, but he hasn't given up his romantic dreams. Even if dejected about not finding work, he still has the air of a melancholic lover. He looked wide-eyed at the open fields of Pakistan and said, 'If only I had a *bigha* of land, I'd show you my true colours. I would plant a mango orchard on one side and dig a wrestling pit on the other for regular jousts of strength. When you visit me in the summers, I would give you such delicious mangoes that you would forget all about the ones from Malihabad.'

I replied, 'Hey, Sheikh Chilli, who'll give you a bigha of land? This land is not for the likes of you and me. It belongs to the *zamindars.*'

But when Pichwa is excited, his feet don't touch the ground. He retorted, 'Aren't zamindars our Muslim brothers? If I appeal to them in the name of Rasoolallah, they'll surely give me a morsel of land.'

That's an example of Pichwa's strange logic—as if zamindars were Hindus or Muslims!

22 April 1950

I seem to be slowly losing my desire to write. Sometimes I blame myself for it, sometimes society. Whenever I pick up my pen, people start shouting, 'Pakistan *zindabad,*' so loudly that the pen falls from my hand. There is a continuous chatter about 'constructive literature' around me. I can't hear anything else in the din. What is this animal called 'constructive literature'? Everything is recognized by its relation to its opposite. I have yet to come across 'destructive literature'. If literature is not 'destructive', how can it be 'constructive'? Literature is neither constructive nor destructive; it is only literature.

A friend of mine went on and on about 'constructive literature'. Irritated, I said, 'I want to write about homosexuality.'

'That's sick,' he shouted.

'Why don't you give me a healthy subject to write about?' I retorted.

'All right, write about Pakistan,' he suggested.

I don't know what to say about Pakistan. It is a reality. I am not imaginative enough to transform reality into fiction. Pakistan is a reality. Qadirpur has already become a fiction and I can write stories about it. I don't know how to describe a real Pakistan; but I can describe Qadirpur because it is already a story. Its soil is red with the blood of its sons. Its soil is red, its air filled with screams, its homes charred, its mosque in ruins, its wrestling pit desolate— each has stories that are eight-hundred years old. I can write with feeling about the sorrows of Qadirpur and write a Mahabharata describing the deeds of its exhausted Arjunas. But writing about the Arjunas of *this* place is a problem I can't solve. Why do I want to write the Mahabharata of Qadirpur? After all the Arjuna of the Mahabharata of Pakistan is a dejected hero. He wanders through its streets and alleys looking for a house and a job. The harder he tries, the more he falls from his status as a hero.

2 May 1950

'Mian, have you seen this damned order?' Pichwa asked, burning with anger. I thought he would chew me up. I was really scared. Then I remembered that I wasn't in Qadirpur, but in Pakistan where Pichwa had no power.

Annoyed, I asked, 'What order?'

'The order that the *mohajir*s here should damn well pack up and go back to India,' Pichwa sputtered with rage.

I didn't know how to respond. Trying to calm him down, I explained to him the difficulties here. 'Bhai, don't be so angry. The problem is that in Pakistan there isn't enough room even for a small sesame seed. How can the new mohajirs settle here? Besides, a few important people who went to Delhi recently reported that the Muslims there were comfortable and happy.'

That made Pichwa even more angry, 'Mian, I have just come from Qadirpur. Am I a liar?'

I knew that Pichwa wasn't a liar. He may be capable of a thousand sins, but he was not capable of telling a lie. But who cares about what I think? It's only what important people think that matters.

3 May 1950

Why does land shrink or food become scarce? The reasons are

simple enough, but I can't explain them to Pichwa who is so thick-headed.

Once upon a time there was a king who got lost while hunting. He was exhausted; his lips were parched. He came upon a garden. He stopped there and asked the gardener for some water. The gardener's daughter plucked a pomegranate and squeezed half of it into a glass. The juice revived the king and he set out to hunt again. On the way, he thought, 'The trees were loaded with pomegranates. Even half a pomegranate filled a glass with juice. Why not impose a tax on it?'

After the hunt, the king went back to the garden and asked for some water. The gardener's daughter squeezed one pomegranate into a glass, then another, but couldn't fill it with juice. Taken aback, she exclaimed, 'Baba, the king has evil intentions!'

Surprised, the king asked, 'How did you guess?'

The gardener replied, 'Maharaj, when the king has evil intentions, the crops fail.'

One doesn't have to be a genius to understand something so simple. Even an ignorant gardener and his daughter could understand it. But, Pichwa's head is full of cow-dung.

4 May 1950

Pichwa says, 'Mian, make me the king of Pakistan for one day and see how I make these people dance. They may own big farms, large houses, or huge factories, but I'll still beat them black and blue. I'll distribute everything so that the mohajirs get their share.' Then he snapped his fingers and added, 'Wait and see, Mian. I'll fix everything in a jiffy.'

I don't trust him. He is a braggart. If he is made the king of Pakistan, he, too, will become selfish. Only those who don't have responsibilities, criticize those who do. Irresponsibility is the opposite of responsibility. Men are not irresponsible by nature; they become so when they acquire power.

5 May 1950

The more I try to run away from politics, the more it pursues me.

Till Pichwa came to Pakistan, he was only a character in my novel. But now that he is here, he is part of a political game. The moment I think about him, I find myself knee deep in the muck of politics. Why hasn't he been allotted a house? Why can't he get a job? Why is he being sent back to India? Every time I think about him, I find myself trapped in a political labyrinth. It's not that I am not interested in talking about politics. In fact, I have a lot to say about the rehabilitation of refugees, minority rights, and abandoned properties. And if I keep my mouth firmly shut, it's not because I am particularly shy. But I see no reason to step onto the political stage. I know that my imaginative energies are being wasted here, but that doesn't mean that I should hold my nose and jump into the political cesspool. A frustrated singer should be content to be a frustrated singer; he shouldn't try to become a singer of *marsias*. Even if someone were to sprinkle kerosene on this earth and set it on fire, I would not interfere.

I am afraid of the real world, and politics is the worst part of it. I shudder at the very thought of politics in the same way as a cow trembles before a butcher. The truth is that politics does to a writer what a butcher does to a cow. The joke is that politics destroys both literature and the writer. Yet, it is politics that gets all the applause.

6 May 1950

My desire to write continues to wane. Pichwa has lost his old magic. He doesn't even seem to be a man. He is a mere pawn on a chessboard. Pushed out of one square, he finds himself in another, only to be pushed back into the first one again. How can he be the hero of my novel? A character in a novel must be alive. Even if I manage to write the novel, it will be worthless. A novel about a pawn would be no better than a move on a chessboard.

7 May 1950

I thought it was an empty threat. But he did go back. What men call conscience is really very shameless. It never dies. It either pretends to be dead, or returns to life unexpectedly.

Pichwa asked angrily, 'Will the leaders also go back with us?'
I laughed, 'If they go back, who will be the leaders of Pakistan?'
That made him so angry that he began to curse Naim Mian.

I tried to persuade him not to go back in a hurry. The
government would make all the arrangements for his return. But
that made him furious. 'Should I take money for my shroud from
here, and dig my grave in India? I don't need charity for my
shroud.'

8 May 1950

Now that Pichwa has left, I have become interested in my novel
once again. But I don't trust him. He may come back and spoil
my plans. It is, of course, possible that he has already been killed.
After all human beings are not immortal. A man can suddenly
drop dead. The heat of Sind can kill a man from the Doab. Maybe,
Pichwa's train was attacked and someone pushed him out of his
compartment. Death, after all, doesn't need an excuse. Allah Mian
can make anything happen. Besides, slaughtering people is an
entertaining game. But…

20 May 1950

Pichwa left nearly a fortnight ago. Who is left in Qadirpur now?
I hear that Subedar Sahib is still there. I wrote him a letter, but
he hasn't yet replied. I wonder if the desert sands of Sind haven't
swallowed that fellow, Pichwa. In fact, I don't believe he managed
to get across the border. Who knows? He may have been enchanted
by the soil of Sind. It is also possible that Pakistan, realizing that
he is upset, has decided to hug him to her bosom. Even if its fellow
citizens are callous, the heart of a country certainly beats for each
of them.

This country is new. Uninvited guests are a strange lot. The
country may or may not have any room, but the mohajirs always
grumble that the people here have no compassion in their hearts.
The people here complain that the guests don't understand their
difficulties. That's why Pichwa left in a huff. He declared, 'I can't
live here any longer. It would be an insult to do so.' I wonder where

that keeper of false dignity is now. No one knows. He was so dignified. He always insisted on wearing a turban. I wonder if he still wears it. When the entire community has lost its dignity, what's the point in holding on to your own? If you can wear your turban, wear it; if you can't, don't. What difference does it make?

21 May 1950

I wait at the door for the postman everyday. He brings many letters, but not the one I am waiting for. I wonder what's wrong. Why hasn't Subedar Sahib replied? Has he too passed away? A man's life is unpredictable, besides Subedar Sahib already had one foot in the grave. And what has happened to that fearless fellow, Pichwa? Has the earth swallowed him or the sky devoured him? Have the winds carried him off? Has a snake bitten him? Man is just a bubble that can burst at anytime. But Pichwa, in his bravado, had set out to fight the storm with a lamp.

23 May 1950

Yeh daur-e-jam yeh ghamkhana-e-jahan yeh rat
Kahan chiragh jalate hain log aye saqi
[This round cup, this world of sorrows, this night,
Where can people light the lamp, O Saki?]

Well, that fellow did finally leave Pakistan. In fact, he travelled miles and miles away from Pakistan—far beyond the borders of India and Pakistan, and reached a country without borders where countless migrants, who found themselves stranded, were instantly 'settled'.

I finally got a letter from Subedar Sahib. I don't know if I should call it a letter or a marsia? Since when has Subedar Sahib, who used to hunt geese and deer, started writing marsias?

'Your letter took a long time to reach me, but I am grateful that I received it. It took time for two reasons: First, it was addressed in a language which, apart from myself, no one else professes to know. And, second, it was sent to Qadirpur, which no longer exists. The new inhabitants of this basti now call it Jatunagar.

'You have asked many questions. I don't know how to answer all of them. You talk about another world. Where is Qadirpur now? '*Ek dhup thi jo saath gai aftab key!*' [That sunny spot vanished with the sun].

'Neither Tidda nor Allah Razi are here now. There is no one here who can fly his own flag on the peepul tree near the Idgah. When Qadirpur became too small for its people, some were buried beneath its soil and others were forced to leave. You wanted to know about the wrestling pit behind the Julahonwalli Masjid. That masjid doesn't exist now. How can a masjid weep for its worshippers or a wrestling pit mourn for its young men if neither of them exists? And as for Allah Razi's shop? Your question reminds me— it now sells *jhatka* meat.

'Your country had no place for Pichwa. He did, however, find a few yards of land in his old country. I didn't get a chance to meet that blessed soul. But one day there was a lot of excitement in the basti, and I saw his head hanging from the same branch of the peepul tree near the Idgah on which Kalwa and Mammad had flown their party's flag.

'It was disturbing to read your letter. At least, you had the graciousness to remember us. Do drop us a line or two when you can. We are not strangers.

Wajh-e-begangi nahin malum
Tum jahan ke ho whan ke hum bhi hain.
[Why do you call us strangers?
We belong to the same place.]

I am old, and like the morning lamp, my light will soon be extinguished. Whom will you write to in Qadirpur then? Remember what I have said about the address.'

Subedar Sahib's letter was shocking. Was it a letter or the last lines of an epic? Perhaps I should end my novel, my Mahabharata about Qadirpur, with this letter.

Poor romantic Pichwa! What a way to meet his end! His death was as dramatic as his life. The only unromantic event of his life was his *hijrat* to Pakistan. If only he hadn't come to Pakistan. By coming here, he humiliated himself and ruined my novel.

25 May 1950

Pichwa is dead, but my novel is still not taking shape. As soon as I pick up my pen, my hand starts shaking. Sometimes I wonder if I didn't murder Pichwa. What got into me to pray for his death? If novels and stories were written like this, writers would be tried for murder everyday.

27 May 1950

Every day, I make a new resolve to begin writing my novel, but I have yet to start. I pick up my pen and put it down. I wonder why I want to write a novel. Who will read it even if I do write it? People here don't care about human emotions—well, leave human emotions aside, they don't even care for literature. Only those who are concerned about humanity love literature. My country doesn't value human beings; why should it bother about literature? Why should I invite mockery? Why debase my creative intelligence?

28 May 1950

I have finally decided to abandon my novel. But how long can I sit at home doing nothing? I am not interested in something as spectacular and disgusting as slave trade. In any case, since the government has got into slave trade, it has decided to make it illegal for private citizens to buy or sell slaves. Naim Mian says that if it had not taken me a such long time to come to my senses, he would have had a large factory allotted to me. Now, he has promised to get a flour mill allotted to me. I must do some work. If I can't get a large factory, a flour mill should do.

29 May 1950

Naim Mian has turned out to be a useful man. He did finally manage to get a flour mill allotted to me. I am now a changed man. As long as I was obsessed with my novel, I felt alienated from my country. Like a *dhobi*'s dog, I belonged neither here nor there. I neither wrote nor did anything else. Now I am a responsible citizen—a responsible citizen of a new nation.

1 June 1950

This is the last entry in my diary. I won't have this kind of leisure from tomorrow. One keeps a diary only if one is unemployed. The flour mill is now mine. Allah willing, it will start functioning tomorrow. In the city, flour is ground at five paise a seer. To attract customers immediately, I have decided to charge four paise for five seers.

Date of publication: 1952

2

Complete Knowledge
(*Poora Gyan*)

Manohar set out on one path, but ended by taking an entirely different one. He was the son of a Brahmin, but was not interested in his studies. He spent his days in fun and frolic. Seeing him so involved in making merry, his father called him and said, 'Son, we are Brahmins. Knowledge is our wealth. Wisdom is our ornament. A Brahmin must be a man of learning.'

His father's words pierced Manohar's heart like a spear. He renounced all his pleasures and bent over his books. He read the Vedas, the Puranas, the Ramayana and the Mahabharata; he read everything. In a short while, he became a learned man. Then he went to see his father, touched his feet and stood quietly before him.

His father asked, 'Son, what have you read?'

He replied, 'I have read everything that has been written.'

'And what about the things that haven't been written?'

The question baffled Manohar.

His father smiled and said, 'Son, there is more knowledge locked in the hearts of people than in books. And, son, one acquires knowledge from books, but only from a guru does one acquire wisdom.'

When Manohar heard that, he left home and wandered from city to city, sat at the feet of pundits and learned men, heard many discourses, but found no enlightenment. He left the cities of men and set out on the path leading to the forests. He touched the feet of hermits and sadhus, served them faithfully, but was still dissatisfied. He walked deeper into the forests; he walked through thick and dense forests; he walked through the summer heat and the rains; he walked through the dark storms and the cold; he continued to walk further and further into the forests. Thorns made his feet bleed, hunger tormented him, and thirst left his lips dry and parched. Unconcerned, he kept walking. His soul was restless.

After walking in this manner for ages, he came to a well under the shade of a peepul tree. A beautiful woman was drawing water from it. The shade of the peepul tree, the cool well and the beautiful woman drawing water—when he saw them, he suddenly became conscious of the fact that he was thirsty. Thirsty and tired. He sat down on the low parapet around the well.

The beautiful woman saw him and asked, 'Stranger, who are you and why have you come here?'

'O woman, I have come from a far-off place and am thirsty.'

'Come, I'll give you water to drink.'

The woman poured cool and refreshing water into Manohar's cupped hands. Once she began pouring water, she forgot to stop because her eyes were riveted on the stranger's face.

'Enough, woman.'

Only then did she realize that he had quenched his thirst, and that she was still pouring water. She stopped and put her vessel aside.

Manohar washed his hands and face, and felt refreshed. He stood up at once to leave.

'Are you leaving?'

'Yes.'

'All right, then go,' she said sounding disappointed.

She watched him till he had vanished from sight. Not once did Manohar turn back to look at her. He was lost in his own thoughts. His soul was restless and the forest was calling him back.

Still lost in thought, he wandered into another dense forest. There, he saw an old man meditating under a banyan tree. His skin was as dry as leather, his ribs could be counted one by one, his hair was long and white, his beard was thick and tangled. His eyes were closed. Manohar thought that he had finally met a great *rishi*. Instinctively, he sat down at his feet. The birds that had made a nest in the rishi's hair, chirped angrily when they saw the stranger, flapped their wings and flew away.

The rishi was the well-known Sampoornanandji. Sampoornanandji opened his eyes, frowned at Manohar, and asked, '*Betey*, why have you come?'

'*Prabhu*, I have come to ask you for something.'

'What?'

'Knowledge.'

'Fool, you can acquire knowledge only if you are at peace with yourself.'

'Then help me to be at peace with myself.'

'Peace! No one can help you to be at peace with yourself. Peace grows and blossoms from within. Go and meditate there.' Sampoornanandji pointed to a green peepul tree in the distance.

Manohar, who had been walking in the sun and was exhausted, suddenly regained his strength. His heart whispered, 'You have found a guru. You shall acquire wisdom.'

He walked to the peepul tree and sat down under its shade to meditate. He controlled his breathing, closed his eyes, and cast all worldly thoughts out of his mind just as one gets rid of the dust on one's clothes. But, the moment he closed his eyes and cast all worldly thoughts out of his mind, his imagination conjured up an image before him. It was the image of the beautiful woman who had offered him water at the well. He was distracted. He tried to concentrate, but the image refused to disappear. It had become a part of his soul.

A year passed, and then another. Years and years went by, but Manohar's heart remained as sorrowful as ever and his soul as disturbed. Finally, admitting defeat, he went and sat at Sampoornanandji's feet.

Sampoornanandji opened his eyes after a long time. When he saw Manohar, he asked, 'Betey, how are you?'

Manohar folded his hands and confessed, 'My mind is perturbed and my soul is in agony.'

'Why?'

'Desire.'

'Kill desire.'

'I can't. It torments me.'

'How does it torment you?'

'When I close my eyes and try to concentrate on God, the image of a woman rises before me and beckons me towards her.'

'Remember, if you go to her, you will be ruined.'

'How?'

'Just as Raja Harcharan was ruined when he saw a woman and was enchanted by her.'

'Guruji, how was Raja Harcharan enchanted by a woman and how was he ruined?'

'All right, then listen to the story of how Raja Harcharan came under the shadow of a woman and how she ruined him.'

A Small Shadow in the Sunlight

Once upon a time there was a king named Harcharan. His kingdom was peaceful, rich and fertile. Rivers of gold flowed through it. The men and women led a comfortable life. The people were fond of their king; the king was fond of his queen. Raja Harcharan was so much in love with his wife, that he had never cast a sinful eye on another woman.

One day the king went on a hunt. Riding through the forest, he caught sight of a beautiful deer. It was an enchanted deer. The king strung an arrow in his bow, and chased the deer. But the deer suddenly vanished. The king rode far into the forest searching for it. After he had wandered for a long time, he saw a small shadow move near a cluster of trees. The king thought it was the deer. He quickly rode after it, but when he reached the trees, he saw a beautiful woman sitting under their dark, green shade. The king was hypnotized by her. He remained where he was, transfixed by her beauty. Indeed, it seemed, as if he had been turned into stone.

When the woman saw him staring fixedly at her, she said, 'Why are you looking at me like that? What do you want?'

The king replied, 'I have travelled for a long time in the sun. I am exhausted.'

'What do you want?'

'Some shade.'

She laughed and said, 'Then why don't you come and lie down—here under the shade?'

The king got off from his horse at once, and lay down exhausted under the shade. And just as dark clouds spread over the sky, that woman spread the shadow of her charm over him. He grew obsessed with her and lost his capacity to reason or think. He didn't realize when the sun had set and that night had fallen.

When the sun rose again the next morning, the king woke up with a start. He rubbed his eyes and looked around, but he couldn't see the woman anywhere. He wandered far and wide in search of her. Sometimes he went in one direction, sometimes in another, but he couldn't find her anywhere. Tormented by his longing for her, he forgot his home and his kingdom; he lost his peace of mind and his sleep. He wandered aimlessly through the forest, calling for her, 'O my sweet shadow, I walk in the sun.'

After Manohar heard the story, he sat still for a long time. He seemed absorbed in trying to solve a difficult puzzle. Later, he said, 'Guruji, I didn't understand anything. My soul is in even greater agony.'

Sampoornanandji said, 'Betey, if you didn't understand it, I'll explain it to you again. Have you heard the story of the student who did exactly what his teacher had warned him against?'

'No, Guruji. What did the teacher forbid and what did the student do?'

Sampoornanandji said, 'If you haven't heard the story, let me tell it to you.'

Then he told him the story of the student and his learned teacher.

The Learned Teacher and His Student

A student went to meet a very learned man and said, 'O learned man, teach me.'

The learned man said, 'Son, I'll teach you, but on one condition. You must not talk to a woman.'

Astonished, the student asked, 'What will happen if I talk to a woman?'

The learned man replied, 'If you talk to a woman, she will smile at you.'

'What will happen if she smiles at me?'

'You will smile back.'

'What will happen if I smile back?'

'She will look at you with intense longing in her eyes, and you will be enchanted.'

'What will happen if she looks at me with intense longing in her eyes and I am enchanted?'

'You will run after her.'

'How will I run after her, O learned man?'

'In the same way as Prajapati ran after Usha.'

'How did Prajapati run after Usha?'

'Prajapati ran after Usha with such intense lust in his eyes that when she saw him, she changed into a deer and ran away. Prajapati also changed into a deer and ran after her. When he caught her, he united with her. Then she turned into a peacock and flew away. He, too, turned into a peacock and flew after her. When he caught her, he united with her. Then she turned into a cow and ran away in fear. Prajapati turned into a bull and ran after her. When he caught her, he pushed her down and united with her. Usha transformed herself into a hundred shapes and a hundred forms. Prajapati also transformed himself into as many shapes and forms, and united with her a hundred times.'

When the student heard the story, he sat in a thoughtful mood for a long time. He could neither understand the meaning of the story the learned man had told him, nor figure out how it could have happened.

Anyway, there was a girl who lived in the house next to the house in which the student lived. Her name was Saraswati. The student had never paid her much attention. But when he saw her that day, he couldn't take his eyes off her.

The student thought to himself, 'I'll talk to her. Let me see what will happen.'

When he talked to her, she smiled at him. He smiled back. When she saw him smiling, she felt shy and hid her face. Then she looked at him with intense longing in her eyes. When he saw her looking at him with intense longing, he was enchanted. When she saw desire in his eyes, she was startled, just as a deer in the forest is startled by the rustle of a leaf. She got up and ran away. When he saw her jump up in surprise and run, he ran after her with desire.

The next day, the learned man waited for the student. But the student did not come because he was pursuing Saraswati.

Saraswati transformed herself into various shapes and forms. But the student was no less agile than her. He took on as many shapes and forms as she did. If she turned into a deer, he too turned into a deer; when she turned into a peacock, he too turned into a peacock.

Once again the story baffled Manohar. He sat quietly for a while and then said, 'Guruji, I didn't understand anything. My soul is still agitated.'

Guruji said kindly, 'All right, betey, I'll try to explain things to you once more. You must have heard the story of how Vishwamitraji's meditation was ruined?'

Manohar said, 'No, Guruji, tell me the story.'

'All right, then I'll tell you the story. Listen!'

Sampoornanandji then told Manohar the story of how Vishwamitra's meditation had been ruined.

How Vishwamitra's Meditation was Ruined

Once Vishwamitra practised his austerities so rigorously that the gods became nervous. They were scared that if Vishwamitra continued to meditate that intensely, he would become a god and their equal. The gods, therefore, called a conference to discuss how they could stop Vishwamitra from becoming a god. After much thought, one of them suggested that only a woman could break Vishwamitra's concentration.

'A woman? How?'

'Friends, man has only one weakness, and that is, woman. Even a man of iron-will turns into wax in a woman's hands.'

The gods understood. They persuaded an *apsara* named Menaka, to go down to earth and tempt Vishwamitra, and destroy his meditation.

Menaka descended from the abode of the gods and went directly to the forest where Vishwamitra sat in meditation. Swaying sensuously, she appeared before him and revealed all the charms of her body in such a way that Vishwamitra's soul was agitated. His long suppressed desire was aroused. He forgot his vows of asceticism. Tormented, he abandoned his austerities and said to Menaka, 'O woman with heavy breasts, let me unite with you.'

She pretended to be hurt, and said, 'What are you saying, rishi? There is neither shelter here, nor privacy. The gods above and the creatures on earth will be able to see us.'

'O beautiful woman, don't worry about that, I'll make a shelter for us at once.' Vishwamitra raised a finger towards the clouds and signalled to them. They immediately covered the sky so the gods could not see them. Then he signalled to them once again. This time the clouds swirled down and surrounded both of them. Vishwamitra united with Menaka.

The result was that Vishwamitra's meditation was ruined, his labour wasted. He lost the godly powers he had begun to acquire.

After telling Manohar this story, Sampoornanandji became silent. He thought that Manohar had finally understood his meaning. But Manohar sat lost in thought for a long time, and then said, 'Guruji, I didn't understand anything. My soul is even more agitated.'

Guruji lost his temper and said, 'Fool, I have tried to explain things to you. You don't understand because your intelligence is distracted by love and desire. If you don't understand, leave me alone. Go to that woman, she will make you understand.'

Manohar interpreted that as his Guru's command. He got up

and left the forest as swiftly as an arrow leaves the bow. He covered the distance of days in a few hours, and the distance of hours in a few minutes.

He headed straight for the well. When he got there, he saw the woman sitting on the parapet of the well as if she was expecting someone. The moment she saw Manohar, her face lit up, and she said, 'So you have returned?'

'Yes, O beautiful one, I have returned.'

'Why?'

'I was thirsty; therefore, I decided to return.'

He sat down next to her, and looking at her with thirsty eyes, pleaded, 'O river of sweet waters, I am thirsty.'

The woman rose like a river in flood and Manohar felt as if he had been washed in the waters of the Ganga. The sun set, night fell; it was dawn once more and night once more; the sun rose and set a thousand times; sometimes the night was dark and sometimes it was lit by the moon; summers passed and winters passed. Days went by, time flew past.

Suddenly one day, Manohar was startled, as if he had been jolted out of sleep. He recalled what his father had said to him. Manohar thought, 'I had set out on one path, but I have ended up taking an entirely different path.'

Full of remorse, he stood up and walked away from the woman in the direction of the forest once more.

Sampoornanandji was in the forest, meditating as usual. But he was no longer at peace with himself. Strange thoughts had begun to torment his mind. 'Why had Vishwamitra been distracted from his austerities when he was so close to achieving divinity? He had already acquired such awesome powers that even the gods had become nervous. Why had he let the glimpse of a woman ruin his chances of attaining godhead?'

Sampoornanandji carried on an angry dialogue with himself. Then he said to himself, 'What Vishwamitra did was not right.' As soon as he said that, he began to doubt his own conclusions. 'Is it possible that Vishwamitra couldn't distinguish between right and wrong? Of course, he could. Then...?'

Suddenly, Sampoornanandji recalled the story of Rishi Parashar who was entranced when he saw Sitavati rowing a boat down the Jamuna.

Parashar called out to Sitavati, 'O woman, your thighs quiver like sinuous fish, come unite with me.'

Poor Sitavati was overcome with shame. She forgot to row her boat. Indeed, her own life's boat was in danger of capsizing. She didn't know what to do. How could she accept Parashar's proposal? Yet, if she refused it, the rishi would feel insulted. What would happen if he cursed her?

With great fear and trembling, she said, 'O rishi, I am your slave. What will the great rishis and sages standing on the banks of the Jamuna think when they see us?'

When Parashar heard that, he called up a heavy mist and united with her.

Sampoornanandji fell into deep thought, 'Great rishis have been ruined by the sight of a woman. They have renounced the world, left the cities of men, spent their lives in lonely forests, expelled desire from their hearts, won freedom from all attachments and illusions, and yet the mere sight of a woman has ruined everything. Why do such things happen?'

Sampoornanandji tried to find an answer to that question, but the more he struggled with the question the more entangled it became. He lost his peace of mind and the tranquillity of his soul. He had been sitting in that forest like a firmly-rooted banyan tree—like an unshakeable mountain of knowledge. Rajas and maharajas, hermits and mendicants, pious men and atheists, men of knowledge and fools used to visit him and take back with them peace of mind, happiness and pearls of wisdom. But now the very roots of the banyan tree had been shaken.

'Guruji, I have returned,' Manohar suddenly stood before him.

When Sampoornanandji looked at his pupil, he couldn't believe his eyes. When Manohar had left him, his soul had been in turmoil and his mind had been full of agonizing doubts. Now he seemed completely transformed. He was self-possessed and calm. Instead of turmoil, there was joy on his face.

Manohar sat down at Sampoornanandji's feet. His mind was clear and free from all doubt. He was ready to receive wisdom.

At first Sampoornanandji was puzzled. He didn't know what to do. Suddenly, he got up from the spot on which he had been sitting for ages like an unshakeable mountain. His face reflected the turmoil in his soul. He said to Manohar, '*Sishya*, you sit here. I am leaving.'

Manohar was shocked. He looked at his guru's face in disbelief. Utterly baffled, he said, 'Guruji, I came here to sit at your feet and acquire wisdom. How can you leave? What journey do you still have to make?'

'The journey of knowledge.'

'The journey of knowledge?' Manohar asked, even more surprised. 'You are a man of wisdom. What journey of knowledge do you still have to undertake?'

Sampoornanandji retorted, 'Who has ever attained complete knowledge? Human beings must search forever.'

Sampoornanandji left Manohar sitting on the spot where he had once himself sat. He emerged from the forest and walked in the direction of the Jamuna. As he walked along the banks of the Jamuna, he saw many rishis meditating on both sides of the river. He didn't, however, pay attention to them. His eyes scanned the boats floating in the middle of the stream.

Date of publication: 1960

3

The City of Sorrows
(*Shahre-e-Afsos*)

The First Man declared, 'I can tell you nothing about that. I am dead.'

Startled, the Third Man turned and looked at him in surprise and fear.

The Second Man, however, didn't react at all. In a disinterested voice, he asked, 'How did you die?'

The First Man replied dispassionately, 'She was a dark girl with long hair which reached down to her waist. She wore a red *bindi*. A dark, young man stood beside her. I asked him—Is she related to you? She is my sister—he replied. I commanded—Strip her naked. When the girl heard that, she turned pale and began to tremble like leaves of a willow tree. The young man pleaded with me—Please don't ask me to do that. I was insistent. I pulled my sword out of the scabbard and yelled—Strip her naked. He shuddered when he saw the naked sword in my hand. Slowly, with shaking hands, he reached for his sister's saree. She screamed and covered her face. Before my very eyes his hands...'

'Before your eyes? Really?' the Third Man exclaimed.

The Second Man was still unmoved. Without a tremor in his voice, he asked, 'Was it then that you died?'

'No, I continued to live,' he replied blandly.

'Continued to live? Really!'

'Yes, that's what I said. I saw all that and continued to live. I lived to see that young man order another one to repeat that incident. He caught a woman in a *burqa* as she was running away in fear. The old man who was with her pleaded—O young man, have pity on us. Do not ruin us. The young man's eyes burned red with rage as he shouted—Is she related to you? The old man begged—Son, she is my wife. Grinding his teeth, the young man ordered—Strip her. Pale with fear, the old man merely stared at the young man. Intoxicated with rage, the young man grabbed him by his neck and screamed – Strip her. When he said that, I…'

'Died?' the Third Man asked eagerly.

'No.'

'Really!'

'Yes. I heard and saw all that and still remained alive. Afraid that the young man might recognize me, I covered my face and ran away. But I was, finally, trapped by a crowd. Just as I was about to throw away my sword, a man forced his way through the crowd and stood before me. He looked into my eyes and said—Don't lay down your sword. That's against the laws of valour. I hesitated. He continued to stare at me. Utterly defeated, I lowered my eyes and said—There is no other solution. I must live. The moment I said that, his eyes began to smoulder with rage. He spat on my face and turned away. Suddenly, a sword flashed above his head. He spun around and fell on the ground. His body was drenched in blood. I washed my face in his hot blood and…'

'Died,' the Third Man said, anxious to complete the sentence once again.

'No. I still lived. I put my sword away, and continued to live. Suddenly, that young man reappeared out of nowhere. He stopped when he saw me. Glaring at me, he snarled—Aren't you the same man? After some hesitation, I admitted—Yes, I am. The minute I said that, he turned around and disappeared into the crowd. Puzzled, I remained standing there. A few moments later, he came back, dragging a young girl with him. He pushed her in front of me. When I finally recognized her grime-and-dust covered face, veiled by her wild hair, I was stunned. She looked at me and wept bitterly. I was utterly shattered. The young man asked venom-ously—Is she related to you? I hesitated before replying—She is my daughter. With a firm voice, he ordered—Strip her. That innocent and helpless girl began to tremble. I fainted and...'

'Died!' the Third Man added with anxiety in his voice.

'No.' The First Man paused. After a while, he whispered, 'I still lived.'

'Still lived? Despite all that? Really!' the Third Man was amazed.

'Yes, despite all that I heard and did...Ashamed of myself, I crept away from there. Terrified, I hid in the shadows, ran across streets and finally reached my neighbourhood. Terror had gripped the street. In the twilight, everything was hazy. The street, normally full of hustle and bustle in the evening, was silent and empty. The street dog, who recognized everyone in the neighbourhood, growled when he saw me. Strange! In the past, he had always wagged his tail and greeted me affectionately. That day there was hostility and fear in his eyes, and his hair stood on end. He snarled at me and backed away as if I were an alien. A wave of fear swept over me. Carefully, I edged past the dog towards my house. The door was bolted from the inside. I knocked softly. No one answered. It seemed as if no one was at home. I was surprised. I knocked again, this time a little loudly.No one answered. A cat, walking on the low parapet wall of the house next door, stopped, looked at me strangely as if I were an enemy and then quickly slunk away.

I knocked again and called out—Open the door. A woman's voice asked cautiously—Who is it? I was surprised that my wife hadn't recognized my voice. Confidently, I replied—It's me. Slowly and carefully, she opened the door, looked at me nervously and said—You? I was crushed. Yes, it's really me. I walked in. There was an eerie silence in the house. It was as dark inside as it was outside. Only a small, dim lamp burned in the verandah. A prayer mat was spread on the floor. My father sat on it, silently telling his beads. My wife whispered anxiously—I thought our daughter had returned. I was shocked. I looked at her closely to see if she had already heard about our daughter. She stared at me appre-hensively. Trying to avoid her gaze, I walked into the verandah and knelt beside the prayer mat. My father picked up the lamp and studied my face for a long time. You?—he asked finally. I replied — Yes, it's me. My father continued to examine my face in the dim light of that lamp. Then, in disbelief, he mumbled—No. I said— It's really me. I am alive. He didn't say anything for a while. He shut his eyes, sighed and said—If you are alive, I must be dead. He then collapsed and died.

My wife said viciously—Your father is dead, your daughter has been raped and dishonoured... You are dead.

At that moment, I realized I had died.'

The First Man fell silent. The Second Man stared at his blank face and vacant eyes for a long time. Then he declared dryly, 'What he says is true. The old man is dead.'

The Third Man was even more bewildered than before. He, too, looked at the First Man and, then, unexpectedly asked, 'Where is your father's body?'

'My father's body?' the First Man was taken aback. He paused, and then slowly replied, 'I left it behind.'

'Why didn't you bring it with you?'

'How could I have carried two dead bodies? You don't know how difficult it was for me to carry my own.'

The Second Man, who had till then listened to everything and spoken in a detached and dispassionate manner, suddenly sat up with a start and said, 'O, I had almost forgotten. My dead body was left behind.'

'Your dead body!' exclaimed the Third Man, who had been curiously inspecting the face of the First Man. He turned to look at the Second Man in disbelief.

'Yes, my dead body,' the Second Man mumbled. 'I should have brought it with me. Who knows how they will treat it.'

'Are you dead too?' the Third Man asked.

'Really!' the First Man exclaimed. 'How did you die?'

'How can a dead man tell you how or why he died? I simply died,' said the Second Man and fell silent. After a pause, he began talking once again. His voice was emotionless. 'The doom that had been hanging over other cities finally reached the ruined city too. I walked about stealthily. I knew that our fate would not be different from theirs.

Passing through a bazaar, I suddenly caught sight of a dark girl, and stopped. Her saree was in tatters, and couldn't cover her nakedness. Her bindi was smudged. Her hair was wild and her face was covered with dirt. She was a very slim woman, but her stomach was swollen. There was terror in her eyes. I watched her apprehensively. When she saw me, she stopped. She was the same girl whom I had...She too recognized me. She covered her face and screamed—No, no! And fled in terror. My blood froze. I was sure she would have me arrested. Averting my face, I ran for a long time. First I hid in one neighbourhood, then in another. Every street I ran through turned out to be a dead end; every neighbourhood I took shelter in was a trap. I couldn't find a way out of that ruined city.

After a long time, I came to a strange town. Dead bodies lay scattered everywhere. There wasn't a single living soul in sight. Surprised and bewildered, I went from one neighbourhood to another, from one lane to another. The bazaars were shut, the roads were desolate, and the houses seemed empty. Occasionally, a window on the upper floor of a house would open cautiously to reveal a frightened pair of eyes and shut at once.

I didn't know what to make of that strange town. It was inhabited, but the people who lived there seemed to be imprisoned in their own houses.

Finally, I came to an open field. A large crowd was gathered there. The children were crying with hunger, the lips of the adults were chapped, the breasts of the mothers were dry, fresh faces had withered, fair women were covered with dirt.

I asked them—Tell me, o people, what city is this? What calamity has befallen you? Why have the houses become prisons? Why does dust blow through the streets?

O unfortunate man—they replied—this is the city of sorrows. We are doomed. Our lives have been destroyed. Now we sit here waiting for death.

I looked at their faces. Every forehead was marked with woe; every face was marked by the shadow of death. Still curious, I persisted—Tell me truthfully, did you not come from distant lands to build your homes in this city of peace?

They answered—Yes, you are right. Now our homes lie in ruins.

Curious, I asked—Your homes lie in ruins now, but tell me, what was the city of peace like before?

They replied—We swear by God, we had to endure the injustices of our own people.

I laughed at that. They were shocked by my reaction. I laughed louder. They were even more shocked. I laughed wildly. They were horrified. I continued to laugh uproariously. They were utterly bewildered.

Soon, the news that a strange man had arrived in the city of sorrow and was laughing spread through the town.

—Even on a day like this?

—Who is this mad man?

—Where has he come from?

—God knows.

—He is not a spy, is he?

—Maybe.

They looked at one another apprehensively.

Then I said—Listen, people, I am not one of them.

—Then where do you come from?

—Where do I come from? I stood lost in thought for a while.

At that moment, an old man stepped out of the crowd and addressed me—If you are not one of them, you should weep.

—For whom? I asked.

—For the descendents of Israel.

—Why?

—Because what happened to them in the past is now happening again. What has happened once will happen again.

At that I stopped laughing. Concerned, I said—Old man, have you noticed that the earth never accepts those who leave their homeland?

—I have learnt that from experience, I have seen that with my own eyes. The earth does not forgive.

—What about the place where one was born?

—No, not even the place where one was born. Not even the land that promises peace and shelter. I was born in a place called Gaya.

The mendicant of Gaya learnt that there is only suffering in this world, that it is impossible to attain nirvana here, and that this earth cannot be trusted.

—And the sky?

—Everything under the sky is an illusion.

I was unconvinced—I must think about that.

—Even to think is an illusion.

—But thought is man's real wealth.

The old man retorted—Even man is an illusion.

—What, then, is the truth? I asked hesitantly.

—The truth? What is that?

—The truth, I said confidently, is the truth!

Calmly, he replied—What you call truth is also an illusion.

I thought to myself—This old man is under the shadow of death and this city is on its way to extinction.

I left those people to their fate and escaped. I wanted to live.

Soon I reached another strange place. The crowd swelled by the minute and people played the drums of victory.

Curious, I asked—O people, what place is this? What age am I in?

Someone whispered in my ear—This is the age of decadence, and here everyone is taught a lesson.

—And who is that man on whose face someone just spat?

He looked at me bitterly and asked—Don't you recognize him?

—No.

—O disfigured one, you are that man.

—Me?—I was shocked into silence.

—Yes, you.

I examined the face of that man carefully, and couldn't turn my gaze away. I really was that man. I recognized myself and died.'

The Third Man said, 'After discovering one's real self it is difficult to live.'

The First Man turned towards the Second Man and asked, 'Did someone really spit on your face?'

'Yes.'

'I thought someone had spat on mine,' the First Man insisted. 'On your face?'

'Yes, that's what I thought. Anyway, I now know that I was mistaken. It wasn't I who was spat upon, but you.' The First Man sounded relieved. Soon, however, he began to feel uneasy again. The thought that someone might have spat on his face made him wince with pain. When he spoke again, his voice was no longer as casual as it had been before. He said to the Second Man, 'You are mistaken. I am sure I was the one who was spat upon.'

Expressionless as ever, the Second Man said, 'I looked very carefully at the face of that man who had been spat upon. His face was exactly like mine.'

The First Man studied the Second Man carefully from head to toe. Suddenly, an idea occurred to him, 'Is it…is it possible…that you are me?'

'That I am you! No, it is not possible. I know myself. I am not under any delusion.'

'How can you be sure you know who you are?' the First Man challenged.

'I know who I am because someone spat on my face.'

'But that is how I know who I am too,' the First Man said. 'That is why I suspect that you are me.'

'How is it possible that every face that has been spat upon is your face?'

'True. It is, however, possible that your face is not your face, but mine,' the First Man insisted.

The Second Man was now really confused. Apprehensively, they asked each other a variety of questions. Finally, the Second Man admitted defeat and said, 'We are dead. How can we possibly recognize each other?'

The First Man answered, 'Did we recognize each other when we were alive?'

The Second Man didn't know how to respond to that question. At that moment, the Third Man came up with an embarrassing question, 'Which of you has brought his body with him?'

'I have brought it with me,' the First Man replied.

The Third Man suggested, 'Instead of shouting at each other, why don't you go and look at the body? That should help you distinguish truth from falsehood.'

His proposal was accepted at once, and the three of them went to inspect the body. When the Third Man saw the body, he was shocked. He exclaimed, 'The face is disfigured. It's beyond recognition now.'

The Second Man said with conviction, 'If the face of the corpse is disfigured, then it is certainly mine.'

'But my face, too, was disfigured,' the First Man insisted.

'When was your face disfigured?'

'When I forced to strip the young man's sister,' the First Man replied.

The other two stared at him. Together, they asked, 'And you continued to live even though your face had been disfigured?'

'Yes. I lived till the moment my father saw me and shut his eyes. Then I died.'

That reminded the Second Man of his own father. 'My father too died the moment he saw me. I went to him seeking comfort. I appealed to him—O Father, your son died today. He looked at my disfigured face and said—I am glad that you died before you came to see me. If you had come to me while you were still alive, I would have cursed you to live and suffer till doomsday. Those were his last words. He died soon after.'

The First Man said, 'Our fathers were more worthy of respect than we are. And yet we mistreated them. I brought my body with its disfigured face here, but left my father's dead body behind.'

Startled, the Second Man said, 'I didn't think of it in that way either. I, too, left my father's dead body behind.'

The Third Man laughed bitterly and said, 'During the first migration, we left the graves of our ancestors behind. This time we left dead bodies behind.' He stopped laughing and grew sad. Memories of the first migration rose before him. In the dim light of the past, he saw a number of faces. A stream of bright faces. Faces that he would never see again, flowed before his eyes. Then he thought of the second migration and the same...

In disbelief, he thought, 'I don't know whether I migrated or not, but all these bright faces have once again vanished from my sight. How many of them have vanished from my sight in the past!

How many bright faces have disappeared again?' Then he thought of the sadness that had clouded those glowing faces in the past, and recognized that the same sadness had cast its shadow over the faces in the present.

Sadly, he turned to the First and the Second Man and said, 'What I said earlier was not true. The same thing happened during both the migrations—each time we left with our faces disfigured, and each time we left bright faces behind.'

The Second Man continued to stare into space for some time and then suddenly stood up. As he was about to leave, the other two asked him, 'Where are you going?'

He replied, 'I should at least bring my father's body here.'

'You can no longer bring bodies from there.'

'Why not?'

'Because all the roads are blocked.'

'Really? Does that mean that my father's body will remain there?'

'What will you do with it?' the First Man asked. 'Look at me. I brought my dead body here. Now I have to carry it around on my shoulder.'

'Why don't you bury it?' the Third Man asked.

'Where can I bury it? There is no place here where I can bury it.'

'You mean there are no burial grounds here?' the Second Man asked.

'No. There are burial grounds here. But they are overcrowded and there is no place for more graves.'

Upon hearing that, the Third Man wept. The other two were puzzled, 'Why are you crying?'

'I am crying because I have yet to die and there is no ground here for new graves. Where will I be buried?'

'Aren't you dead already?' the other two asked, looking at him carefully.

'No, I am still alive.'

The other two stared at him in surprise. 'Do you want to continue to live? Are you sure you are still alive?'

'Yes, I am alive, but...'

'But?'

'But I have disappeared.'

'Disappeared?'

'Yes, disappeared. Do you know how many people disappeared in this calamity?'

'And do you also know how many of them were killed?' the First Man added.

'I know, but I was not among those who were butchered.'

'Many died the way we died.'

'I was not one of them either.'

'How do you know that you are one of those who disappeared?'

'The truth is that it is impossible to find those who are still alive in the city of ruins. But the bodies of those who were slaughtered are found everyday. If I had been killed, my corpse would have been found by now.'

'If you are not dead, you should be among those who were captured. And if you are one of them, you have completed the circle.'

Puzzled, the Third Man asked, 'Completed the circle? What do you mean?'

'I mean that after wandering from one place to another, you have returned to the city you once left behind. The same thing happened to a companion of mine. He was captured and taken to the place where he had been born. When he was contemplating escape from there, his friend asked him—Why do you want to run away from here? What does this soil say to you?

'That man wept—It is the season of *basant*. When I look out of this prison window, I see fields of yellow mustard sway in the wind before me. I was born here, but I am now in a prison and am shattered.

'Basant, the place of birth and captivity…Together they can be painful. That man escaped from captivity and disappeared.'

'Disappeared?' the Third Man asked with a start. 'Are you sure that I wasn't that man? It is possible. When mustard fields bloom, they create a crisis in me too.'

'No, you are not that man.'

'Basant, the place of birth and captivity…' the Third Man

mumbled and fell into deep thought. After a long time, he said, 'No, that man couldn't have been me. I wasn't ever captured.'

The First Man said, 'Isn't it strange to go back to the place of one's birth as a captive?'

The Third Man frowned and answered, 'Yes, it is strange indeed. My grandmother used to narrate stories about the mutiny of 1857. She told me that many people were killed during that uprising. They left their homes and never went back. There was a woman who fought the British valiantly. When her home was destroyed, she left her fragrant city and disappeared into the forests of Nepal. For years, she wandered from forest to forest like the vagabond breeze, and then she vanished.' He paused, took a deep breath and continued, 'Instead of hiding in the cities of torment, it is better for a man to find refuge in some dark and dense forest.'

He stopped talking. Something reminded him of the first migration. Lost in thought, he sat quietly for a long time. Then he sighed, and said in a voice full of regret, 'Alas, if only my hijrat had been in the forests of Nepal.'

All the three men were now silent. Silent and still. They had lost interest in talking. Time passed. They continued to sit like statues. After a long time, the Third Man began to feel uneasy. He looked at the other two. They were staring blankly into empty space. He wondered if he, too, had turned into stone. As if to convince himself that he hadn't, he deliberately raised his arms and yawned loudly. Reassured, he thought, 'I am alive.' Then he turned towards the other two and asked, 'Should we leave?' He wanted to let them know that he was really alive.

At first, the other two didn't respond. Then they slowly turned and looked at the Third Man. Disinterestedly they asked, 'Where should we go? There is no place for us to go to now. We are dead.'

Terrified, the Third Man glanced at their disfigured faces. Their eyes had neither light nor life in them. He said to himself, 'I should leave before I, too, turn into stone.' After hesitating for a long time, he stood up. The other two watched him, and asked without curiosity or emotion, 'Where will you go?'

'I'll go and find out where I am.' He paused, and after some thought, asked, 'I am not among the captives, am I? Have I been taken back there?'

'Where?' the First Man asked.

It appeared, however, that he didn't hear the First Man. Staring at the Second Man, he asked, 'Did he really escape from prison? Are you sure I wasn't that man?'

'No, I am not,' the Second Man said, as he looked at him intently for the first time. With a start, he asked, 'Were you not in the city of sorrow?'

'Yes, you do recognize me. I was in the city of sorrow.'

'It took me some time to recognize you, because your face has been disfigured. But when you were in the city of sorrow, sitting with those who were waiting for death, your face wasn't mutilated. How did it get so disfigured?'

Ashamed, the Third Man replied after some hesitation, 'It was disfigured when I turned my back on those people.'

'It is strange that you managed to escape. All the roads to the city of sorrow were closed. Weren't you caught?'

'How could I have been caught? Who could have recognized me? My face was disfigured.'

'Your disfigured face was your salvation!'

The Second Man interrupted him, 'Don't delude yourself. If he is still hiding there, he'll be caught in a day or two.'

'I am worried about that too. That is why I want to go and find out where I am.'

'Even if you do, what difference will it make?' the Second Man asked.

'I'll try to find a way to escape.'

'Escape?' the Second Man looked at him with pity. 'You have disappeared. Don't you know that all the escape routes are closed?'

'That is true. But how long can I remain among those who have disappeared? I must find out where I am. Besides, who knows, I may be able to find a way out.'

'You are a simpleton. Where will you go?'

'Where? I'll come back here. After all, those who escaped earlier did manage to find their way here.'

The First Man was surprised, 'Here? There is no place here. Didn't I tell you that my body is lying here without a grave?'

The Second Man looked at the other two and said, 'Listen, didn't I tell you about the man from Gaya? The earth is a place of suffering. Everything under the sky is an illusion. Those who have been uprooted can never find a place where they can flourish again.'

The Third Man was overcome with despair. The Second Man stared at him in silence.

At last, the Second Man said, 'Listen. Sit down. Don't worry about where you are. Accept the fact that you are dead.'

Date of publication: 1973

4

A Letter from India
(*Hindustan Se Ek Khat*)

My dear Kamaran,

May God bless you and may you live long! May you continue to be a man of lofty ideals! You are dearer to me than my own life. You cannot imagine how I yearn to see you again and how anxious I am to receive a letter from you. I have often tried to get news about you from others and have attempted to send you letters from here. Unfortunately, however, I have always failed. I addressed a letter to you and sent it to Ibrahim's son, Yousuf, and begged him to forward it to you at Karachi. I also requested him to send me your reply as soon as he received it. He is, as you know, in Kuwait and earning a lot of money. That seems to have gone to his head and made him forget his duty. He did not even bother to inform me whether he had posted my letter and received a reply. When Sheikh Saddique Hasan's son was leaving for England, I gave him yet another letter addressed to you and requested him to post it from London. But, that *haramzada*, too, did not bother to inform me whether he had done so or not.

I am very worried about Imran Mian. I am not sure if he reached Karachi. He should, at least, have informed us if he had.

Imran Mian came by eight or ten weeks after the war. Winter had just set in. I had moved my cot from the verandah back into the room. Late one night there was a knock on the door. Puzzled and anxious, I wondered who had come knocking at that hour. I opened the door and examined the man who stood there from head to toe. At first, I didn't recognize him. But, then, I realized that he was my own flesh and blood, even though he had changed beyond recognition. I embraced him and said, 'Son, we didn't send you to Pakistan in this shape. What have you done to yourself?' I regretted my words at once. Wasn't it enough that the one whom God had entrusted in our care had come back to us? A man should thank God in all circumstances. He must never utter a word of complaint lest it becomes, like the word of an infidel, a curse and rebound on him. Men of weak faith have done such sinful deeds that there is no room left for complaint. We should silently endure everything and be afraid of the anger of the wise and almighty God.

When your *chachi* saw Imran Mian, she was astonished. She hugged him and wept. I had resolved not to question him about anything, but she could not restrain herself. 'Why didn't you bring your wife with you? Where have you left your children?' she asked. Those questions unnerved Imran Mian and he turned pale. Your chachi and I were concerned. Then we decided that we wouldn't bring up the painful subject again.

Imran Mian stayed with us for three days. How strange those days were! He neither talked nor laughed. He just sat lost in thought. On the third day, he decided that he wanted to visit the grave of Mian Jani. I blessed him, 'Son, you should, of course, read a prayer at your grandfather's grave. It has been more than twenty-five years! But it is not advisable to go there in the daytime. You were born here and are a part of this soil. Someone will recognize you.' He laughed bitterly and said, '*Chachajan*, I walked through the basti before I came to your house. Even the soil did not recognize me.'

Well, I took Imran Mian to the graveyard that evening. I showed him all the new graves of the family. He recognized the old graves without my help. As it got darker, it became difficult to identify the graves. When we reached Mian Jani's grave, Imran Mian was overcome with emotion. I, too, had tears in my eyes. The grave was old and in disrepair. The *harshringar* tree that used to grow by its side had withered some time ago. You may remember that Mian Jani used to be very fond of harshringar. He had planted many of those trees in his garden and used to look after them with great care. They always had such an abundance of flowers that the girls of the family used them right through the year to dye their *dupattas*, and the cooks to flavour the *biryani* made on special occasions. But a harshringar tree needs to be tended carefully. And I can no longer look after everything by myself. The tree next to Mian Jani's grave was the last one remaining in the graveyard. It withered in the rains before the war. Now, there are no harshringar trees left either in our garden or in the graveyard.

By the grace of Allah, we still retain the garden. We do so only because it is next to the graveyard and is regarded as a part of it. Over the last twenty-seven years, so many trees have fallen, and with them so many memories have been buried, that one should now consider the garden to be an extension of the graveyard. The few trees that still remain there are like tombstones on the graves of days long past. Anyway, Imran Mian knows what state the garden is in. If he reached Karachi, he must have told you about it.

Imran Mian left early next morning. He had spent the night beside Mian Jani's grave. I, too, sat with him. At dawn, when the birds began to chatter, he stretched himself, stood up and begged me to give him permission to leave. I was concerned, 'Why do you want to go away? Now that you have returned, why don't you stay?' Despondent, he replied, 'No one recognizes me here any longer.' I said, 'Son, your safety lies in your not being recognized.' He wasn't convinced. He had decided to leave. I asked, 'Where will you go, son?' He said, 'Wherever my feet carry me.' I sensed from what he told me, however, that he was planning to go to Kathmandu first and then try to reach Karachi. I was sad. But his insistence, and my concern that the news of his presence would spread, compelled me to give him permission to leave. I took an amulet off my arm and tied it on his. I recited a prayer for his safety. Before

he left, I implored him to send me news about himself as soon
as he crossed the border. Since that day, however, I haven't heard
from him.

Here, one rarely ever gets news from Pakistan. And I don't feel
like believing the news that does trickle across. One day, Sheikh
Saddique Hasan told me that everyone in Pakistan had become
a socialist and that onions were being sold there for five rupees
a seer. When I heard this, my heart sank. But, I told myself that
since Sheikh Sahib was an old Congressee, he couldn't possibly
give me any other kind of news about Pakistan and that I shouldn't
believe what he says. A few days later, I heard something that
contradicted the bad news. I was told that Pakistan had declared
that the Mirzayis were non-Muslims. When I passed on that
information to Sheikh Sahib, he was unable to come up with
anything to counter it. May Allah have mercy on Pakistan and
reward it for its goodness! We live in the midst of infidels here and
can't raise our voices in protest. Non-believers have built a masjid
near our haveli. When they proclaim the *ameen* loudly, we have
to keep quiet.

Oh yes, Sheikh Sahib once brought me news about you too. He
told me that you had built a house; that there was a sofa-set and
a television in your sitting room. I was happy to hear that. Thank
God that everything you longed for here and didn't possess has
been granted to you over there.

The haveli is in disrepair. The wooden beams supporting the
roof are rotting and have begun to sag even more after the last
rains. The *diwankhana* is in such a bad condition that if you look
at the ceiling you can catch a glimpse of the sky. As you well know,
our financial situation is rather bad. If you can send me some
money, I can use it to repair Mian Jani's grave and have some clay
plastered on the ceiling of the diwankhana. There is no need to
undertake any more repairs at present. The court case regarding
the haveli has yet to be settled. My late and respected brother had
placed all the papers regarding the case in my custody before he
left in 1947. With God's help, I have thus far handled all the
appearances in court satisfactorily and have always hired compe-
tent lawyers. God willing, the case will be decided soon and in our

favour. But who can predict the arrival of the angel of death? He may come at any time. I am very worried about who will continue to fight the case after I am gone. No matter where I turn, I see only darkness.

My son, Akhtar…what can I tell you about his character! He has changed his name to Premi, and he goes to the radio station to read plays! Khalida, the daughter of my younger brother—unfortunately my brother passed away some time ago—has married a Hindu lawyer! Now she wears, without any sense of shame, a saree and a bindi! You can, of course, shed more light on the state of our family in Pakistan than I can. But I hear that *Appajan's* daughter, Nargis, has married someone of her own choice, and that the one she has married is a Wahabi! I also hear that Appajan herself sits in her son's car without a veil, and that she shamelessly bargains in public with all the cloth merchants!

Alas, I am the one who has been spared death to witness all this and write about it. My late and respected elder brother and my younger brother passed away at the right time. When I go to the graveyard to read a prayer for Mian Jani and my younger brother, I always remember my elder brother and say a prayer for him too. What times we live in! These days we can't even go and read a prayer for Mian Jani! The graves of our family—a family which had lived in one place and whose dead had been buried under the same soil—are now scattered across three different lands. I had respectfully urged my elder brother to go to Karachi—'Since you are determined to leave us, go and live with Kamaran Mian. That would be the proper thing to do.' But his love for his youngest son drew him to Dhaka. His untimely death was a great shock to all of us. But I now believe that his death is proof of God's mercy. He was a good soul. God did not want him to witness these days of evil and suffering. It is only a sinner like me who has been condemned to live through such days.

Now that the protective shadow of our elders has been lifted from over our heads, and now that our family has been divided and scattered over Hindustan, Pakistan and Bangladesh, and now that I am standing at the edge of my grave, I think that the history of our family, which had been given to me as a sacred trust, should be passed on to you because you are now the oldest member of the family after me. But I can only recall the history entrusted to me from memory. My elder brother had taken the records of the family and the history of our lineage with him to Dhaka. When the members of his family were killed in Dhaka and buried there, the memories of the family were also buried with them.

Imran Mian came back here empty-handed. The biggest calamity for our family is that its history has been lost. Our forefathers, who were the descendents of Saadat-e-Azam, had preserved that history even when the times were bad and they had to suffer a lot of pain and torment. We, however, have to bear the shame and sorrow of losing the history of our family and forgetting our lineage. Now we are a family that has been afflicted by misfortunes. We have neither a place of our own nor a past which we can remember. We are victims of an era where everything has fallen apart. Some members of the family died in Hindustan, some disappeared in Bangladesh, and some wander from place to place in search of a home in Pakistan. Our faith has been corrupted. It has been polluted by un-Islamic rites and customs. Some of us have married outside our community or into different sects. If this continues much longer, our lineage will be completely wiped out and there will be no one left to remind us where our ancestors came from or who we are.

Let me, therefore, tell you, my son, that we are the descendants of the holy and renowned Sayyids. Our family can be traced back to Hazrat Imam Musa Karzan. But, al-hamdulillah, we are not Rafzis. We are Sahihul Aqeeda Hanafi Muslims. The true followers of Ashab-e-Kabar—the followers of Ahele Bait. Mian Jani's practice was to keep the fast during Ashoora and sit on the prayer mat for the entire day. Our family possessed holy-beads which used to turn a deep red during Ashoora. Mian Jani used to tell us that the beads had come from the place where our forefather, Sayyidana Hazrat Imam, had first dismounted from his horse and set foot on earth. As the beads turned red, our grandfather would go into a trance, but he never beat his breast or wept. He thought that it was not proper to do so. However, large pots of *khichdi* were always cooked and distributed amongst the poor and the needy.

After the Partition, we were left with only one large pot. Last year, we lost even that. We could only afford to make a small pot of *channa* for the poor. Allah alone knows what our financial state will be next year. Everything is becoming more and more expensive and our existence is becoming more and more precarious. We know the price of onions in Pakistan. But, son, always remember this. Once prices rise, they never fall; just as once standards of morality decline, they can never be raised again. Pray that you may be spared from witnessing the days when prices begin to rise and morals begin to decline. When such a time comes, those who truly believe in God should do penance and recite the Koran. There are many signs that such a day will be upon us soon, and the wise know how to decipher them.

Anyway, I was going to tell you the history of our family—the family that I had known when it was together and which is now scattered. Mian Jani summoned the three of us when he was on his death-bed and pleaded with God that his grave should always be scattered with the sweet-smelling flowers of harshringar. He told us that his father, Sayyid Hatim Ali, had told him, when he himself was on his death-bed, that his father, Sayyid Rustum Ali, had orally passed on to him the entire history of their family. The written documents concerning our family were partially lost in the tumultuous times of 1857, when our forefathers had to leave their home in Bayees Khala and wander for years from place to place seeking shelter.

It is out of respect for our ancestors that I want to tell you that we originally came from Isphahan. The exiled Emperor Humayun, when he was gathering his forces together to regain his lost dynasty, had invaded Isphahan. Our ancestor, Meer Mansoor Muhammad, was in those days a date merchant. He was known as an ocean of learning. When he came to Hindustan, he was acknowledged as the light of the faith. His grave in Akbarabad is still a place of pilgrimage. When unmarried girls pick up dust from the grave and put it in the parting of their hair, it turns into red *sindhoor* within a year; and when childless wives carry away a bit of that dust in their sarees, they always return with a child to give their thanks and cover the grave with a cloth. During the reign of

Shahjahan, the descendants of our worthy ancestors left Akbarabad and settled in Jahanabad. However, they had to flee from their homes when there was trouble in 1857. Our ancestor, Rustum Ali, didn't take a single coin with him. He did, however, tie the parchment on which the family tree was drawn, to his waistband and clutch the bundle of papers containing the history of the family as he ran. On the way he was, unfortunately, attacked by dacoits. In the ensuing fight, the papers were scattered. He could recover only a few of them, the rest were lost. By the grace of God, the paper containing the family tree was saved and not a single word on it was defaced.

After wandering like haunted fugitives across dusty lands, our ancestors founded this settlement. They discovered that this piece of earth was hospitable and decided to build their homes on it. When the earth is kind, it is as soft and gentle as the bosom of a beloved and as generous as the lap of a mother. When it turns cruel, however, it is more cold-blooded than an emperor and more callous than a hard-hearted miser. The truth is that this land treated our family generously for a long time. It nurtured our family at its bosom, and watched us grow and prosper like a jealous mother who gathers all her children in her embrace and does not let them out of her sight.

Before the Partition, only three members of the family had left home. Bhai Ashraf Ali, Bhai Farrukh and Pyare Mian. Bhai Ashraf Ali was the son of my *chachajan* and a year older than Kibla Bhaisahib. He was, therefore, your *taya*. By the grace of God, he became a Deputy Collector and was posted in different districts. He used to send us all the gifts that were offered to him. Bhai Farrukh, who was his younger brother, was the same age as me. He was in the forest department and spent his youth in the Central Provinces. All the wooden furniture that you saw in our haveli had been made and sent by him. Both the brothers were the pride of the family. They spent their youth outside, but their last days were spent in the comfortable embrace of this soil.

Pyare Mian was the favourite son of our *Phuphi Amma*. He had been so spoilt by the love and affection showered on him that he grew up to be an undisciplined man who couldn't refrain from indulging in all the seven deadly sins. He was the first one in our family to see the bioscope. Once, he even enticed me from the path of duty. After I saw Madhuri, my heart was perturbed for sometime, but I controlled myself and never again accompanied him. Pyare Mian was already addicted to the theatre. But after the bioscope came to town, he became its ardent disciple.

He was so smitten by Sulochana in *Bombai Ki Billi* that one day he stole Phuphi Amma's gold earrings and ran away to Bombay. Mian Jani sent word to him that he was no longer welcome back—'*Sahibzade*, don't ever come back home.' In Bombay, a dancing girl led him to believe that she would help him meet Sulochana. Of course, she didn't introduce him to Sulochana, but ensnared him into marrying her. He spent his youth in Bombay. When he got the news of Phuphi Amma's death, he came back home. By then he was old. He had a long, white beard and a string of beads in his hand. He wept for his mother. All of us urged him to stay back. But he said that he couldn't possibly do so without Mian Jani's permission. Unfortunately, however, Mian Jani had already departed from this earth. So, who could permit him to stay back? He decided to return to Bombay. That was in the year 1947. Trains were being attacked and looted. We tried to persuade him not to travel at that time, but he didn't listen to us. He got into a train. He never reached Bombay. Who knows what happened to him on the way?

Pyare Mian was our family's first offering in the riots of 1947. I have made a list of the names of our family members who have died since then. Thirty-one were embraced by God, twenty-one were murdered, five died of natural causes, seven were martyred by the Hindus in Hindustan, and fourteen were sent to God by their Muslim brothers in Pakistan. Of the last fourteen, one was shot by Ayub Khan's henchmen for supporting Motrima Fatima Jinnah during the elections. Ten died in East Pakistan. In this tally, I have not included Imran Mian. A man should never despair of God's mercy. Deep in my heart, I am certain that Imran Mian, who is my flesh and blood, is alive and if he hasn't yet reached Karachi, he is still in Kathmandu.

Kathmandu reminds me—Bhaiya Farrukh's son, Sharafat, also visited us. He had escaped from Dhaka and was on his way to Kathmandu when he decided to stop here for a while. He is the exact replica of Pyare Mian. Calamity has had no effect on him. During his stay here, he went fearlessly to see the bioscope everyday. When it was time for him to leave, he packed up to go to Bombay instead of Kathmandu. When I asked why he had decided to go to Bombay, he said that he wanted to meet Rajesh Khanna. I said, 'You idiot, is Rajesh Khanna the equal of E. Bellimoria or A. Bellimoria that you should be so anxious to meet him?' But he turned a deaf ear to what I said and left for Bombay. Later, he sent me a letter from Sri Lanka to inform me that he was well. I don't know what misfortunes drove him there. When I saw Sharafat, I thanked God. But his behaviour didn't please me.

I have heard that the girls of our family have become more independent after going to Pakistan. Each one of them, I believe, has married a man she chose herself. Before the Partition, there was one such incident which could have brought a bad name to our family. But it was tactfully dealt with. One day, a kite fell on the roof of our younger *phupha*'s house. Now, as you know, it's not a good sign when a kite flutters over the roof of a house where a young girl lives or when a pebble falls into the courtyard. In those days, phupha's daughter, Khatija, was coming of age. Phupha reported the matter to Mian Jani. She also placed before him the note that had been tied to the kite. Mian Jani boiled with rage. He shouted and screamed, 'How dare Raza Ali's son drop a kite on our roof!' But, after phupha explained the entire matter to him in detail, he cooled down. He had no choice but to get Khatija married to that ruffian and send her to her new home. Raza Ali had never even dreamt of getting a girl from our family as a bride for his son. He agreed at once. But, at the last moment, he insisted that the *sighah* had to be read at the ceremony. Mian Jani had to swallow his pride and accept his terms. But the outcome of that affair has not been happy. Half of Khatija's children are *teetars* and half are *battairs*. One son takes care of the *niaz* of the Gyarveen Sharif, and the other performs *azadari* at Moharrum. Anyway, now our entire family is divided into teetars and battairs.

Our family tree has been lost and our lineage sullied forever. How will our family be recognized as a distinctive one in the future? Indeed, I feel that our family members are like the falling leaves of a tree that have been scattered by the wind and left to crumble into dust.

Azeez, I am now the only one left to mourn over the scattered leaves. I remember those days when this family prospered and flourished, and we could count the leaves that had been blown away.

I have records not only of those who have died, but also of those who are still alive. I have kept a list of the names and addresses of those who went away to other countries and made a home in other lands. I shall soon send you that document because it is full of revealing details.

Who knows what the future has in store for me? I am like a fading lamp in the morning light. The flame has begun to die and my eyes have begun to close. You are the new light of this ill-fated family. It is your duty to light the path of those who wander in darkness. Of course, I know that experience teaches us that leaves which have once been scattered can never be gathered again. A family that has drifted apart can never be united again. But it is man's duty to try. So, try to be a guide to this family of wanderers. Find those who have strayed off the path. The borders are now open again; do visit us at least once. Show us your face, have a look at us. Your *chachi's* command is that you should bring your wife with you. Yes, Mian, don't come alone. That will give us a chance to see your children too—look at their faces, note who is fair and who is dark. And one more thing. There have been many additions to the family in Pakistan. I have included their names in our family history—noted their dates of birth. Of course, I couldn't record what they look like.

There are still a lot of blank spaces left which only you can help me to fill. So please send me a list of all those who were born and those who died in Pakistan during the past three or three-and-a-half years. I can't write separate letters to every family member. There is no censorship of letters these days, but even an ordinary postcard costs as much as a telegram used to. By the way, is it true that Khatija's youngest daughter has divorced her husband and taken up a job in the Population Control Office? She has, of course, ruined her own life, but why must she interfere in the marriages of others? Yes, Mian, I am now convinced that our family's lineage has been lost forever. But I hear that other families are even worse off. The other day, someone told me that Ibrahim had made so much money by adulterating wheat flour that he has constructed another mill. And, that Mian Faizuddin, who used to walk about in rags here, has accumulated enough black money to build a number of houses. I wonder, however, if all the other families in Pakistan have also lost their family heritage. It must be a strange and peculiar country! We had spent generations in the land of Hind. We saw good days and evil days here. By the grace of God, we ruled over it and were also slaves in it, but we never forgot the proud and honourable lineage of our family. But, in Pakistan, people seem to have lost all sense of self-respect and forgotten the entire history of their families in just a quarter of a century. Well, anyway, I hope they are happy.

There is so much to tell you and so much to write about, but I hope that the little I have written is sufficient for the time being. Let us know how you are and inform us about your plans to visit us. I must end this letter because the time for saying the *namaz* is at hand. I still have to put all the legal documents in order because our case is to be heard in court tomorrow. It will be the four hundred and twenty-seventh hearing. *Insha Allah-al-Aziz*, even this one will be handled with the usual care. Sometimes, I feel that I am still alive for the sake of this case alone. Otherwise, there isn't much left in this old body of your chacha's—not even the desire to live. I have lived through so much since I was born.

from your chacha,
Kurban Ali

Dated: 28 Ramzan-ul-Mabarak, 1394 Hijri
Mutabiq: 15 October 1974 AD

Date of Publication: 1978

5

Tortoise
(*Kachuwe*)

Vidyasagar continued to sit quietly. He held his peace, while the bhikshus argued and fought each other. He refused to get involved in their debates. After a while, he got up and left.

In a forest, far away from town, Vidyasagar sat in *samadhi* under a sal tree and meditated on a lotus flower. It blossomed, smiled at the day and then withered. He gazed at another flower and then another. Each flower he looked at blossomed, smiled at the day and then withered. In sorrow, he shut his eyes and sat in deep concentration for a long time.

One day, his former companions, Sundersamudra and Gopal, came to see him and said, 'O Vidyasagar, we are distressed.'

Vidyasagar continued to sit quietly, and at peace. He didn't utter a word in reply.

Tearfully, Gopal said, 'These are dark times. Those who should remain silent talk a lot, and the one who should speak is silent.'

And Sundersamudra added, 'The bhikshus have been corrupted by Subhadra. She told them that Tathagata was no longer among them. That Tathagata used to prevent them from doing what they pleased and was forever ordering them to do this or that. That they were now free to do what they wanted.

'O Vidyasagar, the bhikshus now do as they please and are trapped in worldly desires. They have stopped sleeping on dry grass, and sleep instead on beds and sit on mats. O learned one, O wise one, why don't you say something?'

At last, Vidyasagar opened his eyes. He looked at them thoughtfully and asked, 'Bandhu, have you heard the Jataka story about the parrot?'

'No.'

'Then listen.'

Once upon a time, when Brahmadutta was the King of Benaras, the Bodhisattva was born as a parrot. The parrot had a younger brother. When both of them were young, they were trapped by a bird-catcher who sold them to a Brahmin in Benaras. The Brahmin looked after the two parrots as if they were his own children.

One day the Brahmin had to go out of town. Before leaving, he told the parrots, 'Look after your mother.'

As soon as the Brahmin left, his wife began to indulge in all sorts of sinful pleasures.

The younger parrot anxiously beat his wings hoping to talk her out of committing sin.

The older parrot tried to dissuade him. He said, 'Bandhu, hold your peace and don't interfere.'

But the younger parrot refused to listen to his brother and spoke to the woman about her sinful behaviour.

The clever woman said, 'You are right. I shall not sin anymore. Thank you for reminding me of my duty. Come out, let me hug you.'

The moment the naïve parrot stepped out of his cage, the woman caught hold of him and wrung his neck.

When the Brahmin returned after many days, he asked the parrot who was still alive, 'What did your mother do during my absence?'

The Bodhisattva replied, 'Maharaj, in evil times the wise keep quiet or they risk losing their lives.'

Then he resolved, 'It's impossible to live in a place where one is not free to speak. Let me find a place where I can speak without fear.'

So he beat his wings in order to attract the Brahmin's attention and said, 'Maharaj, I must inform you, with due reverence, that I have decided to leave.'

'Where will you go?'

'Where I can speak without fear,' the Bodhisattva replied. He then left Benaras and went to live in a forest.

Having finished the story, Vidyasagar walked away. He wandered for miles and miles, from forest to forest. At last, he came to a wild and lonely place. He decided to stop there. Sundersamudra and Gopal, who had dragged themselves behind him, also decided to stay with him.

For three nights, Vidyasagar sat quietly in samadhi without eating or drinking anything. On the fourth day, Sundersamudra and Gopal left in search of alms and returned in the evening, their begging bowls filled to the brim with food.

They sat down next to Vidyasagar and appealed to him, 'O Vidyasagar, didn't Tathagata teach us that we should eat to appease our hunger and drink to quench our thirst?'

Vidyasagar opened his eyes. He ate what was placed before him as if it were tasteless, and drank water from the river as if it were neither refreshing nor cool. Then he intoned, 'Dust unto dust.'

Sundersamudra, assuming that the occasion was right, pleaded with Vidyasagar once more, 'O Vidyasagar, all the bhikshus have departed from the path of duty. They no longer follow the rules laid down by Tathagata. Instead of living under the shade of trees, they sleep on beds inside houses. The congregation of monks is divided into innumerable sects which are mortal enemies of each other. Please return and show them the right path once more. You are the only one who is truly learned and wise.'

Vidyasagar asked, 'O Sundersamudra, have you heard the Jataka tale about the mynah?'

'No.'

'Then listen.'

Once upon a time, when Brahmadutta was the King of Benaras, the Bodhisattva took the form of a mynah and lived in a forest.

The mynah built a pretty nest in a tree. One day it rained very heavily. A monkey, wet and shivering, sought shelter under that tree. But even then he couldn't escape being drenched.

The mynah said, 'O monkey, you always imitate man. Why don't you also build a house? If you had a house, you wouldn't have to suffer like this.'

The monkey replied, 'O mynah, mynah, I can imitate man, but I am not wise like him.'

But then he thought to himself, 'This mynah can talk because she is sitting comfortably in her own nest. I wonder what she would say if she didn't have one!' And so the monkey destroyed the mynah's nest.

The mynah realized that to give wisdom to a fool is to invite trouble.

She flew away to live in another forest.

After completing the story, Vidyasagar sighed and asked, 'Do you know what the Bodhisattva did for the monkeys and what the monkeys did to him in return?'

Then he narrated the following Jataka tale.

Once upon a time, when Brahmadutta was the King of Benaras, the Bodhisattva took the form of a monkey. Since he was a very strong and vigorous, he became the leader of a large troop of monkeys who lived in the mango grove owned by the king.

One day the king, full of longing for the flavour of ripe mangoes, went to the grove. When he saw the monkeys there, he became very angry. He ordered his archers to shoot them down. 'Make sure that not a single one escapes.'

When the monkeys heard the order, they ran to the Bodhisattva and pleaded, 'Save us, tell us what we should do now!'

The Bodhisattva reassured them, 'Don't be afraid, I'll find a way out.'

Then the Bodhisattva climbed a tree whose branches stretched wide across the Ganga and almost reached the other shore. He jumped across to the other side and measured the distance between the longest branch and the shore. He cut a bamboo shoot and fastened one end to a bush on the shore and tried to tie the other to that branch. But the bamboo stick fell short by the length of his body. So, he tied it to his legs instead, held the branch with both his hands and told the monkeys, 'I have made a bridge, run quickly over my back and reach the safety of the other shore across the Ganga.'

Thus, the eighty-thousand monkeys, who had been trapped in the mango grove, treading gently over his body so as not to cause him pain, escaped massacre by the archers.

But Devadutta, who had also taken the form of a monkey at that time, was among the troop. He said to himself, 'This is my chance. Let me kill the Buddha now and avenge myself.'

Devadutta jumped so hard on the Bodhisattva's back that he fainted with pain.

Brahmadutta, who had watched everything, quickly helped to untie the Bodhisattva. He bathed him in the Ganga, put fresh clothes on his body, anointed him with perfumed oils and gave him some medicine. Later, he sat at the Bodhisattva's feet and said, 'You sacrificed yourself so that others could be safe, but they treated you cruelly in return.'

The Bodhisattva replied, 'O King, let that be a lesson to you. A king should make sure that his people never come to harm, even if he has to sacrifice his own life to ensure it.'

After instructing the king, the Bodhisattva gave up his life as a monkey.

The Jataka tale made Vidyasagar, Sundersamudra and Gopal feel sad. They sat for a long time in silence, thinking about the innumerable incarnations of the Bodhisattva and the suffering he had endured for the salvation of mankind. They also wondered about evil men like Devadutta who had caused him, generation after generation, misery and pain.

A while later, Sundersamudra asked, 'O Vidyasagar, wasn't Devadutta the brother of the Bodhisattva?'

'Yes, he was his brother,' replied Vidyasagar. Soon after, he laughed and then burst into tears.

Sundersamudra was surprised, 'O wise one, why did you laugh and then burst into tears?'

Vidyasagar replied, 'When a goat can laugh and then cry, why can't a man do the same?'

Sundersamudra was intrigued, 'Why did the goat laugh and then cry?'

Vidyasagar then told them the following Jataka tale.

Once upon a time, when Brahmadutta was the King of Benaras, there lived a Brahmin who was very learned and knew the Vedas well. One day the Brahmin bought a goat to offer as a sacrifice to the dead. He bathed the goat and put a garland around its neck.

When the goat saw the preparations being made for its ritual sacrifice, it first laughed and then cried.

The Brahmin asked, 'O goat, why did you laugh and then cry?'

The goat replied, 'O Brahmin, I too was once a Brahmin who was very learned and knew the Vedas well. I too sacrificed a goat to the dead. For that sacrifice, I was condemned to have my neck slit five hundred times. Today my neck will be slit for the five-hundredth time. I laughed because this will be the last time when the knife shall slice through my neck. I shall now be released from suffering forever. I cried because, in order to atone for killing me, you will have your neck slit five hundred times.'

The Brahmin then said, 'O goat, don't be afraid. I shall not sacrifice you.'

The goat laughed even more loudly, 'I am a goat and my neck will be slit one day. If you don't kill me someone else will.'

The Brahmin didn't pay heed to what the goat said and set it free. He also told his students, 'Look after this goat well.'

His students took good care of the goat. But that which is fated always comes to pass. While the goat was grazing one day, a tree fell on her and killed her.

There was another tree next to the one which had fallen. The Bodhisattva, who had taken birth as a tree, at once assumed the form of the Buddha and appeared before the people. When they gathered around him in surprise, he taught them the following lesson: 'O my people, violence always begets violence; he who kills another, is always killed in turn.'

Sundersamudra and Gopal, who had listened to the tale attentively, bowed their heads in reverence.

After some time Sundersamudra said, 'O wise man, you haven't still answered my question. Wasn't Devadutta the brother of the Buddha?'

Vidyasagar replied, 'O Sundersamudra, don't insist on an answer to that question. If you do, I shall first laugh and then cry.'

'O wise man, why will you do that?'

'I will laugh when I affirm that Devadutta was indeed the Buddha's brother, and I will cry when I recall that he was also a bhikshu.'

Sundersamudra wept when he heard that. Troubled, he asked, 'O Prabhu, why do bhikshus commit sin?'

Vidyasagar stared at him in surprise for a few moments and then pleaded, 'O Sundersamudra, please don't ask me that question.'

'Why not?'

'Please don't insist, because it so happens that the one who searches for evil in others sees a reflection of himself.'

'Why?'

'Well, let me answer that with the help of the following story.'

Once upon a time, when Brahmadutta was the King of Benaras, his wife fell in love with another man. When the king questioned her about it, she said, 'Since I have betrayed you, I shall be reborn as a witch with the head of a horse.'

That was, indeed, what happened. After her death, the queen was reborn as a horse-headed witch. She lived in a cave in a forest. Whenever anyone passed though the forest, she caught him and ate him.

One day, it so happened that a Brahmin, who had studied at Taxila, was returning home through the forest. The witch caught him and carried him away to her cave. There she teased and played with him for a while. The Brahmin was wise, but he was also young. And as you know, learning has its own attractions and youth its own impulses. The Brahmin was aroused. They hugged and kissed each other. Then they had sex. Nine months later the witch gave birth to a son. That child was the Bodhisattva who had chosen to be born into the world as a witch's son.

When the child grew up, he decided to free his father from the thralldom of the witch and return to the world of men. The moment the witch came to know of this, she said, 'Son, since you have decided to return to the world of men, let me tell you something I learnt from my own experience. It is easier to live with witches than it is to live with men. Let me give you, as a gift, the magical power to see footprints as far as twelve miles ahead. It will help you in the world.'

Armed with that gift from his mother, the Bodhisattva and his father left for Benaras. He told the king about his gift and persuaded him to give him a place in his court. The king's counsellors, however, advised him to test the Bodhisattva's claim.

So, in order to test the Bodhisattva, the King stole some jewels from his own treasury and threw them into a lake far from the city. The next day, when a hue and cry was raised about the theft, the king ordered the Bodhisattva to investigate. The Bodhisattva saw the footprints clearly and recovered the treasure from the lake.

The king said, 'You haven't told us who stole the treasure.'

The Bodhisattva said, 'Maharaj, the treasure has been recovered. Please don't insist on the name of the thief.'

But the king refused to listen. He insisted, 'Tell us who stole the treasure?'

The Bodhisattva replied, 'O King, let me tell you a story. As you are a wise man, you will understand what it means.'

Once upon a time there was a musician who, while bathing in the Ganga, began to drown. When his wife saw him drowning, she cried out, '*Swami*, before you drown, please teach me a tune on the flute so that I can earn my living.'

The drowning musician cried, 'O good woman, how can I teach you a tune on the flute? This river, whose water sustains life and nurtures the earth, is also the cause of my death.'

Then he made the following observation, 'Sometimes, the one who nurtures also kills.'

After telling the king that story, the Bodhisattva added, 'Maharaj, a king is like life-giving water to his people. If he who sustains and nurtures life also begins to destroy it, what would happen to the people?'

The king heard the story but wasn't satisfied. He said, 'Friend, I liked the story. But you haven't yet told us who stole the treasure.'

The Bodhisattva said, 'Maharaj, listen carefully to another story.'

Once upon a time, there was a potter who used to live in Benaras. He went to the forest everyday to fetch clay for his pots. Since he dug up clay from the same spot everyday, there was soon a deep pit there.

One day, while he was digging, there was a storm and a tree fell on his head. The poor fellow cried out and made the following observation, 'Sometimes, the earth which nurtures and sustains us can also be the cause of our death.'

The Bodhisattva said, 'Maharaj, a king is like the earth to his people. If he who nurtures and sustains his people begins to steal from them, what would happen to the people?'

The king heard the story and said, 'The story doesn't answer my question. Catch the thief and bring him before me.'

The Bodhisattva said, 'Maharaja, in the city of Benaras, there lived a Brahmin. One day he ate too much food. He felt miserable and knew he was going to die. He wept and said—The food, which nurtures and sustains countless Brahmins, is also the cause of my death. So, Maharaj, a king is like food to his people. If he who nurtures and sustains his people steals food from them, what would happen to the people?'

The king insisted, 'Friend, stop entertaining us with stories. Tell us who stole the treasure?'

The Bodhisattva said, 'Maharaj, there was a tree on a mountain in the Himalayas. It had many branches. Lots of birds used to nest in those branches. One day, two of the branches rubbed against each other and the tree burst into flames. On seeing the flames, one of the birds cried out—O birds, fly away from here at once. The tree which once sheltered us will now burn us, the tree which once sustained and nurtured us will now destroy us. So, Maharaj, just as a tree gives shelter to the birds, a king gives shelter to his people. But if the tree which gives shelter becomes a thief, then what would happen to the birds?'

The foolish king still didn't comprehend the purpose of the Bodhisattva's stories. He continued to intone, 'Tell us who stole the treasure?'

The Bodhisattva finally admitted defeat and said, 'All right. Gather all your people together. Only then will I tell you who stole the treasure.'

The king called an assembly of his people. When they had all gathered there in the court, the Bodhisattva spoke to them, 'O people of Benaras, listen carefully and pay attention. The earth in which you had buried your treasure has stolen it.'

The people, who were intelligent and alert, understood the meaning of the Bodhisattva's speech at once. They attacked the king, placed the Bodhisattva on the throne and proclaimed him their new king.

After Sundersamudra and Gopal heard the stories, they hailed the glory and the wisdom of Tathagata. Vidyasagar watched both of them carefully to see if they were still infected by curiosity.

Then he said, 'O bhikshus, the wise one gave us all the necessary laws for righteous behaviour before he departed from this earth. The best thing for you would be to stop asking for guidance from others and follow the light of your own lamp. That was the last piece of advice Amitabha gave Ananda before he left his mortal body.'

The advice of Tathagata filled Sundersamudra and Gopal with grief. They cried, 'The light that had once guided us is extinguished. There is darkness everywhere. We wander aimlessly, guided by the dim light of our own lamps. Storms rage around us and destroy everything. The trembling flames of our lamps are becoming dimmer.'

Vidyasagar interrupted them, 'Listen, O bhikshus, how can you harbour such thoughts about Amitabha. He is eternal and the light of his lamp can never be extinguished.'

Sundersamudra and Gopal realized their folly. They meditated on the Buddha with great reverence. A bright radiance spread across the earth and the sky. Their eyes filled with tears and their bodies trembled with ecstasy.

Vidyasagar joined them in prayer, 'O Tathagata, O Amitabha, you who are in Paradise and whose body is bathed in the perfume of flowers. O Sakhyamuni, O wise man, we call upon you with profound reverence to come down to us again and give us light.'

Tears flowed down their eyes as they recalled the days when Amitabha had resided in their midst, and every town, village, path, field and forest seemed to glow with the light of his presence.

Vidyasagar said, 'We used to wander with Amitabha even at night. When we walked through forests on moonless nights, we never felt we were walking in darkness. The path always seemed lit by the light of the full moon. Indeed, everything—trees, leaves, flowers, bushes—seemed to celebrate the glory of his presence on earth.'

Recalling those days, Gopal said, 'O *bandhus*, how much we used to walk in those days! We walked everywhere. Through forests and fields, through towns and villages, with a begging bowl in our hands!'

Sundersamudra was startled out of his reverie. He suddenly remembered the present and said, 'The bhikshus have given up walking now. Their feet are sore, their bodies are tired and their stomachs have become much too large.'

When Vidyasagar heard him, he said, 'O bandhu, Tathagata always told us that the man who is fat and eats too much will never be released from the cycle of birth and rebirth. Like the pig, he will be born again and again, and will die again and again.'

Sundersamudra said, 'O learned one, now the bhikshus eat too much, sleep on comfortable beds and laugh when they talk to women.'

'They laugh when they talk to women!' exclaimed Vidyasagar in fear.

'Yes, Prabhu, they laugh when they talk to women. I have also noticed that the women of our congregation smile back at them. They also wear anklets on their feet!'

Vidyasagar closed his eyes and implored in grief, 'O Tathagata, your bhikshus have abandoned the path of righteousness. I am all alone in this vast sea of desire!'

Sundersamudra and Gopal also closed their eyes and implored. 'O Tathagata, we are troubled and surrounded by the rising tides of desire.'

They sat with their eyes closed for a very long time. Then, Sundersamudra opened his eyes and said, 'Gopal, did you notice that, though we begged for alms at every door in the town, no one offered us *kheer*?'

Gopal agreed, 'That is very true. No one offered us kheer; we are rarely offered kheer these days.'

Puzzled, Sundersamudra asked, 'I wonder why people have stopped making kheer as often as they used to?'

'Have people forgotten Tathagata or have the cows stopped giving as much milk as they used to?'

Recalling past days, Gopal said, 'When Tathagata was with us, every man and woman sang hymns in his praise and the cows yielded plenty of milk. There was so much kheer that people ate to their heart's content and still had enough left over for the bhikshus. How tasty it was and how we used to love it!'

Sundersamudra's mouth began to water.

Amazed, Vidyasagar looked at both of them, and said, 'Taste! Fools, you talk about taste! Is that why you eat food?'

Sundersamudra was abashed, 'No, Prabhu, I have never attached any importance to the taste of food. As I ate I always told myself that I was only adding dust to dust. But when I am offered kheer, I always find myself thinking about the kheer Sujata offered Tathagata and my mouth begins to water!'

Trying to make them understand Vidyasagar said, 'O bandhus, forget the past, lest you are trapped once again in the nets of desire.'

Apologetic, they claimed, 'O Prabhu, we have renounced the sense of taste. We only take pleasure in the thought of Tathagata.'

Then, once again, they began to meditate upon Tathagata. They thought of him as one who had preached that the world was an illusion and its pleasures meaningless.

Gopal said, 'Sundersamudra, do you remember the day when Tathagata saved you from the wiles of a woman of pleasure?'

'Wiles of a woman?' said Sundersamudra trying to remember.

'O fool, have you forgotten! I remember that day clearly. Tathagata sat calmly, his eyes shut, while we gazed upon him with love and reverence. After a while, we noticed that a smile had begun to play on his lips. Ananda asked—O Tathagata, why do you smile? Tathagata answered—At this moment there is a contest going on between a bhikshu and a woman. Ananda asked—Who will win the contest? Tathagata replied—It is difficult to tell. The woman is clever. She embraces him and then slips out of his arms. Offers him a glimpse of her body and then hides it. Reveals her breasts and then covers them. Takes off her skirt and then pulls it on again.'

Memories of that day surged through Sundersamudra's mind and washed over him in the same way that the waves of the sea sweep over the land. Then he said, 'Gopal, that was so long ago. Yes, the contest was difficult. What a woman she was! Like a lotus flower! Before I saw her, I used to wander from door to door begging for alms. But her beauty so bewitched me that I forgot every other path and went only to her door. I went to her house every day and called—O gracious woman, give alms to a bhikshu. She was very kind to me and gave me plenty of alms. I enjoyed myself.

One day, she was so generous that I thought I had bathed in the cool waters of the Ganga. She took me inside, bolted the door and fell into my lap like a flower. O Gopal, don't ask me how soft and sensuous her body was! How full and luscious her breasts, how large and heavy her hips and how smooth and supple her waist! Our bodies were about to unite, when Tathagata appeared to me in a vision.' Sundersamudra sighed and fell silent.

'What happened next?' Gopal asked.

'What happened next? I killed desire and pulled myself out of the sweet river of pleasure.'

Sundersamudra closed his eyes once more and sat as if he were lost in some distant memory.

When he opened his eyes again, he whispered, 'I wonder where she is now?'

'Who?' Gopal asked in surprise.

'That beautiful woman.'

'Who knows?'

Sundersamudra stood up. Gopal was astonished to see him walk towards the town.

Gopal called out, 'Bandhu, don't go. Come back!'

But Sundersamudra kept walking as if in a trance.

Gopal called again, 'Bandhu, come back!'

Vidyasagar said dryly, 'Sundersamudra will never come back. He is once again enchanted by the world of desire.'

Gopal appealed to him and said, 'O Vidyasagar, do something to save him from being enticed by worldly desires. Persuade him to return.'

Vidyasagar advised, 'O Gopal, forget him. Save yourself if you can.'

'Prabhu, don't worry about me. I am safe.'

After a brief silence, Vidyasagar laughed bitterly and said, 'The one who spoke the most about the sinfulness of others was the first to go back to the world. Desire swept over him, like flood waters sweep over a sleeping village.'

Confused, Gopal stared at Vidyasagar for a while and then asked, 'O learned one, O wise one, what's the harm in talking?'

'Bandhu, it appears that you don't know the Jataka tale about the one who was very talkative. Let me tell you.'

Once upon a time, the Bodhisattva was born in the house of a king's counsellor. When he grew up, he became an advisor to the king. The king was very talkative. The Bodhisattva wondered how he could admonish the king and tell him that a ruler is great, not because he talks a lot, but because he listens well.

In a lake at the foothills of the Himalayas lived a tortoise. Two wild geese also lived nearby. The three of them became good friends.

Once, it so happened, that the lake became dry. The wild geese said to the tortoise, 'Friend, we have a lovely home up in the mountains. The lake up there is full of water. Why don't you come with us? We'll live in comfort together.'

The tortoise replied, 'Friends, I cannot fly. How could I possibly reach those high mountains?'

The geese said, 'If you promise that you will keep your mouth shut, we'll take you up there.'

The tortoise promised to keep its mouth shut.

The geese brought a stick and placed it before the tortoise. They asked the tortoise to hold it firmly between its teeth. Then each of them took an end of the stick in their beaks and flew up into the sky, the tortoise between them.

They flew for a long time. As they flew over a town, the children who were playing in the streets began to shout and scream when they saw the strange sight.

The tortoise got very angry. It wanted to shout back at them and say, 'If my friends want to help me, why are you jealous?' But as soon as it opened its mouth to speak, it fell to the ground and died.

It so happened that the tortoise fell into the open courtyard of the king's palace. There was a hue and cry. The king, accompanied by the Bodhisattva, went to see the tortoise. When he got there, he turned to the Bodhisattva and asked, 'O wise one, tell us how this tortoise met with such a sad end.'

The Bodhisattva replied, 'Because it talked too much.'

Then he narrated the story of the tortoise and the wild geese to the king and concluded, 'O King, those who talk too much always come to a sad end.'

The king thought over what the Bodhisattva had said and realized that the admonishment was also meant for him. From that day onwards he talked less and listened more.

After Vidyasagar told Gopal the story, he added, 'Bandhu, we, the bhikshus of the Buddha, are like that tortoise. We are only pilgrims on the path to salvation. He who speaks out of turn or without due thought will fall and be left behind. You saw how badly Sundersamudra fell. He will never find the right path again.'

Gopal understood Vidyasagar's sermon. He said, 'How many bhikshus were on the path with us! How many of them fell by the wayside and were left behind!'

After a pause, Gopal resolved, 'From now on, I shall not speak.'

And Gopal abided by his resolution for a long time. He meditated and begged for alms, but refused to utter a word. But one day, when he was in the town begging, he came across his childhood companion, Prabhakar.

Prabhakar told Gopal, 'Friend, I have a message for you. Your father, the king, is dead and the throne is vacant. Your mother wants you to return and your beautiful wife longs for you.'

Gopal replied, 'Friend, there is only suffering in the world. Kingship and power, home and family are all part of the nets of desire. Father, mother and wife—all family relationships are merely illusions. We bhikshus are the followers of Tathagata.'

Then Gopal turned away from his friend and started walking towards the forest.

Prabhakar called after him, 'Friend, I have heard what you have to say. I shall wait for you at this very spot for three days.'

Gopal walked back to the forest, but he was very disturbed and restless. Prabhakar's voice continued to echo in his head. When he finally saw Vidyasagar, he fell at his feet like a withered leaf.

Gopal pleaded, 'O wise man, I have been silent for a long time. But I still feel as if I am falling, as if the stick has slipped out of my mouth. Tell me, what should I do?'

Vidyasagar advised, 'Meditate on that flower.'

Gopal sat down before a flowering bush nearby and began to meditate upon a flower which had recently blossomed. He gazed upon it for a long time. The flower glowed in the sunlight, and then slowly lost its colour and withered.

Gopal seemed to comprehend. He said to himself, 'O Gopal, the world is an illusion.' He closed his eyes. But when he opened his eyes the next morning, he saw another flower on the same branch. It was beautiful. Gopal became anxious once more. He lost his concentration and his eyes began to rove over everything around him.

Suddenly, he realized that it was the morning of the third day. With trepidation, he stood up and began to walk towards the town.

Vidyasagar watched him leave. He didn't say anything. Once Gopal had disappeared from his sight, he laughed bitterly and recalled what Tathagata had once taught them, 'If you can't find a wise companion on a journey, it is better to walk alone like an elephant in a forest.' The memory of that lesson by Tathagata reassured him. He pondered over it and understood how profound it was. 'I can confirm the truth of what Tathagata taught us from experience,' he said to himself. 'A man who travels with a fool suffers much on his journey. It is better to walk alone than to walk with a fool.'

Only then did Vidyasagar realize how much the very presence of Sundersamudra and Gopal had disturbed his own meditations. They were very talkative and they had broken his concentration. Now he felt as if an enormous weight had been lifted off his mind.

Calmer, less tense, he began to wander through the forests again. He walked through tall grass, he wandered over dusty paths and noticed everything around him. He looked at the flowers in bloom and the trees swaying in the breeze, he heard the soft sounds of water flowing in the rivers. He felt as if the sky was filled with music and the air was suffused with perfume. Slowly, he began to pay attention to the infinite variety of physical things in the world and he said to himself, 'Knowledge of the physical world is different from the knowledge of one's soul. Both are necessary.' And the more he wandered, the more knowledgeable he became about the external world. He noticed everything, touched everything, heard every sound and smelt every perfume.

One day, while he was wandering through a forest, his eyes fell on a tamarind tree and he exclaimed with delight, 'O look at that tamarind tree!'

Entranced, he stood in front of the tree for a long time and said, 'I am surprised. I have wandered through these forests for years, but this is the first tamarind tree I have seen.'

The more he thought about it, the more he wondered why he hadn't seen a tamarind tree earlier. 'I have meditated under the shade of many trees. Maybe, I didn't pay sufficient attention. Do tamarind trees usually grow in these forests?'

As he meditated upon that tamarind tree, memories of his youth rose before him. He saw another tamarind tree. Tall, with branches which arched gracefully down to the earth. He recalled a winter morning when waves of shrieking parrots had descended on that tamarind tree.

'I have walked through many forests since then, but I don't think I have ever seen a tree as green and beautiful. Nor have I ever seen so many parrots.'

He continued to gaze at the tamarind tree. Memories rose before his eyes. Dusty roads with carriages, squirrels scuttling up trees, chameleons. 'As a child I used to chase those squirrels. They would run up the tree, sit on its branches with their front paws raised and look down at me. Then they would hide in the leaves.

'Often a creature with glittering eyes and forked tongue would look out of a hole, and then vanish. I would shiver with fear.

'And, yes, Kausambi. We embraced each other one evening under the shade of that tamarind tree like the sea embraces a river. Our lips sought each other. We held each other in a long embrace. Evening disappeared into night.'

As Vidyasagar thought about that day, his body trembled with delight. He felt as if he had tasted the wine of the gods.

'One must have knowledge of the external world!' He was transfixed by the memory of the world he had left behind. He remained in that delightful dream-like state for a long time.

When he finally emerged from his trance, he felt very disturbed. He realized that the bhikshus no longer lived under the shade of trees. They lived in houses, slept in beds and looked into the eyes of women when they talked to them.

He felt very lonely, a lost wanderer in a wild forest. He said to himself, 'Everyone has gone back to his own home, why should I shun that tamarind tree which is a part of my very being?'

The memory of the tamarind tree began to torment him and he decided to go back and look for it. He took the path which lead out of the forest, back towards his home.

When he came out of the forest, he suddenly stopped. Standing before him in the middle of his path was the Bodhisattva. That visionary being urged him to control the ferment in his mind. Vidyasagar recalled the lesson Tathagata had once taught them, 'If you are tormented by sinful thoughts, pull yourself out, the way an elephant pulls himself out of a swamp.'

Vidyasagar struggled to regain control over himself and he turned back into the forest in the same way as an elephant pulls himself out of a swamp.

Full of repentance, he sat down under a peepul tree to meditate. He reproached himself for having taken so much delight in flowers and flowing rivers. Had Tathagata admonished once, 'Bhikshus, why do you smile and take delight in the physical world? The world around you is in flames.' When Vidyasagar looked around, he felt as if he were sitting in the middle of a huge fire. Everything was in flames, flowers, leaves, rivers, his own eyes. He shut his eyes.

He sat in meditation for many days. But his soul was not at peace. His concentration was repeatedly broken. He couldn't forget that tamarind tree. Dejected, he stood up and decided to go on a long journey in search of peace.

He wandered from one forest to another. His body was exhausted, his feet were cut and bruised, his legs swollen. Finally, he reached the Aravalli forests. There he resolved to sit under the bodhi tree and meditate.

The tree stood in all its glory amidst other trees in the forest. He sat under its shade, his hands folded, and pleaded, 'O Sakyamuni, O Tathagata, O Amitabha, this bhikshu of yours is your tortoise and has lost his way.' He closed his eyes and chanted, '*Shanti, shanti, shanti.*'

He sat under that tree for a long time. Days passed. He did not move, as if he were a statue made of stone.

Then slowly he felt as if he had stopped grieving for the past. A new kind of joy stirred within him. At first it sprouted in his soul like a new leaf, then it spread through his whole being like the branches of a beautiful green tree. He recognized it as the tamarind tree of his past.

He stood up. He had finally understood that every one has his own tree in his own forest. To look for it in another forest, even if it has a bodhi tree, is folly. Each one must search for the tree under whose shadow he can find peace in his own forest.

Vidyasagar felt that he had at last deciphered the mystery. He set out towards the tamarind tree in his forest.

But as he came out of the Aravalli forest, he began to be troubled by doubt, 'O Vidyasagar, have you acquired knowledge or have you been fooled my Mara?' He was perplexed, confused. Did he still hold that stick between his teeth or had it slipped out?

Confused, he stood for a long time, one foot in the Aravalli forest and the other on the path leading back to his home.

The world around him was in flames.

Date of publication: 1985

6

The Boat
(*Kishti*)

1

It was still raining outside. Inside, it was warm and humid. Exasperated by the oppressive humidity, one of them opened the window for a moment and then shut it immediately.

'Has the rain decreased?'

'No, it is still raining heavily.'

'Is this the Day of Judgement?'

'Allah! The rain outside is better than the hell in here.'

'There isn't much to choose between the rain outside and the oppressive heat in here.'

'Where can we go? Everything is under water.'

'Why is it still raining?'

'Because we are still alive.'

'How many of us are here? We can be counted on our fingertips.'

'There are also the animals.'

'Perhaps, that's why it's so oppressive in here. How difficult it is to breathe when one is shut in with animals!'

'Yes. And who knows how long we'll have to stay imprisoned in this place. There is no sign of the rain stopping. It's been raining like this for days.'

'When did it start raining?'

'When?'

'Yes. Can anyone remember when it started raining; how many days ago?'

They tried to count the number of days. But no one could remember when it had begun to rain. Neither the day, nor the time.

'That means we don't know how long we have been on this boat or when we began our journey!'

They were bewildered. How long had they been travelling—how many days, how many years, and how many generations? That is what always happens when it rains or when one is on a long journey. When it rains continuously, it seems as if it has been raining and raining for years. It is the same with long journeys. If one travels without a break, one feels as if one has been doing so eternally from one birth to the next.

'We left home the day it started raining. Does anyone remember?'

Home!

That was the first time someone had uttered the word home.

They were startled, 'We had homes once!' Each of them recalled their homes as if they had left them behind only recently.

'Alas, if only she had got into the boat with me! Who knows where she is now and what waters surround her?'

'Who is she?'

'O, she's the one who collided into me as she was descending the stairs.'

And the whole scene flashed before him. That woman, whose eyes were like those of a deer and whose breasts were like ripe and luscious fruit. When he held her in his arms as she rushed down the stairs, he felt as if he were holding a trembling dove. A moment later, she freed herself and ran like a wild antelope with long strides. Then, suddenly, she stopped and returned. The next moment, when the sun was still burning in the sky, she sank under the weight of his body and lay in his embrace under the shadow of the palm tree behind the hill.

Steps, courtyards, meandering paths, hills, tall trees full of fruit and birds. How much he recalled! But why remember houses that had crumbled in the rain and had been washed away by the flood? None of them had accepted the fact that the waters had risen above the peaks of the mountains and had not spared their homes.

'How can we forget our homes? We had spent our days there, sang songs for new brides there, lamented the dead there.'

Their eyes brimmed with tears. They remembered their homes and wept. Slowly, without hope and without doubt, they accepted the fact that their homes had been destroyed.

'O dear friends, those houses were destined to be destroyed.'

'How?'

2

Then Gilgamesh fell on his knees and spoke, 'O fellow travellers, if you have the clarity of vision then consider my fate. Behold how many tumultuous and wild seas I had to cross to reach that land where Utnapishtim was resting. I prayed to him thus: 'O Utnapishtim, I had heard that those who seek, find blessing; that at the end of a journey, there is salvation. But I have searched for a long time. Now I am exhausted. My quest has not brought me blessings; my journey has been pointless. But you sit here and rest in this garden of paradise.'

After I had finished speaking, Utnapishtim said thoughtfully: 'O ill-fated one, I see that this difficult journey has exhausted you and that despondency has seeped into your soul. So, rest here for a while. And listen carefully. I shall tell you how I sought grace and how, at the end of my journey, found salvation. I tore down my house and built a boat.'

I was surprised and said: 'O revered one, what are you saying? Does anyone tear down his house with his own hands?'

Utnapishtim replied sadly: 'That was what my Lord desired. He appeared to me in a dream and informed me that Enlil was angry and could not rest because there was too much noise on earth. So, Utnapishtim, your safety lies in demolishing your house and in building a boat. That is what I did, Gilgamesh. I pulled down my house and built a boat, because my Lord commanded me to do so.'

3

Then they remembered what had happened. The earth had become far too crowded and men had become evil.

The Lord had first created men. The Lord had then created women. The men of the Lord had found the women irresistibly attractive and had taken them as their wives. Those women had given birth to daughters, and the men of the Lord had fallen in love with them and taken them as their wives. Well, that is how the earth became crowded with human beings and a place of evil. When He saw the condition of the earth, the Lord repented. In grief, He said: 'I created the sons of Adam and I shall destroy them for they have polluted the earth and made it an evil place.'

There was, however, among those sinful creatures that crowded the earth, one righteous man who had always followed the commandments of the Lord. So the Lord said to him: 'O son of Lamech, I shall save only you. Make a boat and when the heavy rains begin to fall, take a pair, male and female, of every living creature, into your boat.' The good man did as he was commanded.

Noah was married. His wife had given birth to sons. When they grew up, his sons had married beautiful women.

When that good man's wife saw him build a boat, she taunted him. She gathered her sons together and said, 'Look, what a mess your father has made. He spends his day cutting and hammering to build something useless.'

After a while, when Lamech's son, Noah, couldn't bear her taunts anymore, he said, 'You are my helpmate, the partner of my life. Be afraid of the day when your passion cools and you come to give me news of the approaching storm.'

4

One morning, Manuji was surprised to see that the fish had grown larger than the vessel. It was only the day before that he had found the fish caught in the folds of his clothes when he was bathing in the pond. At that time, it had been no bigger than the length of his hand. He was about to fling it back into the pond when the fish had pleaded with him, 'O Prabhu, peace. Please give me shelter. I am a small fish and the big fish in the pond will eat me if you throw me back.' He agreed to give it shelter and filled a vessel with water so that the fish could swim peacefully in it.

But now he saw that the fish had grown larger than the vessel. Manuji took the fish out of the vessel and put it in a large pot filled with water.

The next morning, however, when Manuji woke up at sunrise for his prayers, he saw that the fish had grown so much larger than the pot that its tail stuck out. He was astonished. How could a fish, that had been so small a few days ago, have grown so big that even a large pot couldn't contain it?

The fish pleaded, 'Prabhu, have mercy on me. The pot is very small and I feel cramped in it.'

There was a pond just outside Manuji's house. He took the fish out of the pot, placed it in the pond and went away feeling happy.

The next morning, however, he was shocked to see that the pond had also become too small for the fish. Its tail stuck out of the pond.

Once again the fish pleaded, 'Prabhu, you promised to give me shelter, but I have not found comfort in your care.'

When he heard that, Manuji pulled the fish out of the pond and carried it to a lake outside the town.

'Here, swim in this lake without fear.'

Leaving the fish in the lake, Manuji went back home. He was relieved that he had fulfilled his promise at last. That night he slept peacefully.

The next morning, however, when he opened his eyes, he was shocked to see that the fish had grown so large that its tail had reached the courtyard of his house. He got up quickly and went to the lake. He saw that the lake could only contain the head of the fish. The rest of its body lay outside on the ground.

The fish pleaded, 'O Prabhu, since the time I asked you to give me shelter, I have been unable to move and breathe freely.'

Manuji pulled the fish out of the lake and carried it on his back to the Ganga. When he reached the Ganga, he released the fish into the river and said, 'There now, I have placed you in the lap of the Ganga. You can either live in it or find another place.'

But, before he could even complete his sentence, the fish began to grow. It grew so large that even the Ganga couldn't contain it.

Manuji was astonished when he saw that. He said, 'You are a strange fish! You keep growing bigger and bigger. The rule of life is that every living creature adapts itself to the space available. But you continue to grow. No water on land can contain you. All right, the only solution left is to take you to the sea.'

So, Manuji pulled the fish out of the Ganga, lifted it onto his back and carried it to the sea. As he was walking towards the sea, Manuji suddenly recalled that a long time ago, Vishnuji had appeared on earth in the form of a dwarf and asked the demon king, who ruled over the earth, for as much land as he could cover in three strides. The foolish king confidently thought that a dwarf couldn't cover much land in three steps. So he agreed to grant the dwarf his request. But Vishnuji, at once, revealed his divine form and, in three large steps, covered the earth, the sky and the heavens.

The recollection of that event alerted Manuji. He looked suspiciously at the fish and thought to himself, in those days, when the earth was in the thrall of demons, Vishnuji appeared in the shape of a dwarf to save it from evil. Why shouldn't Vishnuji appear once again to save it from evil men who roam across it so freely? He can, if he so desires, crush them like ants. Manuji was still lost in thought when he reached the sea.

He pushed the fish into the sea and said, 'Now, please leave me alone. Grow as much as you want to in the sea.'

But even before he had finished speaking, the fish began to grow. It grew so large that it covered the entire sea.

When Manuji saw the spectacle, he was filled with dread. He bowed his head with reverence, folded his hands, shut his eyes and said, 'Prabhu, shanti.'

Then he heard a voice, 'O Manu, the earth is being tormented by evil men. But I will save you. Make a boat. And when the waters of the ocean rise and cover the earth, take a pair, male and female of each of the birds and the beasts that live, into the boat.'

When Manuji heard that voice, he said, 'O Prabhu, when the ocean floods the earth, will the boat made by my hands sink or float?'

The voice declared, 'O Manu, tie your boat to my whiskers.'

Manuji answered, 'I shall obey you. But what shall I tie it with? I don't have a rope.'

Immediately a snake glided through the waves of the sea.

'O Manu, here is your rope. Tie your boat with it.'

5

Suddenly, Noah's wife came running out of her house, her hands were covered with flour. There was fear in her eyes. Terrified, she cried Noah, 'O my husband, the oven is cold, the fire in it is extinguished and water is bubbling from its base.'

Noah immediately understood that those were the signs from God he had been waiting for, and said, 'Listen, the Day of Judgement is at hand. Gather all your children and go to the boat.'

His wife replied, 'I'll place a heavy stone on the oven. Then the water will not gush out.'

So, she went back to the house and placed a heavy stone on the lid of the oven. Then she returned to Noah and said, 'See, my plan worked. Water has stopped bubbling out.' But even as she was speaking, water flooded the courtyard of the house and burst through the door. The lid, with the stone on it, floated away in the water.

At that very moment the neighbour's wife came running out of her house. There was fear in her eyes as she screamed, 'Water is springing out of my oven like a fountain, and the courtyard is flooded.'

Other women too came running out of their houses. Each of them was terrified. They screamed that the fire in their ovens had been extinguished and that water was gushing out.

When water from some outside source floods our homes, we

can try to stop it, but what can we do when it springs from the very foundations of our homes?'

Now, it so happened that the fires in all the ovens in the town were extinguished at the same moment. It was meal-time, and the housewives had just lit their ovens and begun to bake fresh rotis. Well, the fire went out in one oven, and then in another, and in another. Damp patches appeared on the walls, then water started collecting at the base and, finally, it seemed as if the earth itself had cracked—water sprung out of the ground with great force. It burst out of the ovens, flooded the courtyards and submerged all the roads.

And, then, it began to rain. It rained so hard that it seemed as if all the gates of heaven had opened.

Noah said, 'The Day of Judgement is upon us.'

He quickly went to his boat, and took with him a pair, male and female, of every living creature. He pleaded with his wife, 'Listen, the final catastrophe is upon us. The lid on your oven was swept away like a leaf by the flood. Your courtyard is covered with water. Gather all your children and come into the boat.'

His wife, however, remained adamant, 'O my husband, I have lived with you in this very house for more than five hundred years. We have spent all our days and nights in it. Do you remember the days of sorrow we endured together in this house and the days of joy we shared? All my children were born here. I nurtured them with my milk in this very house. We greeted our grandchildren and great-grandchildren with joy here. Tell me, why should we leave our home now?'

Noah answered, 'O companion of my days, that house of yours no longer has a secure foundation. The foundation of the house laid by Adam is weak. Oh, it was my misfortune that I built my house amongst evil people whose misdeeds corrupted the world. Therefore, the Lord has now ordained that the house be destroyed. Before its walls collapse and its roof caves in, it would be better for you to leave it and come into the boat. From this day on, the boat is our only refuge between the earth and the sky.'

But his wife replied obstinately, 'If I can't find shelter in my own house, how will I find shelter anywhere else?'

Noah then turned to his sons and called to them, 'O my children, your mother has chosen to stay back on earth and be with those who are to be sacrificed today. Listen to your father, get into the boat lest you are left behind with the unbelievers and caught in the whirlpools of death.'

His sons decided to accept his advice and got into the boat. Only his eldest son, Canaan, chose to stay back with his mother. He said, 'O my father, why should I leave this house. My umbilical cord is buried here. Why should I turn my back on this earth which has sustained me and enter the boat in which you have collected a pair of every living creature?'

When Noah heard his son's arguments, he pleaded, 'Listen, my son, this is the Day of Judgement. That is why all living creatures, men and animals, are together in this boat. There is no other place of safety in this deluge, no other place where life can survive.'

But his son replied, 'O my father, it is better to die alone than to live with a crowd. I would rather drown in my own house than survive on a boat with strange animals surrounded by flood waters.'

It grieved Noah deeply that his wife and eldest son had decided to stay back on earth and cast their lot with the unbelievers.

The boat began to float on the water. With a heavy heart, Noah turned to bid farewell to the house in which he had lived for five hundred years. He saw that the house with its large gate, which his forefathers had built, was now desolate and surrounded by rising waters. His wife and son had climbed up to the terrace for safety. As he watched, the house slowly disappeared and the waters rose higher and higher.

It rained so hard that it seemed as if the sky had suddenly opened all its gates. It rained all day and all night. It rained day after day. It continued to rain incessantly for such a long time that the distinction between day and night, morning and evening, one day and the next was utterly erased. The land disappeared from sight so completely that it seemed as if it had never existed.

Then it so happened that the crow felt restless in the boat. It flapped its wings, cawed and flew out of the window. But it returned to the boat at once after circling the sky. Its return confirmed that water had covered the entire earth and that there was no dry place left for it to set its feet down.

After a while, the pair of mice on the boat became impatient. They scuttled around the boat to see if they could find a hole somewhere. When they found none, they began to nibble a hole in the bottom of the boat. The other animals realized what the mice were up to. They were terrified. A hole in the boat would destroy the last of the living creatures in the world.

They went to Noah and pleaded with him to stop the mice. Noah regretted that he had invited the mice into the boat and said, 'I am sorry that I gave them a place on the boat. They cannot go against their nature and refrain from nibbling and making holes.'

Noah ordered the mice to stop. But, when they refused to obey him, he waved his hands over the face of the lion and a cat jumped out of its nostrils. The cat immediately pounced on the mice and devoured them. All the animals in the boat praised the cat and thanked her for having saved them from imminent destruction.

After a while, it so happened that the dove beat its wings and flew away. When it came back to the boat with an olive twig in its beak, everyone knew that the flood waters had begun to recede and that dry land had emerged once again. A moment later, however, they were shocked to see that the cat had pounced on the dove and devoured it, before it had time to settle down.

'How could the cat do that?' they asked in bewilderment. 'It even ate the olive twig! Now, who will tell us where the dry land is? We are lost in the flood once again!'

It was very oppressive and humid inside the boat, but the cat seemed quite comfortable.

6

The flood waters were still in an uproar. In the hazy darkness, it seemed as if the sky above had dissolved into the waters below. They could not remember when they had left their homes or how long they had been tossed about in the midst of those thundering waters.

'Will we ever go back?'

'Where?'

'Home.'

'Home?'

They were bewildered and anxious once again. Home. The very thought of home threatened to shatter their sanity just as a storm threatens to uproot trees.

'Which home, friends? Look outside. Do you see any sign of a town or a building? Didn't Gilgamesh tell you that Utnapishtim pulled his own house down and built a boat?'

'Utnapishtim didn't do the right thing.'

'Perhaps. But, at least, he appeased his Lord.'

'And no noise on earth ruined the sleep of his Lord.'

7

Markandeya looked out of the window. There was darkness all around. Darkness and roaring water.

As the hood of Anantnaga spread wide over the waters, Markandeya drew back at once, and cried out, 'Narayana, Narayana!'

There was darkness all around and the spirit of God hovered over the waters; waters which had no shore and seemed to spread far into infinity. In that wild, roaring, infinite flood there was no beginning and no end, no time and no space.

8

They could not remember when they had left their homes or how long they had been floating like leaves in the middle of that vast body of water.

Then the crow became restless again. It flapped its wings and flew away. This time, it did not return.

They looked out of the window. It had stopped raining but water still covered the face of the earth. They could hear no other sound but the roar of the flood waters around them.

There was no sign of the crow anywhere.

'The crow is an intelligent bird. It will not return.'

'Well, at least, we know that there is dry land somewhere. Our boat too will find a shore. O God, show us a place where we can live in your grace.'

'O fellow travellers, do you still believe there is a piece of earth left where there is grace? We are surrounded by deep waters and there is no one who can guide us to that spot of dry land where we can receive God's grace. If only Noah were here, then…'

'Noah?'

'Noah is no longer here.'

'No!'

Fearful, they looked at each other and asked, 'Where is Noah?'

9

Then Hatamtai spoke the following *kalaam*, 'O my dear fellow travellers! O my good people, don't lose heart, be patient and see what lies behind the veil which God has thrown over the face of the earth. Follow my example. I have travelled across many flooded rivers in rudderless boats.

Listen carefully to what happened to me when I was searching for Mount Kohenazha. I was walking along, anxious and lost in thought, when I suddenly saw a beautiful and lofty mountain. I decided to walk towards it. After a three-day journey, I reached the foot of the mountain. When I stooped to pick up a stone, a fountain of blood burst out of the ground. I was puzzled but there was no one who could help me solve the mystery.

I looked around and saw a river flowing at the foot of the mountain. The river was flooded and I couldn't see the other shore. Puzzled, I said to myself: 'O God, how will I get across this river!' At that moment, I saw a boat coming towards me. I thought a boatman was rowing it. But when it reached the spot where I stood, I saw that there was no one in that boat. I was mystified. I took God's name and got into the boat. Then I saw a bundle in a corner. I was hungry, so I reached for the bundle and opened it. There were two hot *naans* and some *kebabs* in it. I was surprised and said to myself: 'O God, from whose *tandoor* could these hot naans have come?' It occurred to me that the boatman had, perhaps, baked them for himself. I was unsure if I had the right to eat food meant for others. But a fish put its head out of the water and said: 'O Hatamtai, these naans and kebabs are your share. Eat them without fear or hesitation.' The fish then dove back into the water and disappeared. I wondered who had brought the boat across the river, who had sent me that food and who that fish was.

10

Fish! Everyone remembered the fish with a start. They had forgotten about it. At first Manuji was completely bewildered, but later he tied the boat to one of the whiskers of the fish.

They looked out. It was still dark and the flood waters continued to roar around them. There was, however, no sign of the fish anywhere.

'We can't see it.'

'Look out for that fish. We are fastened to one of its whiskers.'

They gazed into the darkness. All they could see was the rope rippling in the water. There was no fish in sight.

'Friends, at least the rope is still there, floating like a serpent around the boat.'

'But there is no fish in sight. That is a cause for worry.'

They were apprehensive and filled with doubt. They recalled the events that had happened a long time ago, but they couldn't solve the mystery.

The boat continued to float. There was darkness everywhere and all they could hear was the roar of the flood waters.

Date of publication: 1987

7

The One-Eyed Dajjal
(*Kana Dajjal*)

1

Mohsin sat down on the chair next to *Abbajan*, who was smoking his hookah.

Abbajan turned to him and asked, 'Did you find out anything, son?'

'No, *Abba*, nothing as yet. The news is both confusing and contradictory.'

Mohsin switched on the radio and began turning the dial. After a while, he switched it off and said, 'Now, we'll have to wait for the news at twelve. Abbajan, you can understand Arabic, can't you?'

'I lived for a long time in those parts. Did you think I wouldn't be able to follow Arabic?' Then, he pushed the hookah aside and sighed, 'These are the last days of the earth.'

'What!' Mohsin exclaimed.

Abbajan kept quiet for some time, and then said, 'When our Huzoor ascended to Paradise...'

Ammi, who was sitting on her cot chopping betel-nuts, began to cry. She put the nut-cracker down on the tray and wiped her eyes with the hem of her kurta. Abba's eyes, too, had filled with tears, but he controlled himself, and with great dignity said, 'Yes, Huzoor walked past rivers, mountains and cities, and when He finally reached masjid-e-aqsa, He lay down to rest. Then Hazrat-i-Jibreel appeared before him and said—Huzoor, please come with me. Huzoor asked—Where? Jibreel replied—Huzoor, your sojourn on earth has ended. Now you must undertake your final journey to the heavens above. Huzoor stood up and followed Jibreel up into the sky. He ascended higher and higher. He passed the first heaven, the second heaven and the third. When he reached the fourth heaven, he met Hazrat Issa; then he rose even higher, till he reached the seventh heaven and had only a short distance left to reach Qausain.'

Abbajan suddenly became quiet. Drawing the nozzle of the hookah towards him, he started smoking again.

Ammi continued to cry for a long time. After she had stopped, she wiped her face and said, 'Things were exactly the same when there was a war in Tiblis. That was in the month of Tezi.' She sighed, and added, 'Son, those events happened before you were born. I was in the third month of pregnancy and, may Allah forgive me, *Badi Amma* had just got some new gold bangles made for me. When the war in Tiblis broke out, all the Muslims were outraged. Maulvi Zafar Ali and the Khilafat Maulvi came to us and said— Mothers and sisters, these are difficult times for the Muslims, take off your gold and jewels. I wept, but took off my gold bangles and gave them to the *maulvis*. After that, I took to bed for a month.'

Mohsin looked towards Abbajan who continued to smoke. From the expression on his mother's face, it seemed as if she had finally calmed down and had done her reminiscing.

But she began talking again, 'There is mercy in the heart of Allah Rasool. Before the month of Tezi came around the following year, Father had found a job and I got a heavier set of gold bangles made for myself.' She pointed to her wrists, 'I am still wearing them.'

She picked up the nut-cracker and began chopping betel-nuts again. After a long silence, she asked, 'Mohsin, where is Maulvi Zafar Ali these days?'

'He died some time ago, Ammi.'

'And the Khilafat Maulvi?'

'He, too, is no more.'

'Oh, I see. I was wondering why neither of them had visited us this year.'

Abbajan took a deep breath and said, 'We Muslims left most of our graveyards in Hindustan. There was only one graveyard for us in our village; even that has now been lost. Mohsin, did you ever meet Rais-ul-Ahrar?'

'Rais-ul-Ahrar? No.'

'That's right, how could you have? Even that old man is buried there.' After a thoughtful pause, he continued, 'Who knows how many of us are buried there? We live in strange times. I was deeply moved when I approached Madina because I felt as if I were walking with the earliest followers of the Prophet. When I reached Madina-e-Munnawara—*Subhan Allah, Subhan Allah*—what a place it was!'

Mohsin noticed that his father and mother had tears in their eyes.

Abbajan continued, 'There were hundreds and hundreds of white pigeons on that sacred dome, but there were no bird-droppings anywhere. Allah, Allah, even the birds revere that place!'

Mohsin was taken aback, 'Where do the birds...?'

'They don't.'

'They don't! How is that possible?' he exclaimed. Suddenly, a thought struck him, 'Why do so many pigeons sit there?'

'Why do they sit there? Son, I am sure it is difficult for you to understand why they sit there. The earth is inhabited by devils, by satanic creatures. Satan's brood is everywhere. Madina is a place that is sacred and pure.'

Ammi, still chopping nuts mechanically, added, 'How terrible the sacred dome would look if it were bare!'

Abbajan was quiet for a while. Then he said to her, 'Why don't you tell him about your nightmare?'

Ammi hesitated, as if she were trying to remember it. 'I don't recall all the details. I remember only bits and pieces of the dream. For instance, I recall that I was with you on a pilgrimage. A crowd surged through the holy place. And there were white pigeons everywhere, in the sacred courtyard, on the sacred walls, on the sacred dome. I don't know what happened after that. The only thing I recall is that I suddenly found myself alone and wondering—Where have all the pigeons gone? There were no pigeons in the sacred courtyard and on the sacred walls. Even the sacred dome was bare. I looked here and there, frantically searching for you. Soon after, I woke up.'

There was silence for a while. Abbajan drew the hookah towards him, cleaned the nozzle and began to smoke once more. He seemed to be absorbed in thought.

Suddenly he asked, 'Mohsin, is it true that their General has only one eye?'

'Yes, it's true.'

'Is it also true that he wears a green patch on his other eye?'

'Yes.'

Abbajan sighed and declared, 'They are the signs of the one-eyed Dajjal.'

Ammi was upset, 'Why must you let such evil words escape your lips?'

'Everyone says so. All the signs are there.'

'The Dajjal will appear only when doomsday is near.'

'But, Mohsin's mother, doomsday is at hand,' Abbajan insisted bitterly, as he pushed the hookah aside. 'Nothing can save us now.'

Those words had such a strange effect on Ammi that she began to cry again. Wiping her tears, she asked Mohsin, 'Son, do you still remember Badi Amma?'

'Yes.'

'Whenever a Hindu wedding procession passed down the lane, you used to run out to see it. Badi Amma used to shout after you— Don't go, son. It's the procession of the Dajjal. I used to tell Badi Amma—It's only a Hindu wedding procession. She always retorted—*Bahu*, one day the Dajjal will appear riding a donkey, accompanied by a band. Entranced by the sound of the trumpets and the drums, people will follow him. I would argue—No, Badi Amma, that is not a wise thing to say. How could anyone be entranced by a mere band? She would tell me—*Bahu*, the Dajjal will bring with him many things that people long for. There will be a severe famine in the land that year. People will begin to howl with hunger. The Dajjal will bring tons of *rotis*. He will take out a roti, dig some dirt out of his ear and rub it on the rotis. People will think it is *halwa*. That is all. They will follow him out of sheer hunger.'

When Mohsin heard that story, he began to laugh. Ammi was hurt, 'I didn't make that up, my son. You always laugh at what I say. But that is what your grandmother used to say. She must be lying in her grave and thinking—What a shameless grandson I have, he laughs at his dead grandmother!'

Mohsin was a bit abashed, 'Ammi, I was laughing at something else. It is strange that people will think that the dirt from his ear is halwa.'

Pushing his hookah aside, Abbajan reprimanded him, 'Son, I know that such tales are no more than a joke for an enlightened generation like yours. But, if you think about it carefully, you'll realize that at their core lie some hidden truths. Our Rasool and his disciples knew what awaited us in the future. We were prosperous once. But food has become very scarce today. Do you remember, Mohsin's mother, the cost of wheat when Abba was alive?'

Ammi replied, 'I only know that at the beginning of every month, Abba used to go to the market with two-and-a-half rupees and return home with a sack of wheat loaded onto the head of a labourer.'

Abbajan said, 'Son, that was in the recent past. Now, may God save me from speaking an untruth, but for two-and-a-half rupees you can't even buy a handful of wheat. Indeed, things have come to such a pass that unless America sends us wheat, we can't even fulfil our needs. And what does America give us? What it gives us is no better than the dirt from its ears.'

He sounded bitter. Mohsin didn't have the courage to contradict him, even though he was irritated by his father's tirade. Abbajan had been talking about the one-eyed Dajjal, but had ended his long recital with an attack on American aid. He couldn't bring himself to say anything at that moment because his father seemed very depressed.

Still upset, Abbajan added, 'These are terrible times for the Muslims.' After a pause, he added, 'According to legend, when the one-eyed Dajjal arrives, Muslims will be identified one by one and killed. In the end, only three hundred and thirteen Muslims will be left alive.'

'Three hundred and thirteen!' exclaimed Mohsin.

'Yes, only three hundred and thirteen. Many will be slaughtered; many others will join the procession behind the one-eyed Dajjal's donkey. Only three hundred and thirteen will remain.'

Abbajan sighed, 'May God have mercy upon us Muslims!' He drew the hookah towards him and began smoking once again.

Mohsin sat as if nailed to the spot. Then he stood up and slowly walked towards the verandah.

Ammi called, 'Son, ring up the newspaper office again.'

Mohsin dialed the number. He talked for a few minutes, put the receiver back and sat down on the chair in silence.

Abbajan looked at him anxiously and asked, 'Any news?'

'Yes, a cease-fire has been declared.'

'Have the Muslims laid down their arms?'

'Well, you can assume that.'

Abbajan bowed his head, lost in thought. After a long pause he said, 'We have suffered defeat at the very spot where our Huzoor rose from his grave and ascended to paradise.' Without another word, he covered the *chillum* with a plate, pushed the hookah aside and lay down on his cot.

Ammi continued to chop nuts mechanically. Mohsin was surprised that this time she neither cried nor said anything. She put the nut-cracker down on the tray, put the tray back in the *paandan*, shut it and placed it on the table near her. Then she stood in the middle of the verandah, muttered a few words softly, blew loudly and clapped thrice. After the ritual, she went back to her cot and lay down with her back to Mohsin.

Since Mohsin was not sleepy, he continued to sit as if he had been defeated and would collapse if he tried to stand up. He switched on the radio. He fiddled with the knob for a long time, before he found the channel he wanted. Restless, he began to turn the knob once more in the hope of finding some other channel. Fed up, he switched the radio off and lay down.

He lay with his eyes shut for a long time. When he grew bored, he opened them. The sky was full of stars. As he gazed at them, he saw a dim path winding its way across the sky—a path on which crushed stars lay scattered. A path which led to paradise. Suddenly, he remembered what Badi Amma had told him when he was still a child. 'Son, that path was made by the dust raised by our Huzoor's horse.'

'Did the horse go up to paradise, too?'

'Yes, son. Miraj-e-sharif is in the seventh heaven. Huzoor rode through the other six heavens on his horse.'

He thought about what Abbajan had said: 'We have suffered defeat at the very spot where our Huzoor rose from his grave and ascended to paradise!'

His thoughts drifted away from Badi Amma to the strange stories his father had told him that evening—'the one-eyed Dajjal, dirt from his ear, donkey, wheat, America, dust on the road...Abbajan is an expert at putting together Bhanmati's family. He can find connections between things which are totally unrelated to one another. We may be talking about the present, but he is bound to confuse it with something from the past.'

Mohsin was conscious of the fact that Abbajan's stories had cast a shadow over his thoughts. The past and present had become hopelessly entangled in his mind. With great difficulty, he separated the two, and came to the conclusion that the war was being fought in the present.

'I don't live among the first believers of the Prophet,' he said to himself. 'I live among people who are alive now. I am here, in the present. Abbajan and Ammi live in the past. The one-eyed Dajjal is the dark and horrifying shadow of that past in which they are lost. But what about the imaginative vision of my generation? What is it like?' He was puzzled by the question. After some thought, he concluded that since the present was confused, its visionary projections of the future couldn't possibly have any significance. Unable to think clearly, he gave up and decided that since the night was far advanced, he should go to sleep. He shut his eyes.

As he was about to drift into sleep, he heard Abbajan cough and sigh. He was surprised. 'Hasn't Abbajan gone to sleep yet? He seemed exhausted when he lay down. I was sure that he would sleep at once.' Then he realized that Ammi too was tossing and turning.

Old memories, bits and pieces of their conversation, drifted through his mind. 'Abbajan makes the strangest connections . . . says peculiar things . . . The one-eyed Dajjal, dirt from his ear, donkey, wheat, America . . .' Time and generations once again got muddled in his mind. 'Mohsin, do you still remember Badi Amma?' He was shocked to realize how many years had gone by since her death. He still remembered Badi Amma and his childhood clearly. 'How many marriage processions of the Hindus passed by in those days!' The moment he heard a marriage band, he used to run out. Badi Amma, too, would get up with a start, drag him back into the house and shut the door. 'May you be damned, do you want to become a follower of the one-eyed Dajjal?'

Bade Abba, a tall man with a white beard, would sit with him and explain the signs by which the Dajjal could be identified. He would begin, 'Our Imam . . . ,' and bow his head reverentially; Badi Amma too would say a prayer. 'Then, our Imam will reveal himself again . . .' His eyes would fill with tears. 'He will proclaim himself as the Prophet again. But the Muslims will not testify on his behalf. There will only be, according to tradition, three hundred and thirteen true Muslims left who will acknowledge him.'

Badi Amma would say, 'Arrey, there are lakhs and crores of Muslims. You mean none of them will hear the voice of the Imam?'

'They will. All of them will hear His voice. Indeed, his voice will be heard throughout the world. But there will be no Muslims left. Many would have been martyred; many more would have joined the procession behind the donkey of the one-eyed Dajjal. Only three hundred and thirteen will be left to testify. He will set out with that small number.'

Mohsin turned over on his side and wondered, 'Am I living in the past or in the future?' Past, present, future, dreams, reality— everything was mingled in his mind. He didn't know whether he was awake or asleep. 'Is the number three hundred and thirteen our past or our future?—In the beginning is our end...We had achieved our greatest glory there, but have now been defeated at that very spot...The one-eyed Dajjal will come with his band... The one-eyed Dajjal, the dirt from his ear, donkey, wheat, America...Am I in the past or in the present? Am I awake or asleep?'

When he opened his eyes, he wondered whether he had really been asleep. He looked at the sky; bright morning light had begun to slowly spread across the firmament. Most of the stars had vanished, only a few still twinkled here and there.—And that path in the sky on which star-dust had been scattered? Stars shine in the firmament at night and vanish in the morning...Has the *azan* been called yet? He didn't know. It may have been. But from a house, somewhere far away, he heard the cock proclaim the morning azan. When he turned on his side, he saw Abbajan kneeling on his prayer mat, head bowed in reverence, while Ammi sat with her eyes closed, counting her beads.

Date of publication: 1987

8

The Story of the Parrot and the Mynah
(*Totay–Mynay Key Kahani*)

The argument between the Parrot and the Mynah seemed to be endless. The subject of the debate between the two was the same every night—was man sinful or woman evil? The Parrot always began by narrating a story about an evil woman who cheated and tormented a poor man. In reply, the Mynah countered it with another story about a man who was unfaithful, hard-hearted and selfish, and a woman who was kind, chaste and innocent.

Actually, the popular *quissa* of the Parrot and the Mynah was also about the same debate. This time, however, there was an additional twist to the tale.

Other birds also lived in the tree in which the Parrot and the Mynah sat arguing every night. They were fed up with the unending debate. They came back to the tree after a hard day's work to rest. Some of them had built nests there, while others just roosted in the branches. In the past they had been able to sleep in peace. The moment darkness fell, each one sat quietly in its place. But ever since the day the Parrot and the Mynah had built their nests in the tree, the other birds had lost their peace and quiet. All of them were unhappy.

A Poodna and a Poodni also had their nest in that tree. The Poodni was particularly unhappy with the endless argument between the Parrot and the Mynah. One night, she was so irritated that she said to the Poodna, 'May God damn the Parrot and the Mynah. I am sure that they feed on the brain of a dog during the day so that they can bark through the night!'

The Poodna tried to calm her down, 'They torment each other. Let them be. They don't bother us.'

'O really! They don't bother us, do they? They have destroyed my peace of mind. In any case, what sort of creatures are human beings? Why does the debate about man and woman seem to have no end?'

'My good woman, don't you know anything about man and woman? Human beings are creatures who also inhabit this earth. The male of that species is called man and the female is called woman.'

'But what have the Parrot and the Mynah got to do with those strange creatures?'

The Poodna laughed sardonically, 'There is a profound relationship between them. Both the Parrot and the Mynah have lived in cages built by human beings. Men have invented many things, but the strangest of all their inventions is the cage. My love, a cage is a peculiar thing. Even if one manages to escape from a cage, one always remains trapped within it. So you must understand that the Parrot and the Mynah are still inside a cage. They are haunted by their memories of human beings. That is why they talk about them so much.'

'Then why don't they go back and live with them? Why must they ruin our sleep at night?' the Poodni asked irritably.

'O *nekbakht*, the Parrot and the Mynah are hardly even aware of our presence. Ever since they came here, they haven't even cast a glance in our direction. They carry on with their silly argument by telling each other real or imaginary stories about human beings. They picked up this habit of arguing from human beings. We birds, after all, don't know anything about debating.

It is against our nature to argue. We only chirp, warble and whistle.'

The Poodni interrupted him, 'My *Sirtaj*, I can't continue to live with those accursed ones anymore. My health is ruined because I can't sleep. Please find a solution. Tell them either to keep quiet or to leave the place. There are other trees in the forest. Let them go to one of them and chatter to their heart's content.'

The Poodna was now compelled to pay serious attention to the problem. After pondering over it for a long time, he suddenly fluttered his wings and said, 'All right, I'll go and talk to them.' Then he flew to the branch on which the Parrot and the Mynah were seated.

The Mynah was narrating a tale and was not too pleased with the Poodna for interrupting her so rudely. She said, 'Bhai Poodnay, what great calamity brings you here at such an unearthly hour of the night?'

'Arrey, Bahen Mynah, the two of you have ruined our sleep. Your epic debate about man and woman is so strange that we can't rest at night. The argument doesn't seem to have an end.'

'Yes, I agree,' said the Parrot. 'In fact, it has been going on since the day Eve tempted Adam to eat a grain of wheat. And over time, it has become more complicated. Anyway, I believe that I have finally separated the grain from the chaff and arrived at the truth of the matter. This Mynah, however, is stubborn. She refuses to accept the truth.'

The Mynah retorted quickly, 'You are the one who is obstinate. You keep saying over and over again—I don't agree with you, I don't agree with you. I have explained at length all the faults man has. I have told you about the evil he can do—indeed, is there an evil deed he is not capable of? But you keep repeating the sentence you have learnt from man—man is guiltless, woman is a store-house of sins.'

'O *nekbakhto*, if both of you keep repeating your own opinions, this argument will never end.'

Before the Poodna had finished, the Peacock, who was sitting on the adjacent branch, joined them. Encouraged by what the Poodna had said, the Peacock pleaded, 'Look, it is obvious that the argument between the Parrot and the Mynah is proving to be very expensive for all of us. My wife is restless at night. When she wakes up in the morning, she is irritable. This entire debate has caused a lot of ill-feeling in our family. I want to know how much longer this quissa about the stupid creature called man and the hag called woman will continue?'

When the Peahen heard the Peacock talking firmly, she too spread her wings, flew up from her branch and joined the fray, 'I want to know who these two birds are? Where have they come from? How are they related to each other and why do they talk to each other so intimately? The Parrot belongs to one gender and the Mynah to another. How dare they sit together on the same branch and whisper to each other so intimately throughout the night?'

That remark caught the attention of the Chakvi who was sitting on the tree. She nudged the Chakva and said, 'Arrey, why are you sitting here so quietly? Why don't you go and find out what's going on over there?'

By this time the Parrot and the Mynah had resumed their argument. The debate had become rather heated. That was bound to happen, because wherever human beings are involved there is invariably a fight.

'But, the Peahen said....'

'The Peahen always exaggerates.'

'But we should at least listen to what she has to say.'

The Chakva and Chakvi also joined the debate. The Chakvi spoke in support of the Peahen, 'There is, after all, such a thing as modesty. The Chakva and I are husband and wife, but we have never lived together on the same branch. Indeed, if I sit on one tree, the Chakva sits on another.'

The Poodni had also arrived by then. She too supported the Chakvi. The Poodna was wise. He realized that they were determined to give a different complexion to the entire debate. He quickly intervened, 'In my opinion, the real cause of the problem is that these two started telling stories about man and woman. These stories must end, otherwise we shall have a new problem on our hands and the peace and tranquillity of the kingdom of birds will be destroyed forever.'

The Chakva nodded in agreement, 'You are right, Poodnay. It is in our interest that this debate should end.'

The Poodni, who had become a little more confident by this time, turned to the Parrot and the Mynah, and said, 'O nekbakhto, if both of you continue to defend your opinions obstinately, this debate will never be resolved. Wouldn't it be better if you found someone who could hear your arguments and pass judgement on them?'

'That's a good suggestion,' said the Parrot. 'But do you know someone who will hear us out, consider our arguments carefully and pass a fair judgement?'

'Since you have spent a large part of your lives in cages made by human beings,' the Poodna said, 'I'm sure that you will never trust them to judge fairly. Why don't you entrust the job to one of the birds?'

'All right, tell us whom should we appoint as a judge.'

The Poodna turned to the Peacock and asked, 'What do you think? Whom should we appoint as a judge?'

The Peacock was flustered and confused, but the Chakva thought for a while and said quietly, 'In this forest there is only one wise bird. He is the Owl. He lives quietly by himself and doesn't meddle in the affairs of others. He is also a profound thinker.'

'You are absolutely right,' said the Poodna. 'We should submit ourselves to his esteemed judgement. The Owl will settle this case wisely. What do you think Mynah Bahen and Parrot Bhai?'

Sensing the mood of the birds, the Parrot and the Mynah thought that it was in their best interest to accept the suggestion.

So, with the Poodna in the lead, the birds set out to meet the Owl. When they reached the lonely corner of the forest where he lived, they saw him sitting on the stump of a dead tree with his eyes shut.

When the Owl heard the flutter of wings, he opened his eyes lazily and saw before him a large cluster of birds. He looked at them disdainfully and asked, 'Why have you come to see me at such an odd hour?'

The Poodna said respectfully, 'O wise and all-knowing one, on behalf of all the birds here, I apologize for intruding upon your privacy. We had to see you because we have a problem we can't solve. An endless argument between the Parrot and the Mynah has ruined our peace. O reverend bird, you are wise and just. Please resolve the conflict between the two of them so that we can lead a life of tranquillity once again.'

'What is the argument about, dear friends?'

'It is about who is more virtuous and who is more sinful—man or woman? The Mynah says that woman is virtuous and man is evil, but the Parrot claims that man is virtuous and woman is evil.'

The Owl was visibly upset when he realized that the problem was about human beings. He said angrily, 'O sweet-singing birds, why have you brought an argument about those creatures to me? You want to know who is better—man or woman? Woman is a store-house of troubles and man is the very personification of mischief. Both are of the same kind, both belong to the same species. The sight of a human being is always inauspicious, though they claim that it is I who am inauspicious. Human beings are responsible for all the destruction, yet they think that I am the cause of the evil things that happen to them. Indeed, it is this belief of theirs that has made me lose heart. I hate the very sight of human beings and prefer dark and silent nights.

Unfortunately, those vile creatures are determined to cause more mischief and violate the sanctity of the night. Not satisfied with the noise they make during the day, they have invented machines to destroy the silence of the night. They have also discovered electricity so that they can dispel darkness. Where can we, seekers of darkness and solitude, now hide? Those evil-minded creatures have invaded every corner of this earth.

Only the other day, a swarm of half-dead ducks came here in search of refuge. They were exhausted and trembling with fear. Wondering why they had come so far away from home to find shelter in our forest, I asked—Dear friends, what calamity has befallen you? Why have you left the cool comfort of your lakes and come to this ruin to seek shelter? Here you will be uncomfortable and miserable.

They sighed—What lakes? Our lakes are covered with oil. Human beings, in their greed, have even bored deep into ocean floors. They have poisoned all the waters of the earth.

I was stunned when I learnt that those wretched creatures had not only polluted the air, but had also poisoned the waters. In despair, I looked up towards heaven. They had covered the sky with smoke, choking the birds flying through it.'

The Owl's speech stunned the birds that had gone to see him. After some time the Poodna asked, 'O wise one, what you have told us about human beings is depressing. Will their actions destroy us? Why do they hate us?'

'Human beings hate themselves too. They have also sown the seeds of their own destruction.'

'They should at least think about what they are doing,' the Poodna exclaimed.

The Chakva said, 'How can they? They don't have any intelligence.'

The Owl nodded in agreement and added sadly, 'Those bloody fools have intelligence, but they don't have wisdom.'

'When will they become wise?'

'Poodnay, your question is difficult to answer,' the Owl replied. 'In fact, I can't answer it.'

'Then who can?'

The Owl thought for a long time and then said, 'Far from here is a dense forest at the foothills of the Himalayas. In the middle of the forest is a peepul tree. An old crow lives there. The birds of the forest call him Kaga Muni. Perhaps he has an answer to your question.'

The Poodna turned to his fellow birds and said, 'Friends, let's go to see Kaga Muni. Maybe he can answer our question.'

So, with the Poodna in the lead, the birds formed a caravan and flew towards the foothills of the Himalayas. On the way they met a Partridge who asked them, 'Where are all of you going, friends?'

The Poodna answered, 'We are going to see Kaga Muni to find out when human beings will become wise. Would you like to come with us?'

The Partridge laughed, 'Human beings and wisdom! You want to find out when human beings will become wise! O wonderful are the ways of God!' Then, spreading his wings, he flew away chuckling and muttering endlessly to himself, 'Human beings and wisdom! O wonderful are the ways of God! Human beings and wisdom! O wonderful are the ways of God!'

After enduring many hardships, the birds arrived at the forest at the foothills of the Himalayas. They saw a huge crow sitting on a branch of a tall peepul tree in the middle of the forest. One of his wings was black and the other white. His eyes were shut and his beak was buried in his feathers.

The Poodna approached him and said respectfully, 'O Kaga Muni, we have come from a distant forest to see you.'

Kaga Muni opened his eyes and asked, 'Why?'

'We have come to ask you a question, Kaga Muni. When will human beings become wise?'

Kaga Muni sighed, 'O innocent ones, you have done to me exactly what I did to my father.'

'What was that, Kaga Muni?'

'My father had been meditating for a thousand years. As a result of his meditation the black colour on his wings had been washed away. Only a single black spot remained on one of his legs. I disrupted his concentration and said—Father, may I ask you a question?

He opened his eyes—Ask.

Father, when will human beings become wise? I want to know.

My father glared at me angrily and asked—Son, where have you been?

Father, when I was flying over Kurukshetra, I saw men kill one another. The whole field was soaked with blood.

My father replied—Son, I warned you never to go towards cities where human beings live and never talk about them. Once upon a time, we used to have white feathers. The sins and cruelties of human beings turned them black. I decided to undertake a long penance to wash off those sins and turn our feathers white again. Unfortunately, you didn't take my advice. You went to places where human beings live and you talked about them. You have ruined everything I have achieved thus far through penance. I have now reached the end of my life. If you have the courage, take my place, perform the necessary rites and turn the feathers of your species white again.

My father then gave up his life. I mourned his death and sat down to meditate in his place. Now you have ruined my meditation. I must leave this place and find another forest where I can meditate in peace and will never again hear the name of man.'

Kaga Muni flapped his wings and got ready to fly away. But before he could take to the sky, the Poodna asked him anxiously, '*Muniji*, if you refuse to answer our question, who will?'

Kaga Muni thought for awhile and then replied, 'In the south, on the other side of the river Tapti, there is an old Shiva temple. A Blue Jay lives on its highest turret. He knows about everything that has happened in the world through the ages. Go and ask him.'

So, with the Poodna in the lead, the Peacock and the Peahen, the Chakva and the Chakvi, the Parrot and the Mynah, along with several other birds, flew south and reached the old Shiva temple on the banks of the river Tapti.

When the Blue Jay heard the sound of the wings, and the twittering of birds, he opened his eyes and asked, 'Friends, where have you come from and why?'

'Maharaj,' the Poodna said, 'we have come from a far off forest. We had to ask a number of birds the directions to this place. We want to ask you a question that has been troubling us. Every bird we have thus far asked has turned away from us and flown away. Disappointed, we have finally come to you for an answer.'

'What is your question, my friends?'

'Maharaj, our question is this—When will human beings become wise?'

The Blue Jay looked at the Poodna and his companions in surprise and said, 'O innocent birds, you must be out of your minds to even ask such a question. Don't you see that my neck is blue? Don't you know that it turned blue when I drank all the poison human beings spilled in the sea? But now human beings have polluted the seas again. They have also polluted the forests and the hills and the sky. Human beings, my friends, are fools.'

'Maharaj', the Poodna said, 'that is exactly what's worrying us. Will they ever become wise?'

'My dear birds, like you, all living creatures have their share of wisdom,' the Blue Jay replied. 'But human beings are strange animals. They have the intelligence to conquer the skies, but they have no wisdom.'

The Poodna felt sorry for human beings and wondered, 'Maharaj, if I give my share of wisdom to them, will they begin to act wisely?'

The Blue Jay laughed and said sadly, 'Poodnay, haven't you heard the story of the crow who tried to teach a man?'

The Blue Jay then narrated the following story:

'A long time ago, there was a man called Adam. He was, perhaps, the first man on earth. He had two sons. One of them was very foolish. He killed his brother. After killing him, he didn't know what to do with the body. The foolish son lifted his brother's body on his back and wandered across the entire world searching for a place where he could hide it. He got tired and his back began to ache. A crow took pity on him and said—Foolish man, how long will you carry your brother's dead body on your back? Feeling miserable, the man asked—How can I get rid of this burden? The crow gave him the following advice—Dig a hole in the ground and bury it. Well, that is what the foolish man did.

When the crow narrated this incident to his father, he cursed him and said—Son, you don't know what you have done! You have committed a great sin.

Bewildered, the son replied—I only gave him advice. Tell me, how have I sinned?

The crow's father continued to lament—You have committed a great sin. We were born with white feathers. Now, as a punishment for your sins, our feathers will turn black.

Father, why should our feathers turn black? I only took pity on the fool and gave him advice.

O, my innocent son, to give advice to a fool is like giving a razor to a monkey. Do you know what that fool will now do? He will commit more murders, and as a result of your advice, hide the corpses. We will be tainted by his sins and must bear the consequences. That is why our feathers will turn black.'

The birds thought about the story for a while. The Parrot and the Mynah were shocked.

After a long time, the Poodna asked, 'Maharaj, what should the crow have done?'

The Blue Jay replied, 'Friends, keep your advice to yourselves. No one can give wisdom to another. A fool will always remain a fool. And human beings are fools.'

The Blue Jay's blunt reply made the birds very sad. They returned to their forest and resumed their places on the trees. All of them were silent and morose. The Parrot and the Mynah were totally dejected. Neither of them uttered a word.

The Chakvi, however, couldn't restrain herself for long. She turned to the Chakva and asked, 'O Sirtaj, what's happened to the Parrot and the Mynah? There was a time when they used to talk about man and woman as if there were no other living creatures on this earth. But now it seems as if they have lost their tongues.'

The Chakva smiled, 'O my dear wife, they have finally become wise and escaped their cages.'

Date of publication: 1987

9

Leaves
(*Patey*)

He went back to the same lane the next day. He knocked at the same door. The same woman with soft feet opened the door and stood before him. His eyes lowered, he held out his bowl for alms. When he received the food, he left. That was the rule of the bhikshus.

He had received alms from countless women at countless doors, but he had never raised his eyes to look at them. He knew that, of all the five senses, the eye was the most vulnerable to sin. The eye, easily enchanted by the beauty of the world, led man astray. A man who was caught in the net of *maya* suffered. It was the eye that deceived. The wise man, therefore, kept his eyes shut, refused to be deceived and so saved himself from suffering. That was why he never raised his eyes to see whose hands gave him alms.

Even at the door he didn't lift his eyes to look at the face of the woman who received him everyday. He only saw a pair of soft feet come to the door for a moment and then disappear.

After the first day, he went back to that door the next day and the day after. He went back to it again and again. The woman always gave him alms with great reverence.

It was *Basant panchami*. Yellow sarees fluttered in the breeze in every house, in every lane. It was as if mustard flowers had blossomed in the lanes instead of the fields, and marigolds had filled the houses with their fragrance.

That day he knocked at the same door once again. The same woman with soft feet came to the door again. But that day her feet were painted with mehndi. With his eyes lowered, he looked at those feet and was astonished to see how beautiful mehndi looked on fair feet. The feet of that woman, with mehndi designs, were like works of art. He stared at them as if in a trance. He forgot to beg for alms.

'Bhikshuji, please hurry up! It's a festival day today.'

He had never heard her voice before. As he lifted his bowl for alms, he couldn't resist lifting his eyes. And then he couldn't lower them again. He was fascinated by the beauty of that woman. Her face was like the moon, her hair was dark like rain clouds, her eyes were like the eyes of a doe, her neck was graceful like that of a peacock, her breasts were like ripe pears, her hips were heavy, her waist was slender, her saree was yellow like the flowers of the mustard and she wore a red bindi on her forehead. He was so enchanted that he gazed at her without being conscious of anything else around him.

The woman was shocked. The plate, full of food, slipped from her hand and fell to the ground.

On that sacred day, Sanjaya returned to his monastery with an empty bowl. He was very perturbed.

'Have I fallen in love?' he wondered.

He thought for a long time, but he remained confused. It was as if he had lost his reason. Finally, he went to Ananda and said, 'Prabhu, I am very perturbed.'

Ananda looked at him searchingly and asked, 'Why?'

'Because of a woman.'

'A woman?'

'Yes, a woman.' Then Sanjaya told him his sad story.

Ananda stared at Sanjaya in surprise as he narrated his tale. Then he closed his eyes and remained silent for some time. After a while he opened his eyes and said, 'Bandhu, city streets and houses spread before us nets of attachment. The rule for a bhikshu is that he should wander from street to street and from door to door. One day he should ask for alms at one house, the next day at another. O fool, you didn't obey that rule. You did exactly what Sundersamudra did.'

'What did Sundersamudra do?'

'Don't you know what he did?'

'No, Prabhu, I don't know what he did.'

Then Ananda told Sanjaya the story of Sundersamudra.

The Story of Sundersamudra

It was Janamashtami. The night was lovely and the stars twinkled amidst the clouds in the sky. An old man and an old woman sat in the darkness of their haveli weeping bitterly.

A dancing girl, who was passing by, stopped and asked them in surprise, 'Why are you weeping so bitterly? What misfortune has befallen you? On Janamashtami day, when every man, woman and child is full of joyous celebration, why do you sit here shedding tears?'

They replied sorrowfully, 'Oh, we'll never celebrate Janamashtami or Holi or Diwali again! We have lost our son. Every moment of our lives reminds us of him. We can do nothing but weep.'

'You have lost your son!'

'Yes, we had only one son. We have lost him. Now there is nothing but darkness for us in this world.'

'How did you lose him?'

'One day, Lord Buddha walked through this town. The sermon he preached so influenced our son that he gave up his life of pleasure, shaved his head, put on yellow robes and joined the disciples of the Sakyamuni.'

'What is your son's name?'

'Sundersamudra.'

'I'll bring him back.'

'You don't know what you are saying, woman! Has a follower of the Sakyamuni ever returned?'

Annoyed, the dancing girl said, 'If he is a *muni* of one kind, I am a muni of another kind.'

She made inquiries about the Sakyamuni, discovered the name of the town where he was staying and found out where the bhikshus went to beg for food. She went to the same town and rented a large haveli there.

Sundersamudra used to go to that town every day with his bowl to beg for alms. He wandered from lane to lane begging. One day he happened to pass through the lane in which the dancing girl had rented a haveli. The dancing girl had, of course, been on the lookout for him. She went to the door herself with a plate full of food. She talked so sweetly while she gave him alms that Sundersamudra went back to her lane the next day and stood in front of the door of her house.

He became so attached to that house that he stopped wandering from lane to lane. He would go and stand before her door every day and leave with a bowl full of food.

One day, the dancing girl cleverly suggested, 'Bhikshuji, if the rules of your order permit, why don't you stay here today and eat your food. My home will be blessed and will be filled with the radiance of the four moons.'

Sundersamudra thought for a while and then said to himself, 'Tathagata never turned down anyone's request. He didn't even refuse to eat meat when a fool offered it to him. I, too, should follow the same principle of action.'

So, that day Sundersamudra sat in the verandah of the dancing girl's house and ate his food. The following day the dancing girl made the same request and once again Sundersamudra accepted her invitation. Well, Sundersamudra began to sit in that verandah every day to eat his food.

Having persuaded Sundersamudra to eat in the verandah of her house, the dancing girl bribed the children of the lane to scream and shout near her house the moment the bhikshu sat down to eat his food.

'Raise a lot of noise and dust,' she urged them. 'I shall pretend to be angry and scold you. But you should refuse to obey me.'

The next day the children did as they had been asked to. The dancing girl shouted at them angrily, but they turned a deaf ear to all she said.

When Sundersamudra sat down to eat his food, the dancing girl stood before him with folded hands and said, 'Prabhu, the children of the lane are very naughty. They make a lot of noise and raise a lot of dust, and they don't let you eat in peace. I would be deeply honoured if you were to come inside.'

Sundersamudra once again recalled the Buddha's principles of action and quietly accepted the dancing girl's invitation. From that day onwards, Sundersamudra began to eat his food inside the house.

When he sat down to eat, the dancing girl served him with great reverence. But while she waited on him, she did not fail to reveal her charms and graces. How very graceful she was and how very beautiful! Her face was fair, her cheeks were like ripe pomegranates, her plaited hair swayed with the sensuousness of a snake, her eyebrows were arched like two bows, her breasts were round and full, her waist was slim, and her hips heavy. Whenever Sundersamudra glanced at her, he began to feel weak with desire.

The all-knowing and wise Tathagata soon realized that one of his bhikshus was in trouble. Those days Tathagata was living with the monks of his order in Ananthapandaka's garden on the outskirts of Sravasthi. He called all the monks of his order together to listen to a sermon. When they had all gathered together, Tathagata sat cross-legged under a mango tree with his eyes shut. After some time he opened his eyes and gazed at the assembled monks. Full of wisdom and compassion, he examined Sundersamudra's face. He looked steadily at him for a while and asked, 'Sundersamudra, why is your heart so perturbed?'

Bowing his head, Sundersamudra stammered, 'O Tathagata, I have formed an attachment.'

Tathagata continued to gaze at him and said, 'Attachment causes suffering. Desire ruins man. Even those monkeys, who understood the dangers of enchantment and desire and turned away from it, are superior to men who long for worldly pleasure.'

Curious, the bhikshus asked, 'Tathagata, who were those good monkeys and where did they live?'

'Haven't you heard the story of the good monkeys?'

The Jataka Tale of the Good Monkeys

Years and years ago, far from the realms of man, in a forest at the foothills of the Himalayas, lived a large troop of monkeys. One day it so happened that a hunter wandered into the forest. After much effort, he managed to trap one of the monkeys. He took that monkey to Benaras and offered him to the king as a gift.

The monkey served the king so faithfully that he was granted his freedom. When he returned home at last, all the other monkeys surrounded him.

'O bandhu,' they cried, 'where were you all these days?'

'O bandhu, I was amongst human beings.'

'Amongst human beings! Really? Tell us what they are like.'

'O bandhu, don't ask me that!'

'But we want to know.'

'All right, if you insist, let me tell you. Like us, human beings are also divided into males and females. The human male, however, has long hair on his chin and the human female has large breasts, so large that they bounce. The female, with large breasts, entices the male with the long beard, traps him in nets of desire, and makes him suffer.'

The monkeys covered their ears with their hands and said, 'Enough, bandhu, enough! We have heard enough!'

Then they decided to leave the place where they had heard the tale of evil deeds forever.

Tathagata ended the story and fell silent. Then, a while later, he said, 'O bhikshus, I was the monkey who told that tale and you were the monkeys who heard it.'

Surprised, one of the bhikshus asked, 'O Tathagata, how do women make men suffer? Aren't men stronger and women weaker?'

Tathagata said, 'O innocent ones! So what if women are physically weaker. They are far cleverer than men and can disarm them easily. Haven't you heard the Jataka tale about the clever princess?'

'No, Tathagata.'

The Jataka Tale about the Clever Princess

A long, long time ago, the King of Benaras went to Taxila to acquire knowledge. He became very learned and very wise.

The king had a daughter. He looked after her with loving care and guarded her with great zeal. He didn't want her to fall into bad ways. But a woman, even if she is locked up behind seven doors, cannot be prevented from doing mischief.

Despite all the king's precautions, the princess caught the eye of a singer. The palace, however, was so well guarded that the princess and the singer could never meet each other.

The singer confessed to his old maid-servant that he was in love with the princess. He persuaded her to go to the palace and become the maid of the princess. She waited for the right moment to give the singer's message to the princess.

One day, as the maid was combing the hair of the princess and searching for lice, she deliberately scratched the princess' head with her nails. Familiar with the tricks of enticement and love, the princess at once guessed that the maid had a secret message for her.

She said, 'Arrey, why don't you give me his message. Speak!'

The maid took courage and said, 'He wants to know how the two of you can meet.'

The princess replied, 'What's so difficult about that! Tell him— a trained elephant, a dark and cloudy night, and a gentle wrist.'

The maid gave the message to the singer. He, too, was experienced at the game and understood the message at once.

He trained an elephant and persuaded a young boy to help him. Then one night, when the skies were covered with the dark monsoon clouds, he mounted his elephant, asked the boy to sit next to him, and waited for the princess below the palace walls.

That night, the princess declared to the king, 'Maharaj, the rain tonight is delightful. I want to bathe in it.'

The king tried in vain to dissuade her. But the princess insisted on going out into the dark night to bathe in the rain. She walked up to the parapet of the wall below which the singer was waiting for her on his elephant.

The king, once again, protested, but to no avail. So he followed her out onto the terrace to keep an eye on her. When she began to disrobe, he averted his gaze, but did not let go of her wrist.

The princess, however, was far too clever for the king. She pretended that she needed both her hands to unlace her dress and urged the king to release her wrist for a moment. At once, she placed the wrist of the boy in the king's hand and jumped down to meet the singer waiting for her on his elephant. They disappeared into the night.

In the darkness, the king didn't guess that he had been fooled. He continued to stand with his face averted, holding the wrist of the boy. After a while, his face still turned away, he walked back to the palace. He pushed the boy into his daughter's room without realizing his mistake, and locked it from the outside.

Only the next morning did he learn that the princess had eloped with the singer. The king admitted defeat and confessed that it was impossible to guard a woman. 'She can vanish even as you are holding her wrist!'

After he had finished the tale, Tathagata sat for a long while in silence. Then he said, 'O bhikshus, do you know who that king was? I was the king and had occupied the throne of Benaras in one of my previous births. That princess was my daughter.'

Then after a pause, he added, 'I could decipher the mysteries of nature, but I could never understand the wiles of a woman.'

Sundersamudra suddenly woke up as if from a trance. He realized how dangerous the beauty of a woman could be and resolved to free himself from the trap of the dancing girl. He promised that he would go and tell her never to wait for him again.

When he reached the house of the dancing girl that day, she greeted him with reverence and, as usual, invited him into her house.

That day she had persuaded the children of the lane to shout and play on the verandah of her haveli. She scolded them, but they refused to pay any attention to her. Then the dancing girl stood with folded hands before Sundersamudra and begged, 'Bhikshuji, these children are naughty and cannot be dissuaded from playing on the verandah. They will tease and disturb you. So, please come upstairs and eat your food in peace.'

Sundersamudra hesitated at first. Then he said to himself, 'People are like children. Their wishes ought to be fulfilled. That is the Buddhist principle of action. Besides, I shall never eat food in this house again. Who knows where I'll be tomorrow and who will own this haveli?'

So, he stood up and followed her upstairs. As he climbed one step at a time, he kept his eyes lowered. He didn't pay attention to the woman walking ahead of him. But the dancing girl, who was leading the way, sometimes stopped suddenly as if she was tired. Each time she did so, Sundersamudra bumped into her soft and sensuous body.

When they reached the terrace, she made Sundersamudra sit in an alcove decorated with flowers. Then, pretending that the climb had tired her, she sat down near him.

O bandhu, a woman knows at least forty tricks to entrap a man! The dancing girl knew all of them well! First she yawned and raised her bare arms above her head. Then she suddenly felt shy and lowered them with a coy smile. Then she looked at her nails and played with her fingers. Then she took the end of her saree between her teeth and blushed. Then, for no reason at all, she giggled uncontrollably. Then, immediately afterwards, she covered her face with her hands. Then she spoke loudly. Then she whispered softly.

At first, as if shy, she sat at a distance from Sundersamudra. Soon, she moved up close to him. Once she let the end of her saree slip down her breasts, only to quickly pick it up again and cover herself. Once she lifted her saree to reveal her legs and then quickly pulled it down again. Later she arched her body so far back that her clothes burst open to reveal her breasts, but she hurriedly covered herself up again. Once she leaned so close to him that her lips almost touched his, but she shyly drew back again.

O bandhu, Sundersamudra was completely bewitched! He forgot that he was a bhikshu. She was already burning with passion, and when she saw that he couldn't resist her anymore, that shameless woman tore off all her clothes and pulled off Sundersamudra's clothes too. They hugged each other. Their bodies pressed against each other, their limbs twined around each other, they...

Suddenly, Ananda fell silent.

Sanjaya asked, with a tremor in his voice, 'What happened next?'

'What happened?' Ananda laughed and said, 'Tathagata saw everything from where he sat under a tree. He saw what that shameless woman was doing to one of his bhikshus in an alcove decorated with flowers in a haveli in Sravasthi. Their bodies were about to dissolve into one another, when Amitabha appeared before Sundersamudra in a vision. At once, Sundersamudra came to his senses. He was saved from being drowned in the river of desire.'

Ananda fell silent.

Sanjaya thought for a while and sighed, 'Those were indeed blissful years when Tathagata lived in our midst. He could always lead a man, who was enchanted by a woman, back to the path of duty and truth.'

After a brief pause, he asked, 'Who will now save me from the deceptive charms of a woman?'

Ananda said, 'I will give you the same advice that Amitabha gave me. He said—Ananda, henceforth, you must be your own guiding lamp.'

When Sanjaya heard that, he thought for a while and then said, 'I shall be my own guiding lamp.'

So, the next day, as he left for the town with his begging bowl, he vowed to himself that he would not go to the lane in which that woman lived. But when he reached the town, he noticed that every path led to her lane. No matter which path he took, he felt that it turned back to that lane and led to the door of her house. He stopped walking and stood in thought for a while.

How small Sravasthi seemed that day! He knew every lane and alley of that town. He had begged in each lane, he had asked for alms at each door. But that day he saw only one lane and one door, where she stood waiting for him with a plate full of food. He tried to think of the other lanes in the town. To his surprise, he realized that the lanes of the town were spread before him like a net. And that in every lane there were doors at which women stood with plates full of food for the monks who begged for alms. Lanes, doors, women. He reminded himself that they were all nets of maya. Then he recalled the story of the good monkeys who had not only plugged their ears when they had heard about the deceptive charms of women, but had also left the place where they had first heard the story of sin.

'I should also leave this town,' he told himself.

Then Sanjay turned his back on the town and walked towards the forest. Soon he left all the lanes, doors and women behind. He wandered through thick and lonely forests.

One day, he came across an *ashoka* tree in bloom. He stopped under its shade and sat down to meditate.

It was the season of basant again. The mustard fields were full of yellow flowers. Marigold flowers had filled the air with their fragrance. The ashoka tree was so laden with leaves and flowers that its branches almost touched the ground.

When Sanjaya saw the beauty of the world around him, his heart was filled with ecstasy. He gazed at the ashoka tree for a long time. Then, in astonishment, he said, 'O God, is this ashoka tree so full of flowers because a woman injured it?' Soon, he was attracted by the beauty and delicacy of some mehndi bushes near by. 'Did those mehndi bushes, so lovely and delicate, inspire that ashoka tree?' It was then that the image of that beautiful woman in a yellow saree rose before his eyes. Spellbound, he gazed at the vision for a long time. When he recovered consciousness, he said to himself with a start, 'I am, once again, trapped in the nets of desire.'

He got up and said, 'I had sinful dreams under this tree. I must leave this spot at once.'

Sanjaya went on a long journey again. He wandered aimlessly through many forests. Days passed, years went by, flowers blossomed and seasons changed. Each season brought with it its own splendour, its own delight, and then vanished. Each season caused Sanjaya pain. Each season stirred the river of memories and left traces of sorrow. The fields of yellow mustard flowers, the air trembling with music, the sweet smell of mangoes, the swift wings of butterflies, the hum of the slow bee over honeyed flowers, the call of the *koel* heavy with grief, the fragrance of the *champak* tree, the sad jingle of bells on a dancer's feet. Every moment reminded him of the world he had left behind. And the image of that beautiful woman stood before him always.

Sanjaya began to wonder if every path, in every wild forest, led back to her door. He thought about it for a long time and concluded that the seasons were in secret league with the guardians of the five senses, and that the five senses invited suffering. He also concluded that a man could get trapped in the nets of desire in a number of ways. When he touched a soft petal or heard a gentle tune, when he was carried away on the wings of some delicate fragrance or was enraptured by a gorgeous colour. The truth was that every thing in the world could cause sorrow. When Sanjaya realized this, he was very sad. In his grief he said, 'There are lanes in a town and seasons in a forest. How can I escape the net of desire?'

Sanjaya was still deep in thought when the leaves turned yellow and began to fall. The days became sad. Dried, yellow leaves lay scattered everywhere. With every gust of the wind more leaves fell from the branches of trees and scattered across the earth.

'What is the significance of this season? Why do leaves turn yellow and fall?' Sanjaya once again plunged into deep thought.

Slowly, a dim memory of something he had heard a long time ago began to stir in his mind and excite him. He recalled a story which was entirely different from his own.

The season was the same, the forest was similar. Tathagata had chosen to begin his meditations when yellow leaves lay scattered on the ground. He picked up a handful of leaves, turned to Ananda and said, 'Ananda, have I gathered all the leaves of the forest in my hand?'

Ananda replied, after some hesitation, 'O Tathagata, in this season all the trees in the forest shed their leaves. There are infinite leaves scattered on the floor of the forest. Who can count them?'

Tathagata had replied, 'Ananda, you have spoken the truth. I have picked up only a handful of leaves. The same is true of all that we know. I have only preached as much Truth as I could gather in my hands. Like the leaves scattered on the earth, Truth is also infinite.'

The recollection of that story had such a strangely profound effect on Sanjaya. He stood rooted to that spot for a long time. After a while he sat down, cross-legged in the posture of meditation, under the shade of a peepul tree which was still covered with the splendour of leaves. He began to meditate on the season when the leaves turn yellow and fall, leaves that were infinite like the Truth. He watched them fall in astonishment. Then, slowly, very slowly, he shut his eyes. 'That which is outside me is also within me,' he said to himself.

His eyes shut, he sat in meditation for a very long time. He meditated for days, for years. When he opened his eyes, he realized that countless seasons had passed and that the leaves were falling again. This time his lap was full of dry, yellow leaves. His body had been bathed by a shower of yellow leaves and burnt dry by the heat of the sun. He raised his eyes and saw that the peepul tree was now completely bare. Then he looked all around him. As far as the eye could see, the earth was covered with yellow leaves, and as far as the eye could see, the branches of the trees in the forest were bare.

He looked into his own heart and said, 'I too have shed all my desires. They are now like these yellow leaves.'

After a long pause, he said, 'All seasons pass. Basant, winter, the monsoon. Flowers wither, perfumes scatter in the breeze, trees shrivel, but the season when the leaves turn yellow and fall returns eternally.'

Then his face lit up with a smile. He felt as if his hands were full. He stood up. He was now at peace.

He said to himself, 'My search has come to an end. I should go back.'

Sanjaya entered the forest, his heart despondent and his mind disturbed. He left the forest, his heart full of compassion and his soul at peace.

He walked out of the forest and went back to the town.

Sravasthi echoed with festive-mirth that day. The town had been transformed into a gorgeous garden. The air was heavy with perfume, the lanes were gaily decorated. Birds sang, flowers swayed in the breeze, women wandered through the lanes in sarees of fascinating hues.

For a moment Sanjaya thought that he should stand in the middle of the town and preach, 'O ignorant men, O dwellers of Sravasthi, don't lose yourselves in the pleasures of the senses. Flowers wither, perfumes scatter in the breeze, beauty fades, and youthful bodies sag. The seasons of beauty do not last forever. Only the season, when the leaves turn yellow and fall, returns eternally.' But then he realized how completely detached he felt from all that he saw around him. He felt no desire to speak.

He lowered his eyes and walked in silence through the streets of Sravasthi. He didn't raise his eyes even once to see where he was, before whose door he stood with his begging bowl. 'Why should I look up?' he asked himself. 'My purpose is to receive alms. Why should a monk bother about where he receives them, at which door and from whose hands?'

His lowered eyes fell on the feet of the woman who gave him alms. He was startled. He saw the same fair and soft feet decorated with mehndi.

'Is she the same woman?' He looked up in surprise and saw her standing before him. She had not changed. He remembered her in the same yellow saree, with the same red bindi on her forehead and the same plate full of food in her hands. He couldn't lower his eyes. He couldn't move. He stood as if in a trance.

In that one moment ages and ages seemed to have gone by. It seemed to him as if she had stood, generation after generation and birth after birth, at the same door and in the same manner; and that he had stood, generation after generation and birth after birth, before her, gazing at her in amazement.

Once again, his thoughts were troubled, his soul sorrowful. The season began to change. The trees grew strong and small green leaves appeared on dry branches. Full of doubt, he looked into his soul and asked, 'Have new leaves sprouted within me too?' Puzzled, he asked himself again, 'I followed the light of my own lamp. Where has it brought me? What leaves are these that I hold in my hands now?'

Date of publication: 1990

10

Platform
(*Platform*)

After a while, he was bored. He shut his book, rubbed his eyes and looked casually around him. They had all collapsed in a heap. Bedding, boxes, bundles and bags entrapped some; others sat on their luggage. They were all exhausted. Silent. Still.

Suddenly, one of them saw a man in a white uniform pass by and asked, '*Babu Sahib*, any news of the train?'

'No, none yet.'

'Any hope?'

'Can't say.'

After the man in the white uniform disappeared, another passenger, who was leaning against his bedding, asked, 'What did the Rail Babu say?'

'I asked him if him if there was any news of the train. He said there was none.'

There was silence once again.

The man in the brown bush shirt was very quiet and still. He was surprised to see him sitting like that. Earlier, everyone had been rather agitated by the bad news, but that man had caused the greatest commotion. Suddenly, the entire scene flashed before his eyes again.

'What, the train won't leave today?'

'No.'

'You mean the train won't leave today at all?'

'No, it won't.'

'How is that possible?'

'Sahib, we've given you all the information we have.'

Surprised and worried, the passengers standing nearby stared helplessly at each other.

'That's strange, Sahib. We know that trains are often late, but this is the first time we have heard of one being cancelled.'

At first, the passengers were a bit confused and upset. There was some commotion and consternation. Suddenly a crowd rushed towards the tables where passports were scrutinized and the luggage checked. The clerks were at their seats, but none of them was willing either to look at the passports or inspect the luggage.

The man in the brown bush shirt forced his way through the crowd, and reaching the tables, shouted, 'Mister, my visa expires today.'

'Well, we are not responsible for that.'

'If you are not, who is?'

'Forget these fellows; let's talk to a senior officer,' one of the passengers suggested.

'Where is the Station Master?' demanded the man in the brown bush shirt angrily.

The clerk who scrutinized the passports pointed towards a room on the other side, 'Go there and talk to him.'

The entire crowd turned to follow the man in the brown bush shirt as he rushed towards the room. Everyone wanted to enter the room first and tell the Station Master that the man's visa was going to expire that day.

Suddenly, a new group of passengers, waving their passports at the watchman standing at the iron gate, and followed by heavily-loaded coolies, rushed into the room. They were excited and in a hurry because, according to the information they had, there was very little time left for the train to depart. They pushed and clawed their way towards the passport counter and threw their passports on the table. But they were surprised to see that the table was bare, as if it had been swept clean with a broom. And they were even more surprised when the clerks refused to examine their passports and sign them. At first, they were confused, then they were angry.

'What! Did you say that the train won't leave today?'

'No.'

'You mean to say that the train won't leave today at all?'

'Yes.'

A venerable old man, dressed in an Aligarhi pyjama and a *sherwani*, heard the entire exchange patiently. A teenaged boy standing behind him, wearing blue trousers and a check shirt, was about to step forward and say something, when the venerable old man stopped him, and waving his walking stick, moved up to the counter himself and said, '*Merey aziz*, you shouldn't make fun of people who come from the other side. It's shameful.'

'*Bashao*, we are not making fun of you. All we've told you is that the train won't leave today.'

'Why won't it leave today? Do you realize all these passengers cannot legally stay on here any longer? My visa also expires today. I must, no matter what, cross the border today.'

'All that is fine, *ji*, but the train will not leave today. How can it when it hasn't even arrived from the other side?'

'Oh, so why don't you say that the train is late?'

At that very moment, the man in the brown bush shirt, still fuming with rage, returned with a crowd that was even larger than the one he had left with.

'Sahib, the officers here are pharaohs without power. They don't listen to anybody. They merely repeat themselves.'

'What do they say?'

'They keep repeating endlessly that the train won't leave today.'

'Excuse me, do you have a match?' asked the man who had been sitting next to him on the bench, reading the newspaper for a long time.

He brushed his own worries aside, took a match-box out of his pocket and gave it to the man with the newspaper.

The newspaper reader lit his cigarette, thanked him and returned his match-box. Suddenly, he too felt like smoking a cigarette. He took a cigarette out of his pocket and lit it. Then he opened his book, found the page he had been reading and looked around once more. All those who had been boiling with rage and shouting angrily, seemed to have now collapsed with exhaustion. The man in the brown bush shirt was sitting with his back against his bedding. He had been silent for a long time and was now dozing. His brown bush shirt was wrinkled and dirty. The venerable old man in the sherwani was sitting on his bedroll. His chin was resting on the handle of his beautifully-carved walking-stick, which he gripped tightly with both his hands. Other passengers, too tired to spread sheets under themselves, were sprawled on the bare floor.

Do people cool down so quickly after losing their temper, and do they adjust so easily to circumstances that...But the rising tide of thoughts was suddenly scattered, because just at that very moment more passengers, bewildered and annoyed by the news that the train had been cancelled, arrived on the platform followed by heavily-loaded coolies. Perhaps, another train has arrived from Karachi, he thought to himself.

Every time a train arrived from Karachi, a few confused and harassed passengers, still unaware of the actual state of affairs, would rush onto the platform, learn that the train had been cancelled, get angry, run here and there, corner a customs officer, ask him questions again and again, blow hot and cold and then finally, exhausted and disheartened, somehow make a place for themselves among other exhausted passengers and collapse in a heap like them.

Just as the new group of passengers, after a few sharp exchanges and quarrels, was settling down among the other sprawled passengers, and he had lit another cigarette and opened his book, a passenger with a cigarette dangling from his lips, walked briskly onto the platform followed by a coolie carrying his suitcase on his head. Looking at the passengers sprawled on the platform anxiously, he said, 'There is no sign of a train here.'

'Babuji, I had told you that earlier,' the coolie replied.

'All right, put the suitcase down here.'

After the coolie left, the passenger with the suitcase looked a bit lost, but the moment he caught sight of a man in a white uniform who happened to pass by, he confronted him, 'Excuse me, can you tell me something about the train?'

'We have received no further information.'

'Excuse me, before I left Hyderabad, I had made inquires at your office there and was informed that the train would leave today.'

'You were misinformed.'

The man with the suitcase lost his temper, 'Look here, it's very important for me to be in Delhi tomorrow. If I had known in Karachi that the train was not going to leave today, I would have changed my route or taken a plane. I am sure you don't realise how much I'll lose if I don't reach Delhi tomorrow. I'll sue you for the loss.'

'Sue us for the loss!' Surprised, the railway officer looked at the man from head to toe in contempt and then walked away.

'Well done,' congratulated a passenger who was sitting nearby. He had taken off his shirt, thrown it aside and was sitting proudly in his vest. 'That's the only way to deal with these fellows, otherwise they never give you correct information.'

That conversation over, the man with the suitcase stood around, unsure of what to do next. After some time, he sat down on his suitcase, turned to the venerable old man in the sherwani, and said, 'Pardon me, but you seem to have come from the other side.'

'Yes.'

'Did you also arrive today?'

'No, bhai, we have been in trouble since the beginning of time.'

'That's strange,' said the man with the suitcase slightly puzzled. He was quiet for a while. Then he turned to the man with the newspaper who was sitting on the bench opposite, 'Did you also arrive on the same day?'

'No, I live in Lahore. I thought that the train would leave today and that there would be a lot of rush. So, I got here before sunrise, when it was still dark. I have been waiting since then and there is still no sign of the train.'

The man with the suitcase stared at him for a long time, wondering how he could read a book in the midst of so much commotion.

'Professor Sahib, since when have you been waiting here?'

He looked up from his book and replied, 'Since eternity.' He bent over his book again, but after a pause, looked up and added, 'You are under some misconception. I am not a professor in any college.'

That answer left the man with the suitcase confused. He didn't know what the man with the book had meant or what he should say in reply. After that exchange he didn't have the courage to talk to any other passenger. He fell silent.

He looked up from his book and cast a fleeting glance at the man with the suitcase who was now sitting quietly. He felt that the man had calmed down and was about to collapse in exhaustion.

There were a few more passengers now.

At that very moment the Station Master happened to pass that way. The man with the suitcase jumped up excitedly and asked, '*Janab*, any information about the train?'

'We have no information.'

'You must have some idea when the train will leave.'

'When the conditions are normal.'

'When will the conditions be normal?'

'How do I know? In fact, once the conditions are disturbed, it takes a long time for them to become normal again.'

'In fact, they never become normal again,' he added sarcastically as he turned the page of his book.

'What do you mean?' asked the man with the suitcase belligerently.

'I mean that once the conditions are disturbed they never become normal again.'

That provoked the man with the newspaper to ask, 'Is that a rule?'

'No, not a rule but an observation. Oh, I am sorry, in these matters your observations would be of greater value.'

'Now, look here, Professor Sahib, the fact is...'

But before the passenger with the newspaper could complete his sentence, he cut him short, '*Janab*, I have already told you that I am not a professor. If you call me a professor again, you'll be responsible for the consequences.'

Having been rudely interrupted thus, the passenger with the newspaper fell silent and turned to read his newspaper again.

There was complete silence for some time.

It was broken only when the *Paandanwali Bua* opened her paandan and grumbled with irritation, 'All the damned paan is nearly finished.'

An old woman sitting next to her, whose face was half covered with a burqua and who was fanning herself with a fan made of palm leaves, said, '*Bibi*, give me a bit of paan to keep my wretched mouth busy.'

The Paandanwali Bua made a paan for herself and another for the old woman. Giving it to the old woman, she said, 'Bibi, remember this is the last one.'

'But, Bibi, you have to travel much further than me; you will have to buy more paan. Aren't you going to Sarsi? It is even further than Delhi. You will have to catch the train to Moradabad from Delhi.'

'Arrey, Bibi, I'll worry about that later. Let's first get out of Pakistan. This damned country seems to have put chains around our feet.'

The man folded his newspaper, yawned leisurely and muttered, 'May Allah have mercy on these people.'

The man with the suitcase asked, 'I didn't even have the time to read the newspaper in all the confusion; what's the news?'

Offering him the newspaper, he replied, 'It's Doomsday over there.' After a pause, he added, 'While they chant the mantra of non-violence and have great respect for Gautam Buddha, in reality...Professor Sahib, what do you think? Oh, I'm sorry, I called you Professor Sahib again.'

He smiled, 'You'll be responsible for the consequences... Anyway, what were you saying?'

'Well, you may not want to say anything because no matter what happens you have to live there. But, at least, one of us should ask them.'

'Forget it, Sahib. How many people will you ask?'

'Ji?'

'I mean to say that life is short and there are far too many questions to ask. Where will you go, whom will you talk to, what questions will you ask?'

'That is no answer,' said the man with the newspaper. Then he turned to the venerable old man who had been sitting for some time with his eyes shut and asked, 'Qibla, what is your opinion about violence and bloodshed?'

The venerable old man ran his fingers through his beard and said in tones of deep sorrow, 'What can one say except that there is an ancient curse upon the human race. The legends say that Cain killed his brother Abel. Well, there has been nothing but slaughter and bloodshed since that day.'

'Maulana,' he said, closing his book, 'there was, at least, some reason for that murder.'

'What reason, Sahib?' asked the man with the newspaper with some acerbity.

'Sahib, sometimes one meets a woman who is so voluptuous that one can die for her or kill for her.' As he said that, he noticed that the words 'Ya Ali' were engraved on the ring that the man with the newspaper was wearing. 'Your ring is lovely. What kind of stone is that?'

'Dur-i-Najaf. It is a genuine Dur-i-Najaf. It's very rare. I was lucky to buy it from a jeweller in Mash'had.'

'"Ya Ali" has been carved beautifully.' He paused a little, and then said, 'Pardon me, but wasn't Hazart Ali against mindless violence and bloodshed?'

'Maula Ali is beyond praise,' said the man with the newspaper fervently. 'He offered sherbet to his murderer. There is no other example of that kind in history.'

'Yes, you are right, you are quite right. That's what I also feel,' the venerable old man said. He hesitated for while, and then continued, 'It so happened that last week in Karachi I got into an argument with a Baha'i. He had to run for his life from Iran.'

The man with the newspaper lost interest and said with ill-concealed sarcasm in his voice, 'And now you will tell me that last month you got into an argument with an Ahmadi in London!'

The old man laughed heartily at the jibe, and said, 'No Sahib, I have no intention to engage all the seventy-three sects in an argument. That is why I suggested we drop the subject. At the moment we have only one problem before us.'

'What's that?' asked the man with the newspaper sharply.

'The problem is—when will the train leave?'

Suddenly, the mood of the man with the newspaper changed. 'Arrey, Sahib, this delay is the limit. How miserable we all are! Look at all of us, stranded here, waiting for the train, helpless and without shelter, like homeless refugees from a caravan in 1947. The scene is exactly the same.' Then after a pause, he said in a slightly amused tone, 'But, Sahib, I am quite amazed by you. You seem to be at home here. Ever since I arrived, I have noticed that you have been calmly reading your book.'

'Hazrat, to tell you the truth, I have to travel a lot. The trains there, like the trains here, also run late. So, if I have to wait on platforms, what difference does it make which platform it is, and on which side of the border?'

The man with the newspaper scoffed, 'Of course, there is a difference, Professor Sahib. On a platform in Pakistan, you at least have the leisure to read a book.'

Not far away, a Customs Officer was trying to pacify some irate passengers, 'Bhai, be grateful that you are sitting here peacefully. The conditions on the other side are worse. Even if the train leaves now, it will drop you at Atari and you will be trapped there.'

'Janab, the fact is,' said a young man, 'that we are trapped either way. Why should we remain trapped here? Why shouldn't we be trapped where we are fated to be trapped?'

He turned away from the man with the newspaper and looked at the handsome young man, who was standing at some distance from them, with interest. He listened to the young man with attention and said to himself that the young man's logic was better than his own.

Just then the venerable old man in a sherwani, raised his chin from the handle of his walking stick and said to the man with the newspaper, 'Merey Aziz, we are trapped, but why must you suffer with us when you have a home here?'

Taken aback by the unexpected advice, the man with the newspaper was still thinking of a response when the man with the suitcase intervened, 'You can ask me the same question. But I was misled by the Railway Inquiry Office. Otherwise, do you think I would have rushed here?'

In the meantime, an important-looking officer arrived on the scene. His assistant walked a few steps behind him. The officer glanced at the passengers who were scattered everywhere on the platform, and then turned to his assistant and asked, 'Are there any pilgrims here?'

'We have made separate arrangements for them.'

'Do they have any complaints?'

'No, sir. They are being properly looked after.'

The officer turned to the passengers who were on the platform, 'How many of you are Pakistanis?'

Many passengers raised their hands at once.

'Why don't all of you go back to your homes?'

'Ji? What does that mean?' Asked a few people in dismay.

'We can't tell you for sure when the train will leave. And, since you can go back home, there is no reason for you to wait here without shelter and food.'

The man with the suitcase bristled at that suggestion, 'But I have come from Karachi.'

'Then you should go back to Karachi.'

At this the man with the suitcase lost his temper, '*Janab-i-wala*, it cost me a lot of money to get here. Are you suggesting that I spend some more to go back to Karachi and return?'

'Well, what can we do about that? If you don't want to go back to Karachi, don't. You must have a friend or a relative in Lahore. There should be no problem for those who live in Lahore. Why should they hesitate to go back home?'

When the man with the newspaper heard that, he got up at once, called a coolie, shook hands warmly with the man with the book and said, 'Professor Sahib, please forgive me if I was rude to you. I am sure that you know people in Lahore you could stay with. Why don't you leave with me? Spending the night here could be uncomfortable.'

The man with the book smiled, 'It makes no difference to me. There is always light on the platform. In any case, as you said, there is always enough peace and quiet on a platform in Pakistan for a man to read his book without being disturbed.'

The man with the newspaper didn't know what to say in reply. He took a visiting card out of his pocket and gave it to the man with the book, 'In case you have a problem, call me at this number.' Then he left quickly.

The Pakistani passengers hurriedly loaded their luggage on the heads of coolies and began to leave. Satisfied, the senior officer turned his attention to the remaining passengers, 'My advice to you is that, for the time being, you should also go back to the places where you were staying.'

That made the passengers very angry. Under no circumstances were they willing to return to the places they had left behind.

'I suggested that for your own good. If you don't want to go, you are welcome to stay here and wait for the train. However, we can't tell you anything definite about it.'

One of the passengers lost his patience, 'How long can we wait like this on the platform? You know how hot it is. Besides, we have nearly spent all the money we had.'

'I sympathize,' said the senior officer, 'but you are not our responsibility.' Then he turned around sharply and walked away with his assistants.

The passengers, who had stood up with excited anticipation at the arrival of the officer, collapsed in exhaustion again. No one said a word for a long time. Soon it was evening. Sunlight, which had been sparkling on the platform a little while ago was now shimmering somewhere far away, beyond the railway tracks, on the tops of silent trees, and was slowly fading away from them too. All the passengers huddled together in dejection and dismay. Night would soon engulf them. The teenaged boy in the blue trousers, moved a little closer to the venerable old man in the sherwani, nervous, perhaps, at the thought of the approaching darkness. He sat beside the old man in silence. After a long silence, he asked thoughtfully, 'Abbajan, whose responsibility are we?'

The venerable old man, who had been lost in thought, was startled. He looked at his son, considered a reply for some time, and then turned to the man with the book, 'Professor Sahib, whose responsibility are we?'

The man with the book raised his eyes and stared in silence at the old man. He then turned towards the teenaged boy in the blue trousers and fixed him with his gaze. Unable to come up with a satisfactory answer, he bent over his book again, but he could no longer read with the same calm concentration as before. He soon lost interest in the book. He realised that night had fallen. Sunlight, which had lingered on the tops of distant trees, had now vanished. Everything was lost in darkness. He took a packet of cigarettes out of his pocket. It was empty. He tossed it away, and then called to the teenaged boy in the blue trousers, 'Mian, come here.'

The boy walked up to him.

'Sit down. What's your name?'

'Misbah-ul-Hassan.'

'Are you studying somewhere?'

'Yes, at Aligarh. I am in the first year.'

The venerable old man in the sherwani felt that his son's reply was inadequate. He added, 'Professor Sahib, my son stood first in the Matric exam. I wanted to send him to Allahabad, but the Aligarhwalas put a lot of pressure on me, so I had to admit him in Aligarh. The university gives him a scholarship.'

'*Masha-Allah!* Sahibzade, will you do me a favour?' Then he turned to the old man and said, 'Can I ask your son to do me a favour?'

'Of course, of course.'

'Do you think cigarettes would be available somewhere nearby?'

'Of course. There is a stall on the other platform. I'll go and get them.'

'Thank you.'

'Eh, betey,' pleaded the Paandanwali Bua, reaching for her purse, 'since you are going, will you get me some paan for four annas?'

She opened her purse, counted the change, and said, 'Look, now my purse is empty.'

The young man was about to leave when another passenger asked if there was anything to eat, 'We must find something to appease our hunger.'

'The problem is that we have spent nearly all our money. We'll manage today, but what will we do tomorrow?'

'Let's look after ourselves today, and worry about tomorrow when the time comes. Eh sahibzade, since you are going, ask the naan-kebabwala to come this way.'

After the young man left, the venerable old man in the sherwani said, 'Professor Sahib, my son is very intelligent, but he asks too many questions.'

'At his age, he is bound to.'

'You are right. That's why I never stop him. Sometimes he asks questions which even I can't answer. But I say to myself, it doesn't matter, he'll find an answer to them as he grows older.'

'You are absolutely right. There are many questions which man can't answer, only time can.'

'Don't say that, Professor Sahib. There are some questions that even time can't answer. They remain with us even when we grow old.'

The man with the book fell silent and was soon lost in his own thoughts.

Slowly night fell. Concern about food became more urgent. Just as the passengers were wondering what to do and were ransacking their belongings for something to eat, the naan-kebabwala, who had been summoned by the teenaged boy in blue trousers, arrived. The passengers couldn't restrain themselves. Not having eaten since the afternoon, and finding the smell of kebabs irresistible, they pounced upon the food. Many of them even had something to drink with the kebabs. A bucketful of Coca-cola, Seven-up and Teem bottles was polished off in no time.

The man with the book also ate a little bit, drank a cup of tea and lit a cigarette. Refreshed, he opened his book once again. After eating a few kebabs, the Paandanwali Bua put a paan in her mouth, dozed for a while, woke up and asked the man with the book, 'Betey Professor, do you plan to read that book all night? That book will not absolve you of your sins. If you had recited the Kalma for half the time you have spent on that book, we would have been saved from the calamity which now confronts us.'

The old woman with the palm-leaf fan agreed, 'Bua, my *Taaye-Abba* once wrote down a ritual prayer for me. I am sure that if I had recited it, the train would have been here in an instant.'

'Then, why didn't you recite it, Bibi?'

'How could I have? Before I left home, I packed everything carefully, but I forgot the notebook in which the prayer was written. I suppose all these poor passengers were fated to suffer.'

After some time, when he looked up from his book, he noticed that both the women were dozing, though one was still chewing her paan and the other was still fanning herself. In fact, nearly all the passengers were asleep. The teenaged boy in the blue trousers was lying on his side, his knees drawn up to his chest, and was fast asleep. However, the venerable old man in the sherwani was still awake, and sat with his chin resting on the handle of his walking stick.

'Professor Sahib,' the venerable old man said, breaking his long silence.

'Yes.'

'I know that I am past the age when I should be asking questions, but I am rather anxious to ask one.'

'What is it?'

'All of us are trapped on this platform. We are neither here nor there. Whose responsibility are we?'

Again the same question. He was very disturbed. He wanted to ignore it and turn back to his book, but he had lost his concentration and could no longer read in peace.

The venerable old man gazed expectantly at him for some time and then said, 'Professor Sahib, please answer my question.'

'Answer?'

'Yes, answer. I have to give my son an answer.'

He hesitated, and then said, 'Qibla, I don't have an answer to your question. Maybe time will have an answer...'

'Time,' murmured the old man. 'Perhaps. Who can tell...?'

Date of Publication: 1990

11

Barium Carbonate
(*Barium Carbonate*)

I t had never occurred to any of us here, not even in our wildest dreams that something like this could ever happen. We certainly had our doubts, suspicions and misgivings but they were of another kind and even they came much later. In the beginning, when someone was allotted a house here, he thought he had been admitted into paradise, although in those days, too, there was room enough for complaint. There was no electricity and the road had not been metalled. We had to walk at least three quarters of a mile, over an uneven dirt path to the main road, before we caught sight of the bus stop. And the bus—it rarely came within the range of our vision, even if we stood waiting for it till our legs ached. But Ashraf Chacha brought the news that the construction of the road would begin next month, and that, thereafter, the bus would drive right up to our colony and run every fifteen minutes. In such matters, who could have been more knowledgeable than Ashraf Chacha? We believed what he told us. Besides, even the members of the Improvement Trust were human beings after all. They didn't have Alladin's magic lamp to help them build houses, provide electricity, construct roads and start a bus service overnight. In fact, even Alladin's lamp couldn't have performed a greater miracle. Had we not often seen things being constructed with our own eyes? Day after day, slowly and rhythmically, government workers broke stones and spread gravel; row after row of donkeys laden with bricks, and labourers loaded with trays full of clay, walked up and down. It seemed as if the entire process would never end. Till suddenly, one day, a house stood complete before us. Then, digging started once again, at the same slow and rhythmic pace, for a well. And after a lot of digging, when the water table was finally reached, *batasha*s were distributed, gas-lamps were lit, colourful carpets and white sheets were spread out, *agarbatti*s were burnt and milad was celebrated. Only after that did someone move into the house. But our houses were occupied even before they were ready. Many of them had not been white-washed; some of them had not even been properly plastered with cement. Their redbrick walls looked naked. There were other houses that had door-frames but no doors, and carpenters hammered and sawed day and night in the verandahs. But those who had been destined to move into them had already done so. It was as if in a village settlement, a lamp had been lit even before it had become dark, and then, imitating the first one, another lamp had been lit a few shops further down the lane, and then, other lanterns and lamps with mustard oil had been lit one after another till the entire street had begun to glow before nightfall. Our colony had been inhabited in the same way. Carts loaded with odds and ends, or tongas packed with families, stood before a house one day and then before another the day after.

And so, before our very eyes, our colony began to flourish. Soon we couldn't recall when we had come here or where we had come from, although there were some special events that had left their mark on our memories. For instance, all of us still remember that the first quarrel in the colony took place between Syeddaniji and *Ambale-wali*. Syeddaniji first picked up a fight with Ambale-wali and then with *Dilli-wali*. Unfortunately for Syeddaniji, the other two got the better of her. She sulked for a few days, but then relented, and declared, 'Look here, bibi, how many days do you think I'll live here? I should have gone on a pilgrimage to the Holy Karbala by now, but Mohsin's education has kept me back. The *America-wala* wants him to go to America on a scholarship. Once

Mohsin returns from America, I won't drink even a drop of water in this place. I'll get Mohsin married, and as soon as he utters the two words of consent at the *nikah*, I'll tell him—Look here, son, now lead your own life and let your mother take care of her own future.'

Strangely enough, all of us forgot what she had said about going to the Holy Karbala, only because wherever Ambale-wali and Dilli-wali went they thought it was their duty to tell everyone the second thing that Syeddaniji had said, and so the rumour spread that her son was going to America. It is also possible that Syeddaniji's son was so keen on going to America that we forgot everything else his mother had said. In fact, Mohsin, who was always critical about the condition of the road and the lack of a bus service, never talked about buying a bicycle lest the very mention of it became an obstacle in his path to America. On the other hand, Syeddaniji kept adding things to her household even as she continuously declared that she was going to Karbala. Soon after she arrived here, she bought some hens. Then she planted a neem tree so that, once it grew tall, she could build a *tandoor* under its shade.

All of us were sure that if that particular incident had not taken place, Syeddaniji would have forgotten all about going to Karbala. Life was full of difficulties here, but only Mohsin had to actually face them. As far as Syeddaniji was concerned, her life here was perfectly comfortable. Her greatest source of delight was the fact that she could buy fresh vegetables from the fields of Ramgarh which lay behind her house. Not only were the vegetables cheap, so were all the other items. Take, for example, fine-grained rice. How expensive it now is! Even when Syeddaniji bought rice, it was not cheap. She placed her faith in God, and bought some from a farmer. That rice was bought after a lot of thought and was stored with great care, but that which is fated always comes to pass.

In the beginning, the rice was kept in the kitchen. But when the rats invaded the kitchen, it was taken out of the sack and stored in an earthen pot. The pot was placed in a big wooden box in the storeroom, where some crockery was also kept. The box was then locked and covered with a tablecloth.

How the rats came to our colony and multiplied is in itself a tale. It has a strange beginning and a strange end. It all started with the lower drawer of Syeddaniji's meat-safe that stood in the kitchen. One night, it was left open by mistake. The next morning, Syeddaniji discovered that the lids of some pots had been scattered on the floor and the lids of the other pots disturbed. A little milk, which had not been used up for tea the previous night, and which had been stored in a pot, had been spilled and the pot itself had been overturned. Syeddaniji blamed Ambale-wali's brown cat and all the doors of her house, henceforth, remained shut against it.

Then, one day, as she was pouring milk into the pot, Syeddaniji noticed some black specks in the milk. They made her suspicious. When she looked at them closely, her suspicions were confirmed. The entire blame for them shifted to the milkman. Enraged, she accused him of spreading cholera and of abusing her faith in him. In vain did he plead his innocence, but he failed to convince her. How could Syeddaniji ever believe that there were rats in a house whose floors were made of hard cement and whose walls didn't have any holes in them? It was, of course, true that the land behind her house was overgrown with shrubs and grass, that it was used by her neighbours as a garbage dump and that her hens scratched through it all day for a few grains. In fact, one day, as she was throwing her garbage out of the kitchen window, she had even seen a long-wriggling tail in the bushes. But since throughout her life, she had mistaken the tail of a rat for the tail of a snake, and the tail of a snake for the tail of a chameleon, this time, too, she was convinced that the colour of that particular tail had instantly changed from yellow to red, and that, therefore, she had actually seen the tail of a chameleon. She knew that the chameleon had committed a sin by gnawing through Hazrat Abbas's *mashak* and that she should not spare its life, but she couldn't kill it because it had disappeared into one of the holes in the ground. Anyway, since that was the only tail she had seen after moving into that house, how could she possibly have believed what the milkman had told her?

One day, it so happened that the moment Syeddaniji entered her kitchen, she heard the utensils rattle and saw something flash past her like lightning and vanish under the meat-safe. Syeddaniji moved swiftly, picked up a long bamboo stick from the courtyard, came back into the kitchen and began to hammer on the meat-safe with the stick. The result of all this was that she saw the long tail, which she had noticed a moment ago under the meat-safe, disappear into the drain. That day she realized that evil did not lurk outside the kitchen but inside. Even then she thought that a rat from outside had merely wandered into the kitchen and that the kitchen could be made safe again if the rat were exterminated. So, Ambale-wali's brown cat, which had been reviled till the previous day, was specially sent for and locked up in the kitchen.

When the door of the kitchen was opened the next morning, she couldn't immediately determine whether the cause of evil had been eliminated, but she could clearly see that the brown cat had played havoc with the neat arrangement of the pots and the pans and the plates. So the following night, Syeddaniji carefully locked all the pots, pans and plates in the meat-safe. That night the brown cat did not do much damage in the kitchen. But when let out the next morning, the cat wandered freely through the courtyard and caused panic and fear amongst the hens. The timely intervention of Syeddaniji prevented any loss of life, but the hens continued to cluck in fear for a long time. After that day, Syeddaniji lost all her faith in external aid.

The following day, she gave a rupee to Mohsin and said, 'A damned rat has got into the kitchen from somewhere. Go and get me a rat-trap.' Mohsin disliked the idea of buying a rat-trap and carrying it home. Ashraf Chacha proved useful at that moment. He bought a rat-trap at Nasroo's hardware shop and had it delivered to Syeddaniji. The same night, Syeddaniji spiked a piece of roti on the hook in the trap and placed it in the kitchen. The next morning, she found a fat rat in it. Dilli-wali's son took on the responsibility of getting rid of that rat. As he came out carrying the rat-trap in his hand, a group of urchins surrounded and followed him, and several women came out of their homes to look at the culprit Syeddaniji had trapped, as if it had been caught stealing shoes from a mosque. The platoon of urchins marched far into the fields behind the houses. When the platoon returned, Syeddaniji, of course, came to know about the fate of the prisoner, but couldn't find out what had happened to the rat-trap.

After that it seemed as if peace had been restored in the kitchen once again. Syeddaniji began to keep things carefully in the meat-safe. She was no longer afraid of the rat, but she was still apprehensive of Ambale-wali's brown cat. Once a pot full of cooked *dal* was left outside the meat-safe by mistake. The next morning, Syeddaniji found its lid lying on one side and saw a crisscross pattern over the frozen surface of the dal, rather like a chain-armour. She looked up at the open ventilator and decided that a sparrow must have flown in and made the design with its beak and claws. But later, when she found that Mohsin's shirt, which she had forgotten to give to the washerwoman, had been gnawed through by a rat, she grumbled and cursed the plague-ridden creature who had got into the bathroom and made holes in her son's shirt.

The truth was revealed during Moharram. In a tearful voice, Syeddaniji announced that there would be a feast of *pulao* on the eighth night. She remembered the Imambara which she had left behind; she recalled the golden and silver *alams*, the chandeliers, the *fanoos* and the lamps hanging from the ceiling. She talked about the religious congregations that were held in the past when naan and *keema* were served for ten days. She described the *haazri* of the eighth night when people gathered in large numbers and ate *sheer-maal korma* till they were satiated. It is strange that the Yellow Quarter-wali, who came from the same area, remembered that Syeddaniji had stopped distributing naan and keema the year rationing was introduced. And then, talking about Syeddaniji's haazri and sheer-maal korma, added, 'Mian, as far as I can recall, we only saw pulao being served at Syeddaniji's place during haazri. We had heard that when her father-in-law was alive, he used to serve sheer-maal korma. Anyway, I don't know if those who said so deserved to be punished or rewarded, I am merely repeating what I heard.'

Syeddaniji had arranged dozens of religious congregations since she had moved into the quarters here and had also distributed *jalebis*. None of the congregations were as grand as the ones she claimed were held in her Imambara. For one thing, instead of being male congregations, they were attended only by women, and that, too, by women from the houses in the neighbourhood. Further, the ritual mourning was rather subdued. Still, the fame of the haazri on the eighth night at her place had spread throughout the colony and we had all mentally prepared ourselves for a feast of pulao. That is why none of us had foreseen what happened on the eighth night. Syeddaniji herself was so paralysed by fear that she failed to make alternate arrangements. When it was evening, she sent for Ashraf Chacha and gave him some money to buy jalebis. We tasted one or two for the sake of haazri and left. None of us uttered a word. In fact, all of us were stunned.

The Yellow *Quarter-wali* couldn't believe it. In order to convince her, Ambale-wali gave her an eye-witness account, 'Mian, I saw it with my own eyes. There was a hole as big as my fist in the wooden box.' Then she put her thumbs and two fingers together to form a circle.

'How could they cut through the box with their teeth?'

'*Ai lo!* How could they cut through the box?' Ambale-wali said. 'The box was after all made only of wood. And, Mian, those evil ones are Allah's curse upon us. They can gnaw through and ruin anything that is either edible or useful.'

Dilli-wali was so nonplussed that she couldn't say anything. Lost in thought, Yellow Quarter-wali also sat quietly for a while, and then exclaimed, 'Damn them! Do they have stomachs or mashaks? So much rice…!'

Ambale-wali cut her short and said, 'Mian, I, too, didn't believe it. But Syeddaniji held my hand, dragged me inside and opened the box to show me. I am not lying. There was only a handful of rice left… the rest were droppings'. A shiver ran through her body as she said that.

Dilli-wali shuddered and said, 'May Allah have mercy upon us!'

Yellow Quarter-wali stared at Dilli-wali, but didn't say anything.

That night, even women from distant houses came to attend Syeddaniji's *majlis*. It lasted a long time and there was a lot of ritual mourning. All that had happened to Syeddaniji had alerted the women of the neighbourhood to the danger. Dilli-wali took out her daughter's trousseau the very next day and spread it out on cots in the sun. Her daughter's dowry was intact.

She discovered, however, that her own dupatta, which she had starched and put away in a half-open drawer so that she could stitch silver stars on it after Moharram, had lots of holes in it. And when Ambale-wali sieved her flour, she found that it had more rat droppings than husk. Dilli-wali and Ambale-wali were very upset that the rats from Syeddaniji's house had also invaded their homes. Their suspicions and complaints were just. What was really surprising, however, was that, even though Yellow Quarter-wali's house was at some distance from Syeddaniji's, many of Yellow Quarter-wali's clothes had been eaten through. But what happened to Ashraf Chacha was really astonishing. The papers he had collected, to put in his application claiming compensation for property left behind in India, had grown so large that the clip that had held them together had bent and then snapped in two. He had, therefore, glued the corners together with a paste made of flour. By the next morning, the corners of all his papers had vanished. Shreds of paper were found scattered on the table.

Ashraf Chacha narrated that incident at the shop of Nanva, the grocer. At that time, Maulvi Usman Ali was also there, sitting in a wicker chair. He had his glasses on and was reading the yellowing pages of a book, three-fourths of which Nanva had already used for making small paper packets. He looked up from his book and said, 'What can I say? I had a rare manuscript, *Masnavi-e-Maulana Rum*, published in Tehran. The infidels have reduced it to shreds too.'

From Nanva's shop, Ashraf Chacha went straight to the shop of Nasroo, the hardware man, and bought a rat-trap from him. All of us followed his example and the sale of rat-traps increased tremendously. Nasroo's hardware shop sold so many rat-traps in a single day, that when Syeddaniji bullied Dilli-wali's son into buying her one, its price had risen from a rupee to a rupee and a quarter. Syeddaniji promptly returned the rat-trap and began accusing Nasroo of dishonesty. Dilli-wali tried to pacify her, 'Syeddaniji, rat-traps have become very expensive. I, too, bought them for a rupee and a quarter each. What else could I do, bibi? I bought four rat-traps, one for each room.'

Syeddaniji, however, was so blind with rage that Dilli-wali's advice had no effect on her. But the next day, when she had cooled down, she gave Mohsin a rupee and a quarter and sent him to Nasroo's shop. By then the price of a rat-trap had gone up to a rupee and a half. I am sure that even at this rate Syeddaniji got one rather cheap. For soon the situation became so bad that rat-traps were sold for two and a half rupees. And, God, the crowds! Nasroo, who was by then riding high, declared, 'Form a queue...wait for your turn!' The queue that formed in front of Nasroo's shop became longer as the days passed. Then one day, the queue became so long, that the crowds broke the line and rushed into Nasroo's shop. Nasroo called the police who had to resort to a mild lathi charge to disperse the crowd.

Ashraf Chacha was so critical of what Nasroo had done that he declared that a new rat-trap should be manufactured to catch him too. So, that very day he drafted a complaint against Nasroo, got everybody to sign it and filed it with the authorities. The authorities took immediate action and ordered that rat-traps be sold at a fixed price. The rate for each rat-trap was fixed at a rupee and a half. However, only a few people from the colony succeeded in buying rat-traps at the controlled rate, because Nasroo announced that he had run out of them. Nasroo was, of course, lying because that same evening, he sold a rat-trap to Maulvi Usman at two and a half rupees. He had charged the Maulvi less, out of consideration for his honesty and piety, for subsequently, he sold rat-traps for three rupees each.

We said, 'Ashraf Chacha, rat-traps are being sold in the black-market.'

Ashraf Chacha was already seething with rage. He said, 'What can I say, my son? There is black-marketing outside and smuggling within the house. We are being crushed between the two. I told the officers who settle claims—*Yaaro*, sons of God, don't sanction anything but, at least, accept my application, otherwise all these papers proving my claim will be smuggled out by rats! But they behaved like pharaohs and refused to listen to me.'

Actually, Ashraf Chacha had spoken too soon, for Mohsin had made the rounds of the offices many more times than he had. No action had yet been taken on his application for a scholarship to America. He went to the office everyday, handed a slip with his name on it at the reception, and sat down to read the leaflets scattered on a polished, glass-topped round table. From what he told us, we got the impression that he had met every single officer, but we never found out what they said to him. On the other hand, Ashraf Chacha had managed to meet the clerk at the Claims Office only once. The next day, the peon prevented him from entering the office. To some extent, Ashraf Chacha was himself responsible for his own plight, for though he moved in and out of the office, he wasn't prepared to tip the peon more than eight annas.

During his innumerable trips to the Claims Office, Ashraf Chacha gained at least one thing—he learnt a lot about buses and knew from experience every inch of the dirt road that came up to our colony. He also found out about the construction of houses along the way. He confidently declared that the house contractor had mixed more than fifty percent sand in the cement he had used. Dilli-wali was even less charitable in her estimate than Ashraf Chacha. She tapped the walls with her fingers, and said, 'Arrey bibi, how long do you think these paper-thin walls will stand?' After the first rain in the colony, when her roof began to leak, Syeddaniji said angrily, 'Did the accursed ones lay a roof overhead or simply fix tarpaulin?' And when the Yellow Quarter-wali saw water drip down the yellow walls of her house, she burst out, 'God damn them! They have erected a few reeds and then covered them with kite-paper.'

Ashraf Chacha knew well enough how everything was manipulated; yet he wasn't willing to give a bribe of more than eight annas. Sometimes, we asked him, 'Ashraf Chacha, what has happened to your claim?'

He always said, 'Son, I have set the rat-trap. The rest is in God's hands.'

The funny thing was that soon all our rat-traps were as ineffective as the one Ashraf Chacha had set. In the beginning, we caught quite a few rats with them, but after some time we discovered that the rats refused to touch the food that hung from the hook. The traps remained empty and the rats wandered through the houses fearlessly. Ambale-wali remarked, 'Mian, the rats have become wise; now they refuse to enter the rat-trap.'

Dilli-wali added, 'Ai bibi, it's we who are foolish. We swallow everything we get because we are helpless. Why should rats enter a trap for food that tastes like sawdust?'

Syeddaniji resented that remark. After a lot of running around, she managed to get some whole-wheat flour to make rotis for the rat-trap. The rats were so alert that they refused to be lured even by these rotis. People tried a few other experiments. For example, they mixed blue vitriol in dough, which they rolled into small balls and left under their meat-safes. The trick was successful for the first two days, but failed on the third. The rats sniffed every corner of the kitchen carefully, ate only those things that were fresh, and left the balls made of wheat flour and vitriol untouched.

Mohsin thought that these methods of killing rats were out-dated. He came up with a solution after reading the latest research on the problem by American agricultural scientists. He told his mother that the rats in our colony were nothing in comparison to the epidemic of rats in the farm-houses of Chicago. The enlightened farmers there had wiped them out with barium carbonate in a few days. Syeddaniji was not impressed by her son's opinion. But when Mohsin discussed the matter with Ashraf Chacha on their way back from the city in a bus, he managed to convince him. As soon as Ashraf Chacha got off the bus, he went home and then straight to Munnawar's Medical Store. It is a very large medical store now and Dr Munnawar drives up to it in a shiny big car. In those days, however, it had only a few bottles and packets of medicine, all the other shelves were bare.

Dr Munnawar informed Ashraf Chacha that barium carbonate was not available in his store, and that it was not available in any of the other medical stores in the city, because its import was still restricted although the demand for it had suddenly increased. He confessed that he had already placed an order for it and was expecting the next consignment any day.

When Ashraf Chacha described the new panacea, we thought he had discovered a new 'America'. For us, the discovery of barium carbonate, and the news that it would soon be available at Munnawar's Medical Store, was a great event. The fact is that by then our emotional state wasn't different from that of Syeddaniji's. The rats had made our lives miserable. Neither food nor clothes were safe from them. During the day, everything was always in its proper place. But no one knew what happened at night, because the next morning what was plentiful had diminished, what was less was missing; what had been left in the kitchen was found in the store, and what was in the store was found in the yard outside. Things which were undamaged and intact, suddenly had holes in them; things which were neat and clean, were soiled. The rats stole in under the cover of darkness and disappeared before sunrise. They did, however, leave clues behind: a few droppings in the flour container, a nibbled piece of bread, a small heap of shredded paper in a corner of the almirah that contained papers and books. Sometimes, at night, we woke up with a start, felt something clammy slither off our quilts, jump to the ground with a splat, and squeak in a shrill, moist voice. After that there was always silence, while we ground our teeth and lay huddled under our quilts. Then, we heard a new sound; the sound of someone cracking a nut. At first, it sounded as if a single nut was being cracked, then another and another, till there was a whole series of cracking sounds. Later, it seemed as if someone was slowly, very slowly sawing through the branch of a tree in the distance.

Under the cover of darkness, the sound of a saw cutting slowly, very slowly, through the branch of a tree in the front yard went on and on, and the nights became longer and longer. When we woke up in the morning, it was as if we had lived through a nightmare. As we busied ourselves with the routine of the day, the events of the previous night gradually receded into the past. But then, when night fell again, the saw began to cut slowly, very slowly, through the branch of a tree once more till the first signs of morning appeared again in the sky. Everyday, we found newly dug holes in the front or the back yards of our houses. Often we were startled to see two discoloured whiskers, sharp as tusks, and two shining eyes leap out of some hole, dash into the kitchen and vanish.

Once Syeddaniji picked up a long bamboo stick from the courtyard, chased a rat into the kitchen and banged on every box there. After some time, she gave up in exhaustion. Later, when her eyes drifted towards the drain and she saw the same pair of whiskers and the same set of glittering eyes while she was baking rotis, she merely continued with her work. When the utensils rattled, she turned around only to see a piece of roti being dragged towards the drain. She got up wearily, picked up the piece of roti and put it aside for the hens. Often she saw a single rat, sometimes two and sometimes a whole line of rats run from one room to the next. She continued to sit and watch them helplessly. If ever she was seated in the verandah doing nothing, and her eyes fell on a hole and she caught sight of a long tail disappearing, she merely convinced herself that she had seen the tail of a chameleon. A shiver of revulsion ran through her body. But she always continued to sit as if rooted to the spot. She began to regard her house as polluted and her utensils as unclean. That is why, even though she scrubbed all her pots, pans and plates with ash thrice a day and washed them thoroughly with water, she was still dissatisfied. She washed the floors of her house every Friday with buckets of water and yet never walked on them barefoot. In fact, this wasn't just Syeddaniji's condition; all of us had been reduced to a similar state.

It was during those days that Maulvi Usman Ali, who told us stories from the Bible, and described the history of the Prophet and his disciples, narrated to us the following story of the punishment inflicted upon the descendants of the Pharaoh: Almighty Allah said to the Pharaoh, 'Look, your kingdom shall be invaded by frogs; your rivers shall bring forth frogs in abundance. Frogs shall enter your houses; they shall jump into your beds, they shall find their way into your ovens and live in your kneading troughs. Frogs shall be upon you and on your people and on all your servants!'

When we first heard that story, we felt a strange revulsion, but soon that revulsion became a part of our very existence. Rats emerged from the cracks in barren lands and the filthy holes in cities ruined by sin, entered our homes, our sitting rooms, jumped into our beds, found their way into our ovens and lived in our kneading troughs. Our lives were filled with revulsion.

Syeddaniji often spoke angrily about Mohsin and his dream to go to America. And every day, after saying her fifth namaz, she begged that Mohsin's trip to America and her own pilgrimage to the Holy Karbala be granted. On the other hand, we went every day to Munnawar's Medical Store to find out if the consignment of barium carbonate had arrived. And every day, when Maulvi Usman Ali saw us return disappointed, he shook his head sadly and warned us that, till such a time as the Muslims reformed their character, barium carbonate would have no effect. Then, like a preacher, he told us stories of disciples whose crops had been eaten by locusts, of cities submerged by floods, and of settlements where people had regressed into monkeys. We heard the same tales every day, discussed the same subjects every day. We were so bored that we could no longer tell the difference between one day and the next. Each new day seemed like the previous morning. The sparkle of the day and the colours of the night were obliterated. It seemed as if the earth had stopped rotating on its axis and everything had been stilled—the order for barium carbonate, the promise of electricity, the construction of the metalled road, and even our actions and feelings. Of course, the main road had been constructed and some houses even had electricity. But, to us, it seemed as if the unpaved roads, the partially-built houses and the electricity poles without wires were a part of the architectural plan for a colony which was destined to remain incomplete forever. Longing for something that could make us feel alive again, we often looked beyond our colony towards the black glittering road and at the buses that roared down it at short intervals. When we saw the buses whiz past us, we realized that far away, beyond the horizon, lay another world, more dazzling and exciting than the one we inhabited. Sometimes a strange thought would occur to us, that one day, when Ashraf Chacha returned from his usual round of the Claims Office, he would be shocked to see that our faces had changed, that our eyes had become as small as tamarind seeds and that our whiskers had grown as long as tusks. He would be so terrified and disgusted that he would turn around and get back into the bus he had arrived in. At that moment, we wondered if the evolutionary cycle could be reversed, if men could leave their homes and go live on trees again and, if creatures could get down from the trees and slither back into the holes underground. Our thoughts and feelings moved in a circle; we went over and over the same ideas. Tied to the wheel of a grinding mill, night and day were merely endlessly repeated cycles of darkness and light. The night never seemed to end; somewhere far away a saw continued to cut slowly, very slowly, through the branch of a tree; and somewhere close by, either under the bed or on top of the quilt, something soft and squishy squeaked endlessly. We were overcome with revulsion; we felt suffocated. Night crawled like a slimy thing and vanished when the first streak of morning light moved across the sky like a tail. When the sun rose, we thanked God, crept out of our holes and performed our daily chores reluctantly. The metalled road no longer seemed metalled, and the unpaved lanes seemed even more unpaved. Dusty winds swept across them. Our houses, which used to glow brightly before the rains, now looked discoloured; it seemed as if they were slowly sinking and would disappear under the earth one night, and that the next morning we would have to crawl out of the ventilators on our hands and feet.

Barium carbonate helped us break out of the miasmatic circle of thought in which we were trapped. One day, the consignment of barium carbonate really did arrive. When we got the news, our excitement knew no bounds. It seemed as if the earth had suddenly begun to spin on its axis once more. People from every house rushed to Munnawar's Medical Store. By the time we got there, a crowd had already gathered outside the shop, and Dr Munnawar was telling them, 'We have no more barium carbonate left.'

We turned to Ashraf Chacha and said, 'Ashraf Chacha, barium carbonate has also disappeared into the black market.'

Enraged, Ashraf Chacha pushed through the crowd, walked into the store and asked curtly, 'How could it be sold out in one day? The consignment came only today, how could it be over?

Calmly, Dr Munnawar replied, 'Yes, the truth is that the zamindars of Ramgarh had placed their order a long time ago.'

'The zamindars of Ramgarh!' Ashraf Chacha exclaimed angrily. 'Is this store meant for the inhabitants of the colony or the zamindars of Ramgarh? With this calamity upon us, how could the zamindars of Ramgarh grab all the barium carbonate?'

'Ashraf Chacha there is a greater calamity which has fallen upon them.'

'What calamity?'

'The fields of Ramgarh have been invaded by rats.'

'The fields of Ramgarh...and...rats...!' Ashraf Chacha was so stunned that he couldn't utter another word.

Dr Munnawar calmly sat down on a chair, took out a fountain pen and began to write something. Bewildered, Ashraf Chacha continued to stand in silence for a while. Then he came out of the shop and walked away lost in his own thoughts. Gradually, the crowd dispersed and the road in front of Munnawar's Medical Store was deserted again.

Ashraf Chacha went straight to Nanva's shop. The news had already preceded him. Maulvi Usman Ali sat quietly smoking his hookah. Nanva watched him. Without uttering a word, Ashraf Chacha picked up a stool and sat down on it.

Nanva said, 'Ashraf Chacha, when the *ghee-wala* came from Ramgarh yesterday and said, "You city dwellers have infected us with your disease," I understood at once that something suspicious was in the air.'

Nasroo, the hardware man, who had accompanied Ashraf Chacha to Nanva's shop, added, 'They say that the rats have invaded the fields in large numbers.'

Ashraf Chacha didn't say anything in reply.

Maulvi Usman Ali pushed the pipe of the hookah aside, and said, 'May Allah have mercy upon the Muslims.' He didn't say anything more. He stared thoughtfully into space for some time. Then he proclaimed, 'When the share of human beings is consumed by some other creature, we can be sure that calamity is at hand.'

But Ashraf Chacha continued to remain silent.

Maulvi Usman Ali also sat quietly, his eyes fixed on the ground. After a while, he stood up and said, 'May Allah have mercy upon us,' and went home.

The truth is that at that time none of us could find anything to say. We continued to sit in gloomy silence for a long time and then dispersed one by one. That night was oppressive. Later, Syeddaniji told us that she had felt as if something was gnawing its way through a mashak filled with water throughout the night.

When we woke up the next morning, we heard Syeddaniji scream, 'May the plague infect Nanva. He is dishonest. I bought *urad dal* from him only yesterday. The accursed one has doubled its price overnight.'

Despite Syeddaniji's protest, not only did the price of urad dal go up, the price of other dals rose steeply too. And, as expected, life became more expensive. Syeddaniji declared, 'No, bhai, how long can I wait for that America-wala? I will not live here any more.'

Despite the announcement, Syeddaniji has not yet gone to the Holy Karbala. And Mohsin, anxious to escape like a rat caught in a trap, goes from the colony to the city every day and appears for interviews, but there is still no sign of a scholarship for him.

Date of publication: 1990

12

Hisaar
(*Hisaar*)

I

'D o you remember your father? Even he failed to draw the *hisaar* around himself.'

Yes, he remembered his father. So? He didn't like to remember what had happened to his father. But he knew that Meer Sahib, in order to prove that he was always right, was in the habit of either claiming that he was himself an eyewitness to an incident or knew someone who was...It was the last day. His father had not succeeded in drawing the hisaar. As he counted the beads of his rosary for the last time, his father had felt there was someone standing behind him. Distracted, he forgot which bead he had been counting...Anyway, what did it all mean? He refused to believe the story.

They'll continue to talk like this all day, he thought. I must get away.

'Meer Sahib, has anyone ever completed the hisaar?' Naim asked.

On the verge of getting up, he sat down again.

'Yes, one in a thousand does succeed in the attempt.' Meer Sahib paused, and then added, 'The ritual is a wild gamble—a blind throw of the dice. One can either become wise or go mad... We all knew Banday Ali. Poor man, he tried and went mad. He spent thirty-nine days without making a mistake. He had almost completed the fortieth day without a mishap. Only the last two beads remained to be counted... But as he was counting the forty-ninth, he was distracted. He felt as if he was holding a centipede. Startled, he jerked his hand. The rosary fell beyond the prayer mat... Well, he went mad. He began to jerk his hand all the time.' After a thoughtful pause, Meer Sahib sighed, 'Bhai, it's a blind gamble. If you succeed, you become a saint; if you don't, you go mad.'

He tried to tear himself away once again. This conversation will never end, he said to himself.

'Meer Sahib, are there people with occult powers who can conjure what one desires?' Naim asked.

'Yes, men with demonic powers.'

'Really?'

'Yes, yes. I knew an occultist who had demonic power. He used to sleep next to a dog's grave under an *imli* tree. We were children then. One day, some of us boys went to him and said—Shahji, we want to eat *gulgulay*. Shahji raised a finger and a basket full of hot gulgulay appeared before us. We ate to our heart's content. As we were returning home, we saw Kamia, the sweeperess, screaming and shouting—I made a basketful of gulgulay for the funeral feast, but they were snatched away by a half-naked scoundrel in a loincloth. How disgusting!'

'Really, that's the limit,' said Naim.

He yawned and stood up.

Naim looked at him and asked, 'Leaving so soon?'

'I'm sleepy.' He yawned again.

'Yaar, why don't you sleep at my place tonight?'

'Why?'

'I'll be alone tonight. Everyone has gone out. After listening to Meer Sahib's stories, I am sure I won't be able to sleep tonight. Is there anyone waiting for you at home? Come to my place.'

'No, bhai,' he said quickly and left.

'A man with demonic powers can't distinguish between clean and unclean things. And, bhai, now people only have demonic powers,' Meer Sahib's voice slowly faded into the distance.

He stopped at Nazeera's shop and bought a packet of cigarettes. As he opened it, he casually glanced down the street. The bazaar was still bustling with people. A train must have just arrived because there was a long line of tongas loaded with passengers slowly making their way down the street. Groups of men, sitting on low stools placed on the platforms in front of the shops, were engaged in heated discussions. The atmosphere was warm and friendly. He placed a cigarette between his lips and lit it with the smouldering end of a jute string hanging outside Nazeera's shop.

He turned the corner and walked down the old bazaar. The glittering shops were soon left behind. The noises of the market seemed to belong to another world. The electric poles, which stood far apart from each other, squandered their light on the silent street. As he pulled hard at his cigarette, and then exhaled the smoke into the cold, damp air, he felt a sense of relief. He was glad to have escaped from the oppressiveness of Meer Sahib's conversation. Meer Sahib's stories floated through his mind, but this time he didn't find them offensive. 'Do you remember your father? Even he failed to draw the hisaar.'...Why shouldn't I remember my father? A bright face with a long white beard rose before his eyes. The past was like a dream...Those were days of great poverty. We either had to borrow money or pawn some household goods to make ends meet. Even then we were always short of money. When things didn't improve, Father began to recite awe-inspiring, holy incantations. Day after day, he sat on his prayer mat in the room upstairs. He neither spoke nor laughed. Lost in thought, he came out of his room only for an hour or two, wearing wooden sandals. Having given up meat, ghee and milk, he ate only dal and roti, and then went back to his room and locked the door from inside.

On the fortieth day, some time in the afternoon, when only the parapet wall was partially lit by the sun, Father suddenly came out of the room in his wooden sandals. Bare-headed, he held a copy of the Koran in his hand and clutched a walking stick under his arm. 'Get out of here,' he shouted. Bewildered, the entire household stared at his terror-stricken face. No one had the courage to ask him what the matter was. Without uttering a word, he left abruptly, as if disgusted with everything in the house.

We moved to Naqi Hussain's house in the neighbourhood that day. No one slept till late that night. It was a long time before the stream of conversation finally subsided and people began to retire one by one. In the silence, Naqi Hussain's wife whispered to her mother-in-law in a hushed voice, 'I think he forgot to draw the hisaar.' Then she too drifted into sleep.

That night, he woke up with a start. Everyone else was asleep. His father sat on his prayer mat reciting from the Koran. Timidly, he got out of bed, walked to the drain and pissed. A little wary, he looked into the street below. It was empty. There was darkness all around. In the street, on the terrace, across the courtyard. The door was shut. It was locked from the outside. His heart pounded with fear... Startled, he walked quickly down the old bazaar and turned into the street with the window.

As he turned into the Khidkion-wali Gali, he quickened his pace. The doors of all the houses, except Master Imtiaz Ali's, were shut. There was no light anywhere... Wasn't anyone at home? In that case the door should have been locked... When he looked up˚ at Qadir's room, he saw dim light filter through the window and fall on the opposite wall. If Qadir had not been awake and working for his examinations, the street would have been completely dark. Only his footsteps echoed in the street. Afraid, he began to walk softly.

He walked through the Khidkion-wali Gali and turned into a very narrow lane. A gutter flowed down the middle. There was a street lamp in the distance. In the dull light, he saw a man draped in a blanket walking towards him. The man slid past him like a shadow and then suddenly vanished. He was strangely disturbed. Who was he? He looked back. The lane was empty. How could he have walked through the lane so quickly? Perhaps, I should walk back to the end of the lane and look for him. Immediately, he felt foolish. He began to walk faster.

When he reached Qazionwali Gali, he felt reassured. The street was wider and was lit by street lamps at regular intervals. He had hardly taken a few steps, when he heard the sound of footsteps behind him and the voices of two men talking to each other. He thought of turning around to see who they were, but gave up the idea...No, I don't care. Must be someone...He did, however, strain his ears and try to catch what they were saying. But their voices were muffled by the blankets that covered their faces, and he couldn't understand a single word. Then, the footsteps turned down another lane and were lost in the distance...There was a loud knock on a door somewhere far down the lane. The door opened at once and then shut with a bang. He was surprised to notice that all the doors were shut and he was the only one on the street... It's getting late. I must go home...He started walking faster. His shadow kept pace with him. First, it moved ahead and became longer and longer, then it grew shorter and shorter, till it got entangled in his feet; it slipped behind him and became longer and longer again...Is that long shadow mine? The question crossed his mind fleetingly and then vanished. Lost in thought, he slowed down. He shivered a little in the cold; rubbed his hands together because his fingers were almost frozen...I must wear gloves. The fingers are the first to freeze...He recalled how Banday Ali used to appear suddenly at the end of the lane. Sometimes, he would be seen wrapped in an old and tattered blanket and, at other times, in nothing but a shirt, a pyjama and a dirty cap on his head. But no matter how he was dressed, he would continuously jerk his right hand and keep mumbling something. Lost in his own thoughts, Banday Ali seemed to have no relation with the world around him...How narrow and circumscribed this world of relationships really is! A wrong step and it is shattered! Then a man is isolated in his own world; a world of scattered relationships where a rosary is a centipede and a centipede a rosary...

II

...So the prince suffered from a migraine all the time. The *hakims* and the *vaids* tried their best to cure him, but couldn't. Then the royal hakim, who was the master of all the hakims, said, 'I must open the prince's skull and see what's inside.' He gave the prince a tranquillizer, cut open his skull with a sharp sword and lifted it up like a cap...

'His skull?'

'Yes, son. When the hakim lifted the prince's skull, he saw that a centipede had dug its legs, sharp as needles, deep into the prince's brain...'

'A centipede?'

'Yes, son, a centipede. The hakim was confused. 'How can I remove that centipede? If I delay, the prince will die.' Then one of his pupils said to him, 'Ustad, forgive me for my impertinence. Light a fire, get a pair of tongs, take a piece of burning coal and place it on the centipede.' So, bhaiya, that is what the hakim did. The centipede writhed in pain and released its hold...'

III

He shivered in the cold and began to walk faster.

He was annoyed with himself. Why do I remember these old and forgotten tales that make no sense? Can there be a centipede in one's head? How? Why? It can't be born in the head. It can only crawl in from outside. But how? Through what? Through the ear? That did happen once to a girl who had complained of a continuous headache. A small centipede entered her brain through the ear. Once inside, it began to multiply. The centipede gave birth to another centipede, which gave birth to another, and then another, till there were countless centipedes crawling in her brain...Disgusted with himself, he shook his head a little. *Lahol vila quwaat!* This is an equally absurd story...If only I can put a lock on my brain! But how can anyone lock his brain? A thought has a thousand feet. It crawls silently into the brain, either through the eyes or the ears, and finds a dark corner inside to hide...He was again angry with himself...Why do I sit at Meer Sahib's shop and listen to his absurd stories? Why do I waste my time there?...Suddenly, something dark and huge rose before him. Startled, he almost screamed. He cursed Ramzani for tying his buffalo right in the middle of the lane. Was he shivering because he was cold or because he was upset? He broke into a sweat, and he didn't know why his heart was beating so fast. No, he was not feeling cold now. In fact, he wanted to take off his woollen coat and unbutton the collar of his shirt so that he could breathe a little more easily.

He nearly ran down Qazionwali Gali, quickly walked around the Patharwalla Kuan and past Shekhji's furniture shop, before turning into his lane... But why am I running? He slowed down. He felt as if he had just escaped being caught in a violent storm and was lucky to have reached the shelter of his home. The lane was silent, empty, and well-lit. There was a large circle of light outside his house. Slowly, he began to breathe a little more easily, and his heart stopped pounding. He walked up to the door of his house calmly, unlocked it, and switched on the light.

As he was taking off his clothes, he heard a rustling sound behind him. He turned around and looked at his bed. It was empty. Suddenly, he caught sight of the rat which often used to run through the house either freely or surreptitiously, scampering into its hole in the wall at the foot of the bed. He watched the rat till its body disappeared down the hole. Its tail, however, continued to wag outside for sometime. Finally, that too, vanished. He was so disgusted by the sight that a slight tremor ran through him. He forgot to take off his clothes. Instead, he dusted the bed-sheet and then spread it on the bed again. After that, he shook his quilt vigorously, folded it and placed it back neatly on the bed. He took the pillow-cover off and dusted it before putting it back on again.

He realized that sleep had forsaken him. He pulled a packet of cigarettes out of his pocket. He glanced compulsively at the hole in the wall at the foot of his bed. He sat down in his chair, lit a cigarette and once again recalled what Meer Sahib had said: 'Do you remember your father? Even he failed to draw the hisaar...' Once again, the same anxious white-bearded face bent over the holy Koran rose before his eyes; once again, he recalled his house, locked from outside and lost in the darkness for many days... When they had returned home, they were a little apprehensive. The room upstairs was still locked and dark. They didn't dare shut the window of the room that overlooked the courtyard. On Tuesday evenings, the feeling that someone was pacing about the room upstairs terrified us. That house, whose terraces, rooms and stairs had been so friendly till the other day, had now become a place of dread...

He lit another cigarette, and quickly picked up the book he had left open on the table. But he couldn't concentrate. After reading three pages, he put it aside and got up. As he stood, his eyes drifted towards the hole in the wall once again. He grabbed the coat which he had taken off only a few minutes ago, wrapped his muffler around his neck, switched off the light and shut the door behind him as he went out. By then there were no lights in the lane. He was surprised. When he had walked down the lane only a short while ago, the streetlights had been burning... Why have they been switched off so soon, he wondered? Then, it occurred to him that it was a moonlit night.

Wrapping his muffler around his neck more tightly, he began to walk down the lane. There were no lights anywhere. But, since it was misty, the refracted light of the moon cast a strange white radiance over everything. The night was much colder now. His fingers were frozen. He rubbed his hands together and clenched his fingers repeatedly... The fingers and joints are the first to freeze. I must remember to carry gloves... He thrust his hands into his coat pockets.

He turned into Qazionwali Gali and glanced at the door where Ramzani's buffalo sat as usual. When he walked past the buffalo, she neither got up with a start nor shook her head. She just sat there, a huge and inert dark mass. It seemed as if her mouth had been sewn together and her eyes glued shut.

All the streetlights had been turned off. The lane was silent and empty. Everything was shrouded by a misty moonlight. A white cat sat hunched at a door, staring at him. She continued to stare at him with her round, yellow, glassy eyes till he walked past her. He was about to turn into the narrow lane, when he saw the shadow of a cat in the moonlight creep slowly over the opposite wall and then disappear. Walking down the lane slowly, he once again thought about the man who had earlier slid past him like a shadow. Who was he? He felt that what had happened earlier was happening all over again. He began to walk faster and deliberately took a sharp turn into another lane. He looked down the lane. It was empty. At the far end, in the dim moonlight, he saw a dog, with a long muzzle and a curled tail, sitting like a watchman…Stray dogs are a nuisance at night. I should have brought my stick with me…He slowed down again. The lane was silent. Master Imtiaz's door was now shut. There was no light in Qadir's room upstairs… Perhaps, he has gone to bed early today.

He turned the corner of the lane and suddenly emerged from darkness into moonlight. Where had the dog disappeared? He looked around, but didn't see it anywhere. He was surprised, but also relieved. Dogs bark without reason at every innocent man who walks past. The thought of the man who had walked past him earlier, drifted through his consciousness like a shadow and then vanished. Another question occurred to him. Did Banday Ali ever sleep at night? Maybe, he never did…

The moment he heard the whistle, he took off his sandals and began to run. The whistle seemed to come from close by, and as he ran he thought to himself, 'Salay, if they don't catch you, they'll think that you are a thief and will look for you all night. On top of it, you'll be thrashed at home. Anyway, I am sure the door will be locked.' He clutched a sandal in each hand and ran faster. But the moment he turned the corner of the lane, he froze in surprise. His feet felt so heavy that he could not run. Banday Ali stood facing the door of Master Sahib's house, mumbling softly. The door was shut and the street was empty. The moment Banday Ali heard his footsteps, he turned with a start, stared at him apprehensively, jerked his hand violently and walked quickly down another lane. He stood there unable to move. Trapped between the high walls on either side of the lane, he felt as if he had fallen into a dark abyss. He tried to call out to Rafia and Munna and Dinoo with all his strength, but his voice got stuck in his throat and he felt as if there was a heavy weight pressing down on his chest…

His train of thought snapped suddenly. A misty moonlight spread over the silent street. He started walking as fast as he could.

He was no longer cold. In fact, he began to feel that the woollen coat was a burden. He loosened the muffler around his ears and neck, and unbuttoned his coat. The sound of his own footsteps was so loud that it frightened him. He slowed down. His shadow, which clung to him, also slowed down. He examined the entire lane from one end to the other. It was empty. In the misty moonlight, the blank gaze of the street lamps startled him. The lamps seemed to be unrelated to each other. He wondered why there appeared to be a relationship between them when they were lit from one end of the street to the other...Do relationships produce light? Or does light create relationships? Does light create the relationship between the body and its shadow or does the relationship between the body and its shadow create light? And, what is the relationship between the sound of footsteps and feet? Are footsteps the shadows of feet, or feet the shadows of footsteps? He was bewildered...How many feet does a meaning-less thought have? In order to escape from meaningless thoughts, one must draw a hisaar around oneself, otherwise doubts and apprehensions would draw a hisaar around one like a thousand centipedes...He turned quickly into the street that led to the bazaar.

The bazaar, which had been bustling with activity only a short while before, was now asleep. He felt as if he had returned after ages. There was not a single light burning anywhere. The street was empty. It seemed to be split into two distinct halves. One side was lit by moonlight and the other half was in shadow. With the result that shops on one side were lit while those on the other side were lost in darkness. He avoided the moonlit side and began to walk down the side that was in shadow, as if he wanted to hide from someone. He had hardly taken a few steps, when something black jumped at him from a ledge in front of one of the shops. Terrified, he stepped back, but quickly recovered his balance. A dog, which stood in the middle of the road, barked at him. He realized that his legs were shaking violently and his heart was beating with fear.

A voice, muffled by a blanket, shouted at the dog. It stopped barking, but continued to watch him carefully and growl till he walked past the shop. He tried to look unconcerned, as if he wanted to prove to the dog that he wasn't afraid. When he reached the shop, he noticed that it was locked. There was a cot outside, under the awning of the shop. Someone was lying on it wrapped in a dirty quilt. He couldn't tell who it was because his face was covered. Who could be sleeping outside on such a cold night? Maybe the shopkeeper. But why couldn't he sleep inside? Who could it be? Why bother? To hell with him! He resolved not to indulge in wild speculation. His steps, too, became more resolute. After some time, he felt that he was being followed. His heart sank...It must be the same dog. Sometimes, a dog walks so cautiously that its footsteps sound like the footsteps of a man...He wanted to look back, but he stopped himself...To look back is to admit one's fears, which will torment one later. But supposing it was that man who was lying under the quilt on the cot? No, that's not possible. Why should he get out of bed and run after me like a rabid dog? Why should he?...He stepped out of the shadows and began to walk on the side that was lit by the moon. He turned to look back in the direction of the man sleeping on the cot, but by then he had walked so far ahead that he couldn't see anything.

When he reached Meer Sahib's shop, he recalled his father— the same terror-stricken face bent over the holy Koran; the same lonely voice echoing through the house in the silent night...That voice now belongs to another world, far removed from the everyday voices of men. And the house, though full of the hustle and bustle of daily life, was strangely silent...He turned away from Meer Sahib's shop and glanced up the street. There was a faint light at the farthest corner of the street...

So, Maulvi Tuntay's shop is still open! He remembered the old days when the shops in the street were open till late at night and there was always a group of people hanging around Meer Sahib's shop. Of late only Naim and he met there to listen to his stories. He felt sad...What has happened? Where have all the festive nights gone? Why have all the shopkeepers, who used to be awake through the nights, pulled down the shutters and disappeared? Now, only Maulvi Tuntay...but even Maulvi Tuntay...He remembered the rumour that Maulvi Tuntay's shop was open till early in the morning because jinns and fairies came there after midnight to buy paan, *ittar* and agarbatti. He thought the tale was absurd...Why do people try to make a fool of a perfectly sane man? He dismissed the idea, increased the pace of his walk and heaved a sigh of relief when he saw Maulvi Tuntay—a dark hunch-backed man, with wizened cheeks, a large mouth and two gaping holes for front teeth. Since he chewed paan and tobacco continu-ously, Maulvi Tuntay only answered questions with his eyes and hands. His large eyes, which were staring at him, now frightened him. A thought flashed through his mind like lightning...Isn't Maulvi Tuntay himself a...No, no, what nonsense! But he wasn't reassured. He stared at Maulvi Tuntay apprehensively...I still have a cigarette, he said to himself, as he reached for it in his pocket. Maybe, I should eat a paan? 'Paan,' he ordered loudly. Maulvi Tuntay turned his eyes away and began to concentrate on making a paan for him. He took out a cigarette. As he turned to light it with the smouldering end of the jute string hanging from the shop, his eyes fell on Maulvi Tuntay's right hand. Three fingers of the hand were missing, and three-fourths of the forefinger was also cut. Only the thumb was intact. He remembered that Maulvi Tuntay used to make crackers during *saab-i-barat*. Once, while he was stuffing a cracker with gunpowder, it had accidentally rubbed against the pestle and exploded, and blown away part of his hand. After lighting his cigarette, he released the rope, which swung on the nail for a while and then stopped. He took a long puff, exhaled, and extended his hand to take the paan from Maulvi Tuntay. As he put the paan in his mouth, he felt his fingers were wet and clammy. He walked up to the light and looked at them. They were stained with *kattha*...Perhaps, the kattha was too thin. That's why my fingers are so wet...He wiped them with a piece of cloth already stained with kattha. He placed his cigarette between his fingers, took a deep puff, and turned towards the lane where Naim lived.

If we call our Maulvi, Maulvi Tuntay because he lost his fingers, then why shouldn't we call the prince, who chopped off his fingers so that he could keep awake through the night and catch the Phool Princess, Prince Tuntay? Really, princes in ancient times were strange creatures. They could only think of one way to keep awake through the night—chop off their fingers and sprinkle chilly powder on them! Couldn't one stay awake without doing that? Besides, do jinns and fairies appear only to those who stay awake at night? And do jinns really go to Maulvi Tuntay's shop to buy ittar, paan and agarbatti? And are Banday Ali's fingers really...? Countless other bizarre questions began to crawl like centipedes before his eyes. Suddenly, Chandi Halwai came out of his shop holding a yellow snake with a red mouth by its tail. As he held the snake away from his body in his outstretched hands, the snake's tongue flicked in and out of its red mouth like sparks of fire. Chandi Halwai walked in a stately manner up to the dark well in the old temple, stood on its parapet, leaned forward a little, and slowly let the snake slide out of his fingers. The snake slithered out of his hand, writhed in the air and vanished into the darkness of the well. That strange spectacle sent a shudder down his body as he recalled the day when, following Nanhe's example, he had grabbed the tail of a rat trapped in a wire cage and released it in disgust. He had washed his hands immediately afterwards with soap, but had continued to feel the squishiness of the tail for days afterwards. Now, he felt the same disgust, and a shiver ran down his body. He slowly jerked his head. He wanted to escape from the circle of memories closing in around him so that he could walk calmly. Suddenly, he felt cold and wrapped his muffler around his neck and ears more tightly. He clenched and released his fingers a few times and then thrust his hands into his pockets. He said to himself—At least, I have a muffler...If one's ears are not exposed to the cold winds, one is safe from a thousand calamities. I should buy gloves, because one's fingertips are the first to freeze.

Naim's house was near. By then he had nearly succeeded in making a list of things he needed for winter. But, he failed to regain his composure. Fear, with its thousand feet, had crawled into the darkest corner of his brain. He felt anxious and distraught, as strange and disjointed thoughts and memories continued to haunt him. It occurred to him that an absurd thought has a thousand feet, and that it slowly crawls into the brain through one's ears, eyes and fingertips. He came to the conclusion that one's senses are a curse...Who was that sage, who advised his student to follow in the footsteps of a tortoise? The shell of a tortoise is like a hisaar that it carries on its back, and it is, therefore, saved from sorrows and calamities. Is a tortoise shell a hisaar or is a hisaar a tortoise shell? Is a wise man a tortoise or is a tortoise a wise man? And man? Is man cruel and stupid because he wants to live without a hisaar?...Questions with needle-sharp legs began to crawl through his brain once more. He walked as fast as he could till he reached Naim's house and knocked at his door loudly.

Naim opened the door and came out running his eyes. 'Arrey, what are you doing here?'

'I couldn't sleep, yaar. Sitting alone at home, I felt depressed and decided to come here.'

'Yaar, I am sure there is a worm with a thousand legs crawling in your brain too!'

'What?' he was startled.

'I am sure. Why didn't you come with me, instead of waking me up in the middle of the night? Anyway, come in.'

He followed him inside.

'Take off your coat and go to sleep. I am very sleepy.'

He unbuttoned his coat, and then took off his muffler and put it aside. He was about to take off his coat, when he stopped suddenly. Absorbed in his own thoughts, he walked towards the light and began to examine his fingers.

'What's the matter?' Naim asked in bewilderment.

'Nothing,' he said. He continued to examine his fingers and then whispered, 'Maulvi Tuntay's kattha was too thin today. It stained my fingers.'

A shiver ran through his body as he recalled the feel of wet kattha on his fingers. He clenched his fingers and thrust his hands into his pockets. What Meer Sahib had said floated through his mind once again—'Do you remember your father? Even he failed to draw the hisaar around himself.'

Date of publication: 1990

13

The Staircase
(*Seediyan*)

I

For a minute or so Bashir Bhai sat in such deep silence that Akhtar was a bit nervous and worried. Finally, when he stirred and sighed softly, Akhtar was relieved but still afraid of what Bashir Bhai would say.

'Do you remember the exact time?'

'Time?' Akhtar mused. 'No, I don't remember the exact time.'

'One must always note the time,' Bashir Bhai said, still deep in thought. 'Without knowing the exact time, I can't say anything. If it was during the first half of the night, there is nothing to worry about; you can dismiss it as demonic temptation. If it was in the latter half of the night, you must give alms.'

Akhtar's heart began to beat faster. Razi, however, continued to sit in silence; only his eyes were open wide in surprise and wonder.

'I always make a careful note of the time,' Bashir Bhai said testily. 'Besides, I am the kind of person who can always foresee things before they actually happen. Sometimes, I wake up with a start before dawn and feel as if I have seen something...When I first came here, I wandered hopelessly for months looking for a job. I was very worried and didn't know what to do. Then, one night, in a vision, I saw my late grandfather coming out of a mosque with a bowl full of *peda*s. He took a peda from the bowl and gave it to me...I woke up...I heard the azan. I got out of bed, performed the morning ablutions and stood up to say my prayers...Well, it so happened that three days later I got a job.'

Razi and Akhtar listened to Bashir Bhai very attentively. Syed, who was trying to sleep, continued to lie with his eyes shut and his back towards them.

'Bashir Bhai,' Akhtar asked, 'why do I see countless dead bodies in my dreams?'

'Dreams of dead bodies are signs of grace. They promise a long life.'

'But...this...' Akhtar hesitated.

'Yes, this time it was different,' Bashir Bhai added casually, as if there was nothing to worry about. 'It's inauspicious to dream of a corpse sharing food with you—that is a sign of famine.' He was silent for a moment, and then added irritably, 'But you don't even remember the time. I can't interpret dreams unless I know the time. Anyway, to be on the safe side, give alms.'

Syed was annoyed. He turned around and sat up. 'Yaar, you are weird. I am sure Akhtar Bhai never sleeps. He tells us about his dreams till midnight, and then he starts dreaming again. Tell me, Akhtar Bhai, do you ever find time to sleep?'

Akhtar retorted, 'What's wrong with you? You think everything is a joke.'

'There is something wrong with you, yaar. You dream every night. Tell me, why don't I ever have dreams?'

'It's in our nature to dream. Everyone has dreams. Some dream more, some less,' Bashir Bhai said.

'But what about me? Is it not in my nature to dream? I never have dreams.'

'Never?' Akhtar asked with surprise.

'Not since the day I came here.'

'You are the limit! There is something wrong with you!...Did you hear that, Bashir Bhai?'

'No, there is something wrong with you,' Syed replied. 'I am surprised that anyone who sleeps on such a narrow terrace can have dreams. What an incredible terrace! Four cots cover the entire surface. When I wake up at night, I am terrified to get out of bed. I am sure I'll fall into the lane below!...Now, the terrace of our old house was...' He paused abruptly and then quietly added, 'Why weep over the past? I am sure there is nothing left of that house, not even charred bricks.'

Syed got up and drank some water from the *surahi* that stood on the low parapet wall. He said, 'The water is warm. When was the surahi filled?'

'In the afternoon,' Bashir Bhai said. 'The surahi is old. We'll get a new one tomorrow.'

'Can I turn the wick in the lantern down a little?' Syed asked. 'The light hurts my eyes.'

'Yes, and place it in the corner...The moon will be out soon,' Bashir Bhai replied.

Syed shook the lantern as he lowered the wick. 'There is very little oil in it. I hope it lasts through the night,' he muttered to himself. He picked up the lantern and set it down on the floor near the parapet wall. The dim light of the lantern retreated into the corner and darkness spread over the rest of the terrace.

The cots of Razi and Akhtar were covered with sheets, but in the darkness it was Syed's cot which shimmered in the moonlight. Bashir Bhai lay on his cot with a cotton bed-sheet folded under his head. Earlier in the evening, while washing the terrace, he had sprinkled a mug of water on his cot strung with coarse jute which now felt cool on his bare back. The jute filled the surrounding air with sweet fragrance.

'Bashir Bhai,' Razi, who had been sitting quietly for some time, spoke up. He paused, cleared his throat, and continued, 'Bashir Bhai, if one sees the big *alam* in one's dreams, what does it signify?'

Bashir Bhai thought for a while and then answered, 'It's a very auspicious sign. But tell me about your dream.'

Akhtar listened attentively to Razi. Syed turned his back towards them slowly, shut his eyes and tried to sleep once again.

'Bashir Bhai, do you remember the morning when you woke up to say your prayers and asked me why I was up so early? Well, I just couldn't sleep that night. I don't know why. I spent the night tossing and turning in bed. I was troubled by all kinds of thoughts. Then I dozed off a little before dawn. I dreamt that...' Razi's voice faltered and a cold shiver ran through his body, 'I saw our Imambara and...our Imambara and...the big alam rising from it...the big alam...like the one we have...with the fluttering green flag and the swaying silver *panja*. The panja shimmered brightly, so very brightly that my eyes were dazzled. And, then, I woke up.'

Bashir Bhai, who was lying on his cot, suddenly sat up. Akhtar was so overwhelmed that he was unable to move. A tremor seemed to run through Razi's body...Even Syed turned toward them; his eyes were wide open as if to let the clear sharp rays of light stream into the dark caverns of his brain. He had the vision of a dimly-lit *aza-khana*, filled with the fragrance of burning frankincense. Then he saw glittering alams and panjas shimmering in golden and silver light, banners of green and red silk with sparkling designs in gold and silver brocades, and chandeliers with crystal beads glowing with white light...He no longer remembered where he had found the crystal bead of a chandelier. It was only a glass bead, but when he looked at it closely he was sure there was a rainbow deep inside it.

'A very strange dream,' Akhtar muttered.

'It was not a dream,' Bashir Bhai said softly.

Akhtar and Razi turned to stare at him.

'Were you asleep, or...?' Bashir Bhai asked.

'No, I wasn't asleep. I had only drifted off...'

Bashir Bhai thought for a while and then slowly said, 'It was not a dream; it was a divine vision.'

Razi stared at him in silence. At first, he was surprised, and then his eyes were filled with ecstasy. Soon, however, his sense of deep joy gave way to anxiety.

'That year,' he said in a hushed voice, 'the big alam was not carried in the procession from our Imambara.'

'Why not?'

Bashir Bhai and Akhtar seemed very perturbed.

'All the members of our family had migrated here. Only my mother stayed behind. She had vowed not to leave the Imambara as long as she lived. Every year she used to make preparations for Muharram. The big alam was always carried in the procession with dignity and splendour.'

'Then?'

'She grew old and weak. We came here. I couldn't even reach her bedside in time…' His voice choked and his eyes filled with tears.

Bashir Bhai and Akhtar lowered their heads.

Syed sat up.

Bashir Bhai sighed. There was a long silence.

'We have lived in this house together for quite some time and you never even told us!' Akhtar complained.

'There was nothing to tell.'

Bashir Bhai and Akhtar were quiet again. They didn't know what to say; they felt empty.

II

Like a bolt of lightening crashing through the darkness, an old memory startled Syed…The aza-khana was locked throughout the year, except during the ten days of Muharram and the few days of Chehlam. Sometimes, as a child, when Syed couldn't resist the temptation to find out what lay in the mysterious darkness behind the wooden door, he would steal up to it and peep through the cracks in the wood. Still unable to see anything, he would put a foot on the iron bolt, grasp the chain-hook hanging from the frame and pull himself up so that he could look into the room through the iron grill above the door. He would stare into the darkness till his eyes could make out the crystal beads of the chandelier gleaming in the room. He would stare at them in awe for a fleeting moment and then, jump down nervously and run away.

The underground vault of the house, whose window opened onto the ill-lit staircase, was even darker than the aza-khana. Its darkness never filled him with awe. It merely terrified him. Even though his mother assured him that the speckled snake, which lived in the vault, never attacked anyone unless it felt threatened, he never had the courage to look through the window of the vault. She had told him that one night, as she was climbing the stairs, her hand had touched something slimy, but the snake had slithered away without hissing at her, and had disappeared through the window. He had never seen the speckled snake himself, but after listening to that story, he didn't have the courage to stand on the staircase and peep through the window of the dark vault.

Bundi swore that she had seen the snake with her own eyes.

'Liar.'

'Fine, don't believe me.'

'Swear by Allah.'

'I swear by Allah.'

He still didn't believe her. 'Tell me, what did it look like?'

'Black. Black with white dots...When I looked through the window, it was crawling up the wall. I slammed the window shut.'

A shiver ran through their bodies. They looked at each other. There was fear in their eyes. Their hearts pounded. Both of them jumped up simultaneously, ran down the stairs, dashed across the courtyard, and then went outside and sat on the low parapet surrounding the well.

Leaning over the parapet, they gazed down into the deep well. In the fading light of day, shadows slowly gathered in the depths of the well as it became darker and darker. Occasionally, a streak of light fell on the rippling water, making the darkness seem even more profound.

Suddenly, they saw two shadows floating on the dark surface of the water.

'Jinns!'

'Don't be stupid. Jinns don't live in wells.'

'Then, where do they live?'

'Nowhere,' he replied confidently, sounding like an adult. 'You are an idiot...Wait, I'll shout to them.' He leaned over the wall and called out, 'Is anyone there?' The darkness echoed back, 'Is anyone there?' Scared, both of them quickly jumped off the parapet.

'There is somebody down there,' Bundi said trembling.

'There is no one,' he assured her carelessly, as if he were not afraid at all.

They stood there quietly for some time. Slowly, their fear began to dissolve. Then Bundi suddenly asked, 'Where does all the water come from?'

He laughed at her ignorance. 'Don't you even know that much? There is nothing but water under the earth. That's why the well is never dry.'

'If there is nothing but water under the earth,' she asked thoughtfully, 'where do snakes live?'

'Where do snakes live?' He was puzzled. Snakes are the lords of the earth, not of water, he said to himself. But if there is nothing but water under the earth, then where do the snakes live? And how was Raja Basath's palace ever built?

Suddenly, Bundi confronted him with another question. 'Syed, didn't the snake live in paradise once?'

'Yes.'

'If he lived in paradise, how did he come down to earth?'

'He sinned. God punished him. His legs fell off and he crashed down to earth.'

'Sinned?' There was fear in Bundi's eyes. They looked at each other nervously.

Bundi said, 'I am thirsty. Let's go home.'

He grabbed the bucket lying on the parapet wall of the well. 'Let's drink water from the well; it's very cool.' He quickly lowered the bucket into the well. The rope slipped through his hands so fast that it nearly peeled the skin off his palms. He was startled to hear the gentle sound of water filling the bucket. A pleasant thrill ran through his body. As they pulled up the bucket together, their bodies shivered with pleasure and delight.

When the bucket, overflowing with sweet cool water, emerged from the well, Bundi held it and poured water into Syed's cupped hands. He drank till he was satiated. Then, he took the bucket from

Bundi and poured water into her delicately cupped hands. The water in her cupped hands was deep. Her palms were as white as pearls; her lips were soft... Deliberately, he allowed the water to flow more freely. She didn't notice it stream down her hands and wet her clothes. She nearly choked...

III

'Actually, the alam was in fulfillment of a vow,' Razi said. 'My mother couldn't conceive a child. So she went to the holy city of Karbala...Anyone can ask for a boon at the Imam's shrine... He is very patient. But...but my mother used to say that there was such divine radiance at Chote Hazrat's shrine that the moment one entered it, one was filled with reverence. There wasn't a day which was not witness to a miracle. When my mother entered the shrine, something strange happened. A man was coming out of the shrine. The moment he tried to cross the threshold, his legs were paralysed. He could neither go back in nor come out...His body seemed to be on fire as if he had been struck by lightning...His mother wept helplessly. After a long time, one of the keepers of the shrine went to her and said, 'Bibi, your son must have done something sacrilegious. Chote Hazrat is offended. Go to the Imam's sanctuary; he alone can pacify Chote Hazrat.' Crying bitterly, she went to the Imam's shrine and clung to his mausoleum.' Razi added in a hushed voice, 'Suddenly the shrine was filled with a strange radiance and the man was released.'

'Amazing,' Akhtar whispered.

Bashir Bhai yawned and then seemed lost in thought once more.

'It turned out that the man had taken a false oath,' Razi said quietly.

Taking advantage of Bashir Bhai and Akhtar's silence, Razi continued, 'So, my mother said, 'Come what may, I shall not leave without a boon...I must be granted a child.' She lay next to the Imam's mausoleum all night, prayed and wept. In a vision, she saw a lion enter the *dargah*...She woke up with a start. Her eyes fell on the alam. There was a halo of golden light around the panja. A fresh jasmine flower dropped into her lap...'

'Yes, there is no doubt about His saintly powers.' Bashir Bhai said, a bit emphatically.

'That alam,' Razi whispered reverentially, 'is the real alam. It rose out of the Euphrates. It still stands at the head of the shrine in all its majesty. On the tenth day of Muharram, it is as resplendent as the sun. One can hardly look at it...'

IV

Syed felt as if there was an explosion of bright light before his eyes—that it had filled the dark caverns of his brain with radiance...Every corner of the dark underground vault glowed with bright light...Luminous shadows, a glowing face, burnished alams, and kites floating in the clear sky...The string suddenly snapped and the kite drifted away...Bundi turned away from him in anger; and when he saw her turn and walk away from him, it seemed as if the kite was floating further and further away into the distance...He dreamt that he was climbing an endless flight of stairs which unrolled before him like an infinite white cotton tape and vanished into the distance...That the string of the kite floated just beyond his reach. The stairs went through a tunnel, and then suddenly swirled high into the air. He continued to climb them. He went higher and higher. He was afraid that he would plunge into the dark abyss below. Then he fell into a well. He kept falling, slowly, very slowly. Terrified, he struggled to rise...At that moment, he woke up in panic...

'*Ammaji*, I dreamt that I was climbing a staircase.'

'It's a prophetic dream, son. You will do well; perhaps you'll become an officer.'

'Ammaji, what if one sees a flying kite in a dream?'

'No, son. One shouldn't dream about kites,' she said. 'It's not auspicious to dream about a kite. Such dreams are omens of aimless wandering and suffering.'

'Ammaji, I dreamt that I was climbing up an infinite flight of stairs. I climbed higher and higher. At last, I came to a terrace.

Suddenly, the stairs vanished...I found myself alone on the terrace and the kite...'

'No, son, that was not a prophetic dream,' his mother said, interrupting him. 'You spend your day hopping from one terrace to the next. That's why you see kites in your dreams...You must not have such dreams.'

'Ammaji, I dreamt that a monkey was sitting on the parapet wall of our terrace...'

His mother interrupted him sharply, 'That's enough. Now go to sleep.'

'All right, Ammaji. But you must first finish the story you were telling me.'

'Certainly. God bless you. Now, where did we stop?'

'The princess asked him, 'Who are you?''

'Oh, yes...The princess asked him, 'Who are you?' He tried hard to dissuade her, 'O blessed one, don't ask. It will do you harm.' But the princess was adamant, 'I shall not talk to you unless you tell me.' 'All right, Bibi, if you insist. Let's go to the river, I'll reveal my identity there.' They started walking. When they reached the river, he pleaded with her once more, 'Please don't ask me who I am.' She replied, 'I want to know.' He walked into the river. When the water reached up to his chest, he said, 'O blessed one, listen to me. Don't insist.' She said, 'I must know.' When the water reached up to his neck, he once again tried to dissuade her, and once again she refused. The water reached his mouth. 'There is still time,' he pleaded. 'You will be sorry later.' 'I want to know,' she insisted. The man disappeared under the water. Suddenly, the hood of a black cobra rose from the water and then plunged back into it...'

V

'So, she got an alam made of silver, and had it blessed with jasmine flowers. I was born the same year...'

'The alam, I am sure, is auspicious,' Bashir Bhai said.

'But...' Razi stammered nervously. 'But, that...'

'What's the matter?' Bashir Bhai asked.

'That alam disappeared.'

'How?' Bashir Bhai and Akhtar asked in dismay.

'No procession was taken out that year,' Razi said in a hushed whisper. 'We had a neighbour. He told us that no one had lit a single lamp in the Imambara that night, but when he woke up the next morning to say his prayers, it seemed as if the Imambara was flooded with light from gas-lamps...When I went across later, I noticed that while all the other alams were there, the big one had disappeared...'

VI

The morning mist lifted and sunlight spread over everything. Sitting on the parapet of the well in the bright light, they suddenly saw the shadow of something floating above them. 'A kite!' Both of them shot across the courtyard like arrows, raced up the staircase and reached the terrace.

'Where is it?' he asked, looking frantically all around.

Bundi replied confidently, 'I saw it fall on the terrace.'

'Where is it then?'

Suddenly, Bundi grabbed his sleeve and clung to his arm. 'Syed...a monkey!'

He was frightened, 'Where?'

'There!' she said, looking towards the parapet wall.

A big fat monkey was sitting on the wall. He was sleeping, but the moment he saw them, he jumped up and the black hair on his body bristled like porcupine quills. Bundi and he were paralysed with fear. The monkey stood there for a while and screeched at them. Then he walked leisurely along the wall, climbed down to the lane below and disappeared.

When they reached the staircase, their hearts were still pounding and their bodies were dripping with sweat. Bundi wiped her face with her shirt, rubbed her neck dry and brushed back her dishevelled hair. Then both of them sat down on the staircase. Still very frightened, he looked at Bundi and saw terror in her eyes. In fact, in the half-lit staircase, her eyes looked even more terror-stricken. 'Let's go,' he said, and got up at once. They ran down the steps. When they reached the first landing, he stopped at the window to look at the vast open space below which was surrounded by trees. It seemed as if the scene outside belonged to a different world.

'Don't look!' Bundi warned him.

'Why not?'

'A sorceress lives there,' she said, her eyes wide with fear. 'She has a magic mirror. Whoever looks into it is bewitched and becomes her slave.'

'Liar!'

'I swear by Allah.'

Fearfully, he looked out of the window once again. 'I don't see her.'

'Let me see,' she said, as she stepped up to the window.

She tried to peer out, but the window was too high for her. 'Syed, help me up so that I can see,' she pleaded.

He lifted her up till her feet were off the steps and her face was level with the window...He felt as if he was holding a bucket full of cool and sweet water in his arms...

VII

A ray of light broke through the shadows and scattered. He rolled over in his bed and sat up. Akhtar, Bashir Bhai and Razi were asleep; Bashir Bhai was actually snoring. The moon had risen in the sky. He rose from the bed and walked up to the drain in the dark corner of the terrace. During the monsoons it served as an outlet for rainwater and, at other times, as a convenient urinal. Having relieved himself, he poured out a glass of water from the surahi and drank it. The water was cool. He noticed that the lantern was no longer burning. As he was about to lie down again, he realized that Razi wasn't asleep.

'Razi?'

His voice heavy with sleep, Razi murmured, 'Yes...'

'Are you still awake?'

'I was about to fall asleep when I heard your footsteps.'

Both were silent for a while. Razi's eyes slowly began to close.

Akhtar and Bashir Bhai continued to sleep. Akhtar had also begun to snore softly.

Syed yawned, turned on his side, nudged Razi and asked, 'Razi, are you asleep?'

Razi opened his eyes. 'No, I am awake,' he replied drowsily.

'Razi,' he asked in a voice that was both innocent and sad, 'why don't I have dreams?'

Razi laughed and replied, 'There is no reason why people should dream every night.'

Both fell silent again. Razi's eyes were heavy with sleep. He wanted to turn on his side and shut his eyes, but Syed called him again and said, 'When I was a child, I used to dream that...that I was running up a flight of stairs chasing a kite and the steps...'

'That's not a dream...It's just one of those stray thoughts that crosses your mind before you go to sleep at night,' Razi laughed.

Was it really not a dream, Syed wondered? Have I never had a dream in my life? Memories of past life floated across his mind, but when he tried to grasp them they fell like shimmering snowflakes through his fingers. Then he realized that they were not dreams but recollections of real events. He looked back over his entire life. Every event, every shadowy corner had the hallucinatory quality of a dream. But he couldn't recall a single dream. It seemed as if his dreams were entangled with his actual life in the past; they were like particles of mica mixed in *gulal* which sparkled in the light but could never be separated from the red powder, or like the rainbow colours trapped inside the glass beads of the chandelier in the Imambara, or like sparks of fire scattered across the dark surface of water in a deep well.

'Razi, are you awake?'

'Yes,' Razi replied, his voice heavy with sleep.

'After such a long dreamless life, I can't hope to dream now,' he muttered to himself. 'Even our old home seems like a dream. As we climbed up its dark stairs, we always thought we were in a steep and dark passage. After one turn of the stairs there was another, and then another. As if we were winding our way up an infinite spiral, till we suddenly found ourselves on a bright and open terrace. We felt that we had walked into a strange world...Sometimes, it seemed that the terrace was a sad and desolate place. We often saw a monkey sleeping on the highest parapet wall. At first, it appeared that he would never stir again. Then he would suddenly wake up, stretch his body, jump down and walk leisurely towards the stairs. As we watched him slowly walk down the steps, our hearts pounded with fear. We often followed him, and hid behind the pillars to watch him cross the courtyard. Sometimes, he went and sat on the low wall around the well. He would sit there quietly...and then disappear...perhaps down the well...'

Sleep vanished from Razi's eyes. Puzzled, he looked at Syed. Quite oblivious of him, Syed continued to speak softly, 'We leaned over the wall, looked into the well and shouted, 'Who's there?' The well resonated with our shouts. Spirals of light rose from the deep waters, spilled out of the well and spread over the surrounding courtyard. It seemed as if the night was ablaze with fireworks...A shadow floated over the shimmering surface of the water. A kite! I turned to look up at the sky and saw a black-and-white kite wheeling down in ecstatic circles. It crashed against the parapet wall, slid towards the courtyard and swung above my head. I jumped up to catch it, but it swung out of my reach. I shot up the staircase like an arrow...But, the moment I reached the window, my heart began to beat frantically with fear. I shut my eyes, ran past the window and continued to climb the winding stairs. I ran past one turn, then past another and another; I climbed one flight of stairs, then another flight of stairs and then another...a whole century passed as I climbed and climbed...till, at last, I found myself on an open terrace...But, then, I found myself once more in a labyrinth of stairs, stairs and more stairs...'

'Yaar, you are talking as if in a dream,' Razi said, looking at him in wonder.

Syed fell silent.

The moon climbed up the sky and moonlight spread from the foot of his bed to the very edges of the parapet wall. A few beams of moonlight were trapped in the glass next to the surahi which shimmered with light. Bashir Bhai and Akhtar were still fast asleep.

Since it was cold, Bashir Bhai had removed the cotton sheet folded under his head and had covered himself with it. Akhtar's blanket, which had earlier covered his legs, now lay bunched up on his chest.

Razi shut his eyes and tried to sleep. After some time, he gave up and opened his eyes.

'Syed?'

'Yes?' Syed asked drowsily.

'Are you asleep? Yaar, I can't sleep.'

Syed looked at Razi and whispered mysteriously, 'Yaar, my heart is beating with excitement. I may have a dream tonight.' And his eyes, heavy with sleep, began to close.

Date of publication: 1973

14

The Jungle of the Gonds
(*Gondon ka Jungle*)

'Has he returned?'

'No.'

'Who rang the bell?'

'A servant from the house across. He wanted the newspaper.'

She grumbled, as if she hadn't heard him, 'I wonder where he is?' Looking worried, she turned around and went inside.

'Betey Mobeen,' Bawa Jaan said, 'Sajid Mian is waiting. Make some tea for him.'

Mobeen was about to get up when Sajid stopped him, 'Not yet. Tea can wait. Let Moin get back.'

'If only he came back home,' Bawa Jaan said despondently. 'You can see how worried his mother is.'

Amma, still worried, looked into the room once more as if she had suddenly remembered something, 'Sajid Bhai, what did he tell you?'

'Ji...Actually...I had complained to him—that the evenings are very boring. One can't go anywhere. There is a curfew every evening. He replied—I am always at home these days. Come over after work. We'll invite Rasheed too. Both of you can spend the night here. We'll gossip. Maybe, even see a film...'

'Yes, he has been at home for several days. He has no work.

Where can he go? But, early this morning, there was a telephone call for him. He left at once. I said to him—Betey, don't go. The times are bad…He replied—I have some urgent work. I'll take care of it and be back in about an hour…He is yet to come back! It's almost evening and there is no sign of him.'

Amma continued to stand for a while in silence then went inside. That was the fourth time she had come into the room since Sajid had arrived. And Sajid hadn't been there for long. *Bawa Jaan* hadn't even started his usual commentary on current affairs.

The telephone rang again. Mobeen picked it up, 'Hello…ji…ji…He hasn't yet come back.'

Amma rushed into the room, 'Is he asking for Moin? At least ask him…'

'Ask him what? I don't even know who he was…'

'I don't even know who he was! How casual can you be? I wonder who he was. There was a call for Moin in the morning soon after he left. And another in the afternoon. And yet another now. Someone asks for him and disconnects immediately after…I wonder who he is…an informer or some…' she fell silent before completing her sentence and walked out of the room.

As soon as she left, Bawa Jaan began to talk freely, 'You can at least step out of your house. Was it peaceful in the city today or was there any…'

'I didn't hear anything. We'll know from the newspaper tomorrow.'

'Yes, we'll find out from tomorrow's newspaper. There was a time when the most insignificant news used to spread through the city at once. Now the times are such that if there is a calamity in one locality, other localities hardly even get to hear about it. For instance, last Friday, we were at a wedding feast. There was firing in a locality, a few steps away from the marriage hall. The police arrived. A curfew was imposed. But we knew nothing about it. We continued with our feast.'

'But, Syed Sahib, rumours spread very fast.'

'Yes, that's true, Mian. The times are very bad. That's why I tell both my sons—stop wandering around. But Moin can't sit still.

I especially warn him—Betey, the times have changed. You can't roam through the city day and night. Finish your work and return home at once. But he refuses to listen. You can see how worried his mother is.'

The telephone rang again. Bawa Jaan stopped talking. 'Mobeen Betey, see who it is. Perhaps…his…'

Mobeen rushed to the telephone, 'Hello…all right…I'll get him.' Then he called out, 'Nadeem, phone call for you…'

Nadeem picked up the telephone, spoke for a few minutes and then returned to the drawing room.

'What's the score?' Mobeen asked.

'163.'

'Only? That's very slow.'

'Their bowlers have caught us in a noose. No one has hit a boundary for a long time.'

'I hope we won't lose.'

'Let's see what happens,' he said as he left the room.

Amma continued to stand in silence. Sajid's statement had no impact on her. Suddenly, she felt strange standing there. She quietly left the room.

There was silence for a while.

Mobeen grumbled, 'Bhai Jaan knows that Amma gets worried quickly. Not only does she worry, she makes us tense too. But, Bhai Jaan…'

'Betey, her concern is understandable. These days one is even afraid to step out of one's house.'

'Saiyyad Sahib,' Sajid said, 'why speak of the world outside? One isn't safe even inside one's house.'

'You are right, Mian. One should always be cautious when the times are bad,' Abba said. Then after a pause, he added, 'Let me tell you something. There was a time when I wasn't afraid of anything. I worked in the forest department. I was young. I got a job soon after my matriculation. My Phupha was a forest conservator. He got me a job in his department. I was posted to the Central Provinces. The jungle there…may God protect us…was so dark even during the day that one could walk for miles on end without seeing a ray of light or coming across another human being. My orderly and I were nearly always alone. I had a rifle and a belt full of cartridges. The orderly carried a lantern in one hand and a stick in the other. We had to deal with the Gonds. They were a wild tribe. Very dangerous. They stole logs of wood at night. The forest guards were afraid of them. They didn't want to risk their own lives. But if a Gond fell into my trap, I never let him escape. When I came home during the vacations, *Taya Jaan* said—Why did your Phupha condemn you to that place? The whole area belongs to the Hindus...and you also have to deal with the Gonds, the Bhils and the animals of the forest. Aren't you afraid? I replied—No...Indeed, I wasn't afraid of anything in those days, even though I was the only Muslim around. Believe me, I wasn't afraid of anything...But now I am. I am afraid of the Muslims.' He fell silent. Then he sighed, 'How things have changed! A Muslim is afraid of other Muslims!'

'Syed Sahib,' Sajid asked, 'aren't the Central Provinces in the south?'

'Perhaps. But, Mian, we weren't concerned about north or south. We didn't care about where we were or where we were going. In a forest, one loses all sense of direction. There is nothing but the jungle everywhere...with tigers, panthers, leopards...and men known as Gonds or Bhils—wilder than the animals. I am surprised at myself when I recall those foolhardy days. How could I have wandered so fearlessly? I suppose, I had faith in Allah above, and confidence in my rifle, as I walked through the forest down here. Mian, the rifle was a great help. The Gonds knew I had a rifle...Even during the riots, it was my rifle that saved our locality. We weren't attacked. People knew there was one house in the locality which had a rifle...' Bawa Jaan paused, took a deep breath and said, 'It's sad that I had to leave my rifle back there. Now, Mian, we are unarmed. That is why we are so afraid...'

'Bawa Jaan,' Mobeen asked, 'how can a rifle protect you now? These days, a rifle is no better than any country-made weapon.'

'Did you hear that Sajid Mian? Whenever I talk about my rifle, my sons laugh at me. They tell me people use Kalashnikovs these days. Maybe they are right. But, still, Mian, a rifle is a rifle...'

Nadeem looked into the room and asked, 'Hasn't Bhai Jaan returned yet?'

'No,' Mobeen answered curtly.

'Where could he be? Amma is worried.'

'Allah knows where he is. I wish he would realize how worried Amma gets.' Mobeen paused for a moment and then asked, 'What's the score?'

'The run rate is a bit better now. We have a fifty-fifty chance. Let's see what turn the match takes after the tea-break.' Then he exclaimed with a start, 'The tea-break is over,' and left the room in a hurry.

Bawa Jaan heaved a sigh of relief. He didn't like being inter-rupted.

'Sajid Mian, the boys are crazy about cricket. In our days, we weren't so crazy even about kite-flying.'

'Yes, these days there is a craze for cricket,' Sajid replied briefly.

'Mian, all these are games which fate plays with us. Once upon a time, a sword was a sign of manliness, now it is mocked at. But, to tell you honestly, Sajid Mian, these modern times have yet to find an alternative to the sword. Modern weapons are only machines. Press a trigger and the machines begin to fire. And what's so great about a trigger? Anybody can press it. It's not a test of manliness. But a sword...'

He was interrupted by the sound of the doorbell. 'Mobeen, go and see who it is. Perhaps...'

Mobeen went to open the door.

Amma quickly came in, and asked, 'Did the doorbell ring?'

'Yes,' Bawa Jaan replied calmly. 'There is someone at the door.'

'Who else can it be? I know it's him...' As Amma turned to go towards the door, Mobeen returned.

'Who was it?' asked Amma and Bawa Jaan together.

'The man who lives upstairs.'

'The man who lives upstairs?' Bawa Jaan looked puzzled.

'The one who lives in No. 63.'

'What did he want?'

'He wanted to know if Bhai Jaan was at home.'

'Why?'

'He didn't tell me.'

'You should have asked him. You should have found out what he wanted.'

'I don't know him. I don't even know what he does.'

'He is a lawyer.'

'A lawyer?' Bawa Jaan asked suspiciously.

'Arrey, he has never asked about Moin earlier. I don't think Moin even knows him.'

'Sajid Mian, do you know him?'

'No.'

'That's funny. None of us know him.'

'In fact, I hardly ever socialize with these flat-wallahs,' Sajid said, as if trying to explain himself.

'As if we do, Mian. Apart from you, we don't know anyone else who lives here or what they do.'

'But why did that lawyer come here? Why did he ask for Moin?'

'Amma, I think the lawyer is a decent man. You shouldn't unnecessarily suspect him.'

'You keep quiet. You think every petty thief is a decent man.'

'What strange times we live in!' Bawa Jaan said. 'Men are afraid of men, and neighbours don't trust their neighbours. Indeed, how can they? All sorts of people have now come and settled in the city. Consider our flats, for instance. People from all walks of life live here. They are all strangers. Who knows what they do? That is why they can't share each other's sorrow. Once upon a time, neighbours shared each other's pain, consoled each other. Now, we can't go and cry before anyone; now we can't tell anyone that our son left home in the morning and hasn't yet returned, that he is in trouble...'

Amma, who seemed lost in thought, suddenly got up and left the room.

'Bawa Jaan...'

'Yes?'

'I am really getting worried. It's time for the curfew and Bhai Jaan...'

'Yes, Betey. I don't know what to do,' Bawa Jaan said anxiously.

'Perhaps we should ask someone,' Mobeen said, wondering whom he could contact.

'Moin should have come back by now,' Sajid said. 'I really don't understand why he hasn't. He asked me to come here at this time and even invited Rasheed. Perhaps, Rasheed has delayed him, and they'll come together.'

'We are all anxious about the boy,' Bawa Jaan said. He looked very perturbed. 'I wonder whose inauspicious face I saw in the morning. The whole day has been spent worrying about something or the other. First, a letter from Basharat Bhai upset us. Sajid Mian, Basharat Bhai refused to migrate. He still lives back there. He wrote about the conditions in Khurja. They are very bad. He thinks, however, that people in Pakistan live comfortably.'

'Yes, it's hell over there,' Sajid said.

'Mian, earlier I used to get very angry. At the Hindus, the Sikhs, the Jews. After all, the Jews have also tormented the Muslims a lot. I used to get very angry. Now I don't. Perhaps, I've grown old...or, perhaps, I've witnessed so much that...I can't even tell you. Yes, I used to get very angry. Now I don't. At anything...If I ever get angry, it's at myself.'

'Yes, the times are bad.'

'No, Sajid Mian, that's not the reason. The truth is that we have no compassion. My father, for example—may his soul rest in peace—was such a fine person that when he read *Shikwa* and *Jawab-i-Shikwa*, he would weep inconsolably. Compassion disappeared with people like him, along with all sense of *Mussalmani*.'

Nadeem entered the room looking very nervous. 'Mobeen Bhai, Amma is standing at the door. Go and take care of her. The match is in the last stages. I'll be back soon. Bhai Jaan has caused us a lot of anxiety,' he said as he ran out of the room.

Mobeen rushed to the door. Bawa Jaan seemed to have lost his voice. Somehow, Mobeen managed to cajole Amma back into the room and persuaded her to sit on the sofa.

'Please, Amma Jaan, don't worry so much. Maybe, something urgent has detained him. He'll be back.'

'No, he won't come back. I know.' Amma seemed to have given

up all hope. 'How can he come home now? The curfew has already been imposed.'

'Not yet,' Mobeen said, contradicting her.

'He will never come back,' Amma sobbed.

Bawa Jaan sat in silence for a while. Then he said to Mobeen, 'Betey, take her inside.'

Mobeen tried to console Amma. She wiped her tears and stopped sobbing.

'Come. Let's go in,' Mobeen said.

She stood up and silently walked out of the room. Mobeen followed her.

'Pakistan has won!' Nadeem ran into the room shouting with excitement.

'Really?' Sajid asked enthusiastically. 'It would have been embarrassing if we had lost.'

'No one could predict the result till the last moment. The last ball settled the issue. Had that boundary not been struck, we would have lost the match.'

'Well, at least, we have saved our honour,' Sajid seemed very satisfied at the victory. But he wasn't as ecstatic as Nadeem.

'Now that you are no longer anxious, go and see how your mother is.'

'So, Bhai Jaan hasn't yet returned...that's the limit...Where could he be?' He walked out muttering to himself.

'What's the time?' Bawa Jaan asked Sajid.

'The curfew would have been imposed,' Sajid said, looking at his watch.

After a pause, Bawa Jaan grumbled under his breath, 'Something must have...' His voice trailed into silence.

'I don't understand.'

'What don't you understand?'

After a while, Sajid said, 'Maybe I should go.'

'You have waited long enough. Now...' Bawa Jaan didn't complete his sentence.

Sajid was about to get up when the doorbell rang again. Startled, Sajid said, 'I think he has come.'

'He...how can he come at this time?'

They watched Mobeen and Nadeem run to the door. Tense with apprehension, they continued to sit where they were. When the other two returned, Moin was, indeed, with them. Bawa Jaan looked at him reproachfully.

'Arrey, Sajid, you are still here! What happened was that...'

Bawa Jaan interrupted him and said, 'Tell us later. See your mother first.'

'All right. Sajid, wait for me here. I'll be back soon,' he said, his face tense with fear.

'Allah is merciful,' Sajid said, as Moin left the room. Then after a pause, he added, 'We thought that...' He didn't complete his sentence.

Bawa Jaan, lost in thought, continued to sit in silence.

Trying to resume the conversation, Sajid said, 'Life these days is completely unpredictable. Riots have a logic of their own. A man walks through a crowded bazaar. Suddenly a shot is fired from somewhere. The man falls dead. This could happen to any one of us. Death may strike while one is out for a walk. Anything can happen.'

'Yes,' Bawa Jaan sighed. 'One shouldn't say such things, Sajid Mian, but since you have raised the subject, I must tell you that Pakistan...is lost.'

Nadeem walked in with a packet of sweets. 'Have some sweets, Sajid Bhai.'

'Sweets! Oh well...all right. But what's the occasion?'

'To celebrate Pakistan's victory!' Then he extended the packet towards Bawa Jaan and said, 'You have some too.'

'No. You know I avoid eating sweets.'

Nadeem left the room as quickly as he had come in.

Bawa Jaan's mind was fixed on the same subject. He whispered, as if to himself, 'How funny! Pakistan hasn't fought a war but has lost...lost to itself.'

Moin returned. His face was still marked with fear. He sat down quietly. Tea was served.

'Have some tea, Sajid...Yaar, you had to wait a long time.'

Bawa Jaan got up and said, 'Well, you carry on with your conversation. I must go.'

'Syed Sahib, tea has been served. Won't you have some tea with us?'

'No, Mian, it's time for my *namaz*.'

'Yaar, Sajid, sorry.'

'But, yaar, you have upset everyone in the house. What happened?'

'I'll tell you. Drink your tea.'

'You look upset. Did something happen?'

'No, nothing happened. Drink your tea, yaar. It will get cold.'

Puzzled, Sajid looked at Moin's face for a while and then began to drink his tea. He wasn't in the mood to talk because the entire episode had exhausted him. Moin too was tired at the end of the day.

'I am sure you were bored out of your mind today. Bawa Jaan must have really bored you.'

'Not at all. I was very impressed by his conversation. And, well...' He stopped as if he had suddenly recalled something, 'Wasn't Rasheed supposed to come with you? Didn't he turn up?'

After some hesitation, Moin replied, 'No.' Then in a broken voice, he added, 'He won't come now.'

'Yes, how can he come now? He would have, if he were planning to. Didn't he meet you?'

'He did meet me. We were together.'

'Then?'

Nadeem, looking rather pleased, walked into the room, and said, 'Sajid Bhai, let's see a film tonight to celebrate the victory. What do you say? Bhai Jaan, you also wanted to see one.'

'A film?' Moin asked with surprise. 'Sajid?'

'No, yaar, not tonight. You are tired and I am not in the mood. Besides, Rasheed's absence has upset me.'

'Rasheed,' Moin said in a whisper. 'It's strange that a man is here one moment...and gone the next.'

Utterly confused, Sajid looked at Moin who seemed to be lost in his thought.

'Strange...'

'You haven't yet told me what happened.'

At that moment, Mobeen walked in and said, 'Sajid Mian, there was a telephone call from your home asking when you would be back.'

'Didn't you tell them?' Moin asked.

'I did. But Ammi worries a lot.'

'I told them that you would be late,' Nadeem said. 'We are going to watch a film to celebrate our victory.'

'Oh no, not today,' Sajid said and got up quickly. 'Some other time.'

Moin didn't try to stop him. 'Yes, some other time.'

Sajid went back to his flat. He entered his room and collapsed into a chair as if he had walked a great distance. Soon his mother entered the room.

'It's good that you are back. I was worried. When I called you, Nadeem told me that you were celebrating. When I asked him—Betey, what are you celebrating? He said that you were celebrating our victory. When I asked him—Victory, whose victory?—he replied, Pakistan's victory!—Pakistan's? And Betey, who lost? But suddenly the telephone was disconnected...All right, you rest. I won't disturb you. Should I send you some tea?'

'No, I have already had some.'

From outside came the sounds of whistles.

'Strange, why are people blowing whistles today?' Sajid's mother said anxiously as she left the room.

Sajid got up and began to pace up and down. He didn't know what to do. He flipped through a few books. Rearranged the ones that were lying scattered on the table. Tore up some old papers and threw them into the waste-paper basket. He didn't know what to do after that. Once again, he heard the sounds of whistles being blown somewhere in the distance. He went and stood out on the balcony. From the balcony of his third floor flat, it always seemed as if the entire city lay spread out before him. Glowing with lights, it used to look beautiful at night. That night there was something different about it. Only a few scattered lights were burning and they too seemed dim and lifeless. He looked at the street below. Normally busy, it was now desolate. Suddenly, several jeeps, packed with policemen, roared through the street shattering its silence. Then once again an eerie silence settled over the street.

'Let's celebrate our victory...' Nadeem's sentence echoed in his mind for no reason. Going back to his room, he shut the balcony door and the windows facing the street. Still unable to find anything to do, he collapsed into his chair and closed his eyes.

Many disjointed and meaningless thoughts flashed through his mind—'Where are we? Where are we heading? One loses all sense of direction in a jungle. The jungle is everywhere. It is all around...Fierce Gonds armed with spears...Dark nights...He will not come now. Really?...'

Sajid got up with a start. He wanted to call Moin at once and talk to him. He should at least have asked Moin what...what...? But then he was overcome by another thought—Why should he ask? Slowly, he sat down in his chair and closed his eyes. He was once again in the jungle of the Gonds...

Date of publication: 1990

15

A Chronicle of the Peacocks
(*Morenama*)

Allah alone knows why this evil spirit is after me! I am shocked and upset. I had actually gone there to inquire after the well-being of the peacocks. How was I to know that this evil spirit would grab hold of me?

It was by chance that I came across that small news item; otherwise, in the midst of all that turmoil, I would never have found out what had really happened. Tucked away in the middle of the terrifying news about India's atomic bomb was a small note about how the explosion had so frightened the peacocks of Rajasthan that they had flown up screaming into the sky and scattered in all directions.

Immediately, I wrote a column expressing my sympathy for the peacocks, and thought that, having done my duty, I was free from all further obligations. But had I really done my duty? Was I actually free? That insignificant piece of information disturbed me in the same way as that small fish had disturbed Manuji. Manuji had once caught a fish no longer than his little finger and had placed it in a pot. He, too, had thought he had done his duty and was free. But the fish started to grow and grow. It became so big that he had to take it out of the pot and release it into a lake, and then take it out of the lake and release it into a river. The fish, however, became too large for the river, and Manuji had to carry it to the sea. In the same way a news item, which journalists thought deserved no more than two lines, overwhelmed my imagination.

The news reminded me of the peacocks I had seen in Jaipur. *Subhan Allah*, what a beautifully-planned pink city it was! I reached Jaipur late in the afternoon. At first, I did not sense their presence. But, in the evening, when I opened the window of the guest house, which was as lovely as a new bride, the view outside was breathtaking. Everywhere I looked—in the courtyard, on the parapet around the fountain, over the balconies—there were peacocks; peacocks and more peacocks; peacocks with bright blue tails! They had a quiet dignity and a royal grace and a calm elegance. I felt as if I were in the very cradle of beauty, love and peace.

The next evening, as I was about to leave the city, I saw peacocks on every tree, rock and hill. Their movements had the same peace, the same grace and the same beauty. As the evening shadows deepened, the air was filled with the song of peacocks. I thought they were there to both welcome and bid me farewell.

Whenever I recall that trip, my mind is filled with the images of those peacocks. I am surprised. Did I really see so many of them? Did the peacocks of Rajasthan actually come out to greet me? I wonder how they are now.

I try to imagine that city now, but all I can see is a picture of desolation. Shocked and disturbed, I am neither able to see the peacocks nor hear their song. Where have they all disappeared? In which corner of the world are they hiding? Suddenly, I have a vision of a lonely peacock on a distant hill. He seems battered and bruised. I walk quickly toward him but, before I can reach the hill, he rises into the sky screaming with terror and disappears.

Where has he gone? Where are his companions, those countless peacocks? Why is he sitting alone on that hill, the very picture of desolation? Why is he so despondent, so terrified? The sight of that dejected, bewildered peacock suddenly brings to mind another image of desolation that I had forgotten. On the far edge of a dark, oil-soaked sea, I see a forlorn duck covered with foul effluents, watching the waves in disbelief. Till yesterday the sea was ambrosia, today it is poison. The wings of the duck are so heavy with slime that he can no longer fly. Poison flows though the veins in his body. The weary bird is a symbol of the horrors of the war between the United States and Iraq. It is sad to see a bird in so much pain. The poor duck seemed to have taken upon himself all the crimes human beings commit against each other—Saddam Hussain against his countrymen, the Iraqis against the Kuwaitis and the Americans against the Iraqis. It is strange that whenever apocalypse is at hand, the rich and the powerful rarely ever pay for their sins: instead, the poor and weak take upon themselves the burden of suffering so as to redeem their times. The duck is symbolic of those prophets who, according to all religious texts, think of suffering as a sacred duty.

At that time, I didn't recognize the duck as a symbol of our times. I lacked the visionary insight to see that he had the grace of a prophet. It never occurred to me to write a story about him. I forgot about him completely. He was only a poor, small duck, and not a gorgeous peacock about whom I am so anxious to write a story now. What if he had been a royal swan instead of a mere duck? But there are no royal swans in the world now. Once upon a time, it was difficult to decide whether the royal swan or the peacock was the king of the universe. In those days, royal swans used to swim in lakes that were as translucent as white pearls. And princesses used to scatter pearls across palace courtyards to tempt their swan-lovers. In our times, there are no swan-lovers who can be seduced by pearls. Nor are there any royal swans that swim in the shimmering waters of Mansarovar. Now, no one even knows where Mansarovar is. The lakes are dry, the rivers polluted and the air thick with the dust and smoke of bombs. The royal swans have flown away in search of clear air and pure water. They exist only in the world of fables and myths. Only the poor ducks and geese have been left behind to bear the burden of our times.

Till recently, the peacock, in all his grandeur, was a link between the past and the present. When the monsoon breeze cooled the evening, the song of the peacock used to fill the air. I remember that once a peacock came and sat on the parapet of our terrace. I quickly ran up to the terrace, tip-toed along the wall, and was about to grab its tail, when a shudder ran through his body and he flapped his wings nervously and flew away.

You should never trouble a peacock, son. He is the bird of paradise,' *Dadima* reprimanded me.

'The bird of paradise?' I asked in wonder. 'What is he doing here?'

'He is paying for his mistake.'

'What did he do to be so punished?'

'O my son, he is innocent, but he got trapped in the wiles of that wretch, Satan.'

'How did he get trapped in the wiles of Satan?'

'That wretch disguised himself as an old man and went to the gates of paradise. He pleaded with the gatekeepers to let him in. But the gatekeepers saw through his disguise and recognized that the old man was Satan himself. So they refused to open the gates. A peacock, who was sitting on the wall surrounding the garden of paradise, felt sorry for the old man. He flew down to him and said, 'Bade Mian, I'll help you across the wall.' Well, what does a blind man need but the guidance of someone who can see? Satan jumped onto the peacock's back at once. The peacock flew over the wall of paradise and helped Satan enter the Garden of Eden. When Allah Mian found out, He was very angry. When He exiled Adam and Eve from the Garden of Eden, He also asked the peacock to get out.'

I was upset when I heard the story and felt sorry for the peacock. Once upon a time, he used to sit on the wall of paradise, and now he sits on the wall of our terrace. When I told Dadima this, she replied, 'Yes, son, that is what happens when we are exiled from our own courtyards. Now, all he can do is find something to sit on—any wall around any courtyard—or any tree or hill where he can find a foothold.'

When I walked through Sravasthi, I saw a peacock sitting on a green hill lost in thought. It seemed as if he was waiting for someone. I had reached Sravasthi late in the afternoon. Mahatma Buddha had lived there a long time ago. The *vihara* where he used to stay with his monks during the monsoons is now in ruins. Only a few scattered bricks mark its place. The peacock on the hill was, perhaps, the last of the survivors from the days of the Buddha and still carried images of those days in his eyes. Due to the presence of that one peacock, Sravasthi seemed a place of great tranquillity.

I didn't stay long in Sravasthi. I had to get back to Delhi. But, that evening, Delhi was a sad and desolate city. At least, the basti around Nizamuddin was. Only a few days earlier, a caravan of migrants, whose homes had been looted, had left the area. On that rainy day, it seemed as if the silence and the gloom would never lift. Even Nizamuddin's tomb, in the middle of an unpaved courtyard, looked dismal. The tomb was surrounded by tall grass. As I walked through it, I heard a peacock call from somewhere behind the tomb. When I turned around to look, I couldn't see him, but I heard him call once more. It was a strange call, resonant of millenniums past.

As my imagination moved further down the ages, I was once again startled by the call of peacocks. '*Ya Moulla*, where are those peacocks, in which garden?' Surprised, I walked a little further, and found myself in a city whose outer walls touched the clouds. Beyond the walls were orchards filled with a variety of fruits. The garden echoed with the music of birds of different hues. Two notes were more distinct than the others—the whistle of the koel and the call of the peacock...Arrey, this is Indraprastha, the city of the Pandavas! Have I really travelled so far from home? I must get back.

I have travelled far and long. I have seen peacocks—peacocks from different ages and lands. I have heard their song. Now, it is time for me to write my *Morenama*—my Chronicle of the Peacocks. But, before I go back home, I must make another trip to Rajasthan and find out if the peacocks that had flown away in fear have returned.

The peacocks had actually returned in great numbers. Strangely, the moment they saw me, they were so terrified that, screaming in terror, they rose from the hills and trees and scattered in the sky. At that moment, I sensed that I wasn't alone. Someone else was walking beside me. When I looked to my left, I was so shocked by what I saw that I couldn't turn my gaze away... What! Is that Ashwatthama, the great criminal of Kurukshetra? Why is he here? Why is he walking beside me?...I don't know when he attached himself to me. Perhaps, he began to follow me when, on my way back from Indraprastha, I stopped at Kurukshetra. Yes, I am sure this evil creature attached himself to me there. But Kurukshetra was desolate. I had seen no living being there. Where had he been hiding? Had he been wandering there ever since the war?

War transforms man utterly. Take Ashwatthama, the son of Dronacharya. Dronacharya was a man of such profound learning that all the great warriors of the Pandavas and the Kauravas used to bow down to him and touch his feet. Ashwatthama, his son, had inherited many of his father's qualities, but he didn't have his wisdom. He was the most damned and accursed man of that war.

It is said that Dronacharya, guru of all the great warriors, possessed the most dreaded of weapons, the Brahmastra. In appearance, it was no different from a blade of grass, but its power was so great that it could reduce everything to ash; destroy all living things far and wide in an instant. Dronacharya had passed on the secret of that weapon only to his favourite disciple, Arjuna. War is so awful that in Kurukshetra, the teacher and his disciple found themselves in opposing camps fighting each other. Both, however, had taken a vow never to use the Brahmastra because it would destroy the whole world.

Before his death, Dronacharya revealed the secret of the Brahmastra to his son, Ashwatthama, but warned him sternly never to use it. After Dronacharya was killed there was no one left to restrain Ashwatthama. So, during the last days of the war, he decided to stake everything and release the Brahmastra.

The last days of war are always the most fearful. They are dangerous and unpredictable. During those days, men are tempted to use weapons that are only meant to threaten. It doesn't matter then if a city like Hiroshima burns; at least the fighting comes to an end. The victors are satisfied; the defeated are lost in their sorrow. At Kurukshetra, it was Ashwatthama who acted foolishly and used the Brahmastra.

When Shri Krishna heard what Ashwatthama had done, he said to Arjuna, 'O Janardhan, Dronacharya's foolish son has released the Brahmastra. Now, all living things will be destroyed. Only you can counter that weapon. Act quickly before everything is reduced to ashes.'

Arjuna took out his Brahmastra and released it to neutralize Ashwatthama's weapon. It is said, that when Arjuna released the Brahmastra, the fire was so intense that its flames singed all the three worlds. Its heat even scorched the distant forest where Vyasa Rishi sat in meditation. He was terrified. He abandoned his meditations at once, went to Kurukshetra, stood between Ashwatthama and Arjuna, and raising both hands, shouted, 'O evil ones, what great injustice is this! The entire world will be destroyed. Recall your weapons.'

Arjuna touched the feet of the great soul, and at once recalled his weapon.

But Ashwatthama was unrepentant, 'Maharaj, I have released the weapon, but I don't have the power to take it back. All I can do is change its direction. So, instead of falling on the Pandava army, it will fall on their women, strike their wombs and destroy their foetuses. The Pandavas shall have no heirs and their clan shall come to an end.'

Then Shri Krishna said angrily, 'O son of Dronacharya, you are a great sinner. By killing children you have committed a great crime. I curse you to wander alone in the forests for three thousand years. May your wounds never heal, may pus and blood flow from them always, may they stink so much that people everywhere run away from you in disgust.'

Even I wanted to run away from him as far as possible, but he clung to me like a shadow...Ya Allah, where can I hide; how can I get rid of him?...I suddenly remembered that Meerabai's *samadhi* was also nearby. I wondered if I should seek shelter there. Then, it occurred to me that the dargah of Khwaja Moin-ud-din Chishti was also in the same vicinity. If I could find it, I would easily get rid of this evil spirit. Who would let him enter the dargah? Other thoughts raced through my mind. But I didn't know how to cast him off. No matter what path I took, he followed me like a shadow.

Peacocks screamed with fear on one side; women of the Pandavas wept on the other. There was mourning in every home. In every family, a child had died. There was calamity even in Arjuna's house. Subhadra was crying bitterly. The Kauravas at Kurukshetra had killed Abhimanyu, the son born from her womb. She had mourned for him. She had hoped that Abhimanyu's wife, Uttara, would give birth to a son and ensure the survival of the Pandava lineage. But Ashwatthama's prophecy had been fulfilled. Uttara collapsed after giving birth to a stillborn child. There were no celebrations in any other Pandava household either. The Brahmastra had rendered the wombs of all their women barren. Subhadra remembered the promise her brother had made to her. Shri Krishna had promised, 'Sister, I shall not let your daughter-in-law's womb remain barren.' And, so, because he was an incarnation of Vishnu, he instilled life in the body of the dead child once more. He also predicted that Uttara's son would sit on the throne of Hastinapur and bring honour to the Pandavas.

But when Uttara's son, Parikshit, was on the throne, he asked Vyasaji, who had come to the palace to give him his blessings, a very strange question. Parikshit washed Vyasaji's feet in a bowl of rose water, stood before him with folded hands, bowed his head and said, 'O wise one, with your permission, can I ask you a question?'

'Ask, son.'

'Maharaj, all the elders of our family were present at Kurukshetra. There were wise and knowledgeable men amongst the Pandavas and the Kauravas. Why didn't they understand that in war everyone has to pay a heavy price? That war destroys everything? Annihilates everything?'

Vyasaji sighed and replied, 'Son, during times of war, even the best of men lose their heads. Besides, that which is fated must come to pass.'

Then, Vyasaji went back to the forest.

In those blessed days, rishis used to live for thousands of years. Arjuna's grandson wasn't a rishi. He died when a snake bit him. But the question he asked Vyasaji, continued to live long after his death. I suddenly remembered that question when I was wandering through Rajasthan. Indeed, I encountered it at the same time Ashwatthama began to follow me. I felt as if I were walking between two shadows.

At first, I was surprised to see Ashwatthama. 'Oh, this cursed man hasn't yet completed his three thousand years.' When I remembered the question Parikshit had asked, I was even more surprised. 'Was that question still alive?' In fact, it seemed to be even more urgent in the present. It hung over India and Pakistan like a sword. But that which is fated must come to pass. Vyasaji evaded the question and refused to answer it. That is why it still hovers over us, demanding an answer. Ashwatthama's shadow was bad enough, why must I be tormented by Parikshit's question too?

I had to get rid of Ashwatthama. I tried to deceive and evade him. I changed my path suddenly and was sure I had lost him. But, after some time, I realized he was walking beside me once again.

He couldn't follow me forever. I had to get back to my country. He was the evil spirit of this land. He could follow me only up to the border. Who would let him cross it and go any further? I had to deceive him, escape from his clutches and get back home. I would be safe there.

I did finally evade his vigilant eye. I fooled him, and before he realized it, I crossed the border and heaved a sigh of relief when I reached my country. I thanked God that I had finally escaped from that evil spirit. I recalled a story from the *Baital Pachchisee*. But that was only a story. It is only in stories that evil spirits continue to cling to living beings. Anyway, I was free at last and very relieved.

I thought of peacocks from different epochs and different lands. I recalled their song. Now, I could sit in the tranquillity of my home and write my chronicle of the peacocks. I was ecstatic. All the peacocks I had met began to crowd my imagination. Their lovely songs echoed through my brain. Then I had a vision of one divine peacock. It spread its tail like a fan over the entire universe and danced. I walked in its shadow.

As I approached my house, I heard soft footsteps behind me. I quickly turned around. I was paralysed with fear. Ashwatthama had followed me home. 'Oh, the evil spirit has found me here too! How can I ever be rid of him?'

In despair, I cried out, 'O my Creator! O my Protector! When will this evil spirit complete his curse of three thousand years? When will I be able to write my *Morenama*, my chronicle of the peacocks?'

Date of publication: 1999

Partition, Exile and Memories of a Lost Home
(*Interview with Intizar Husain*)

AB: The Partition left the lives of people of your generation in shreds. Like other writers of your time and age, your stories invariably speak of life before and immediately after the Partition. In your fiction there is a sense that, after 1947, there was a profound rupture in the civilization of the subcontinent and in the psyche of its people. Since a majority of your stories and novels (particularly *Basti*) describe in great detail a culture and a life–world that migrants to Pakistan left behind in India, I am interested in your memories of life in your father's basti. It is quite obvious that they are a rich source of inspiration for your stories and continue to haunt your present social, political and religious concerns.

In your fiction they function at three different levels. At one level, many of your stories seem to be based upon your personal experiences. The opening section of *Basti*, for instance, is surely a transparent record of your childhood in Dibai, a village near Bulandshahar in Uttar Pradesh. At the second level, you weave into your stories your memories of, or your feelings for, the cultural and political life of the subcontinent before 1947. For you, as for many other Hindu and Muslim writers, 1947 was a sad year when all that was worthy in our civilization was suddenly lost. What makes your stories even more fascinating, however, is that they function at yet another level. They seek to imaginatively recreate the shape of the entire civilizational history of the subcontinent by finding analogies for your personal memories and for the historical events of the region in the foundational stories of the Muslims, Hindus and Buddhists. For example, the stories of exile acquire a strange resonance as they weave into their texture accounts of the hijrat of Hassan and Hussain and the wanderings of Hindu sages and Buddhist monks.

Let me begin by restricting myself to your recollections of your early life in Dibai and Hapur, near Meerut. Perhaps you could tell me something about your father. What did he do? How did he find himself in Dibai? Why did he move to Hapur?

IH: My father's life story is interesting. He was an idealistic sort of man. As a Shia Muslim, he was a religious and orthodox man who was always conscious of what was right and what was wrong. When we were children, he always told us that we should never do anything that was wrong. I still remember a particular concern of his. He was against charging interest on loans because he thought it was un-Islamic. He used to insist that both were un-Islamic. On this issue, he was always at odds with the people of our community who were zamindars and moneylenders. Anyway, he always conducted his own business with great honesty. The result was that he always failed in whatever he undertook (*laughs*).

My father's life changed when Saudi Arabia was established as a state. Let me explain. In Saudi Arabia, the *mazars*, which were of great importance to the Shias, were destroyed. My father was very upset by that and decided to join a movement of protest against the Saudi Arabian government. The movement was of particular interest to the Shias, though others, too, protested.

Unfortunately, after the protest movement was over, my father discovered that he had nothing more to do (*laughs*). His Mamu, who used to live in Hapur, and to whom everyone in our family used to go to for help, said to him, 'Now that you have nothing to do, why don't you come to Hapur?' That is how we left Dibai and moved to Hapur.

I was nine years old when we moved to Hapur. As far as I am concerned the first nine years of my childhood that I spent in Dibai were, perhaps, the most important and the most formative years of my life. What I experienced in those years, and what I learnt then, was so significant that I still consider those nine years as the happiest of my life.

AB: You describe those years in *Basti*, and in many short stories, in idyllic terms.

IH: Yes, the opening section of *Basti* contains a description of an ideal community. I can't say how much of the novel is based on memories of real experiences and how much of it is imagined. It does, however, describe the years I spent as a child in Dibai in the pre-Partition India. I can say that it was during the years I spent as a child there that I experienced what a genuine community could be like. Indeed, I can assert that the foundation of everything I was to learn later was laid during those years; everything that I was ever to experience was experienced then. It still seems to me that in Dibai, I lived through the experiences of a lifetime.

AB: Could you elaborate upon the kinds of experiences that left such a deep and permanent impression of an ideal community on you? In *Basti* you write about the Muslim and Hindu myths and legends you heard from the village elders, about the songs you learnt...

IH: My descriptions of the town in *Basti* are drawn from my memories of the peculiar geographical location of our house in Dibai. Our house was located near the boundary separating the Muslim locality from the Hindu. In fact, the houses of the Hindus surrounded our house. As is often the case in small bastis, our terrace merged with the terraces of other houses inhabited by Hindus. I could always walk across from the terrace of our house to those of our Hindu neighbours. During Diwali, for instance, it was difficult to tell if the *diyas* were lit on the parapet of our house or on that of our Hindu neighbours. As a child, I would climb to the terrace of our house and gather as many diyas as I could. The next morning I would count the number of diyas I had picked up (*laughs*).

The same was the case with kites. You know, in those days, children were crazy about flying kites. Along with other children, I would run across rooftops trying to 'loot' as many kites as I could even as the women screamed at us to be careful.

When there were festivals—Holi, Diwali, Janmashtami, etc.—I would invariably climb up to our terrace and watch the rituals being conducted in the courtyards of Hindu households.

AB: Did you also participate in those festivals?

IH: No, not really. But I always watched the celebrations with great interest. I should, however, add that on Holi night I simply had to go out to watch the bonfires being lit in the village square. I didn't play Holi, but I always watched it being played.

AB: Were you ever told not to play Holi?

IH: No, there wasn't any prohibition. It was just that, since I didn't go to the school in the village, I felt that I didn't know anyone well enough to play Holi.

I didn't go to school because my father insisted on teaching me at home himself. He was rather obstinate about that. He was convinced that if I went to school my education would be ruined (*laughs*). My interactions with other children were restricted because of my father's eccentricity.

My father began my education by teaching me Arabic. He said that I didn't need to study Urdu. So, my education started with my being made to read the Koran.

In my father's library there were lots of books on Islamic culture, in addition to books published by the Arya Samaj. I read everything I could find. I don't know how I learnt to read Urdu! But I do recall that there was a copy of the Urdu translation of the Bible in the house (perhaps the first Urdu translation of the Bible). I used to find its Urdu a bit strange. It was only later that I realized how different its usage of the language was from the one that was spoken by us.

AB: In *Basti,* you emphasize the fact that as a child, apart from Islamic stories, you also grew up listening to stories from Hindu mythology.

IH: Yes, the atmosphere was such that as a child I grew up listening to all kinds of stories. Don't forget that our neighbours were Hindus. Like everyone else, they too used to sit outside their homes or shops and tell stories.

I must tell you that I was also very fond of going to see the Ram Lila. I never missed the chance of watching Ravana being burnt on Dussera. There was a Ram Lila performance in our immediate neighbourhood every year.

AB: Were there any tensions between your Hindu and Muslim neighbours?

IH: As I have said, the houses of the Hindus surrounded our house. Our nearest Muslim neighbour was three houses down the lane. I suppose, if there had been riots, we would have been in great danger. But I can't recall any instance of tension between the Hindu and the Muslim neighbours. I do, however, remember that there was often tension between the Shias and the Sunnis, but, never between the Hindus and the Muslims. No, there was never any tension between the Hindus and the Muslims. It is strange to think about all that now...

Let me tell you something interesting. When I was in Delhi recently in October 1997, I made it a point to go and see a performance of the Ram Lila. As soon as I reached Delhi, I told my friend, Reoti Saran Sharma, 'I haven't seen Ram Lila for a long time. I must go and see one, now that

I have the chance.' The Ram Lila to which Reoti took me was a modern production. It was performed in the contemporary style with all the artistic and technical sophistication available. It was nice, but I felt sad because it did not have the authenticity of the old Ram Lila performances, which I remembered from my childhood days. The Ram Lila of our basti was the real Ram Lila. The one I saw in Delhi was an artifice which could only appeal to an artistic sensibility. Of course, I must also admit that I, too, had changed. I was seeing the Ram Lila performance as a grown-up man who had studied the Ramayana as an epic and analysed it critically. But as a child, I didn't know the text and went to see the performances of Ram Lila with all the wonder and naïveté of a child. I recall that I used to feel personally involved in the story—involved as an actor in the performance. It used to affect me deeply. When I saw the performance in Delhi again after many years, I responded to it as an intellectual who was no longer emotionally involved in the lives being enacted. I was, of course, still interested, but as a slightly distanced observer.

AB: What you have said, thus far, is significant. You have said that your house was surrounded by Hindu families, and that you participated with emotional fascination in all the Hindu festivals. Were your Hindu neighbours equally interested in Muslim festivals? Did they celebrate Moharrum with you for instance?

IH: In fact, my Muslim friends used to go to see Ram Lila performances more often than I did. I couldn't go every evening because my father used to object. All of us used to participate in the Diwali festivities too. Holi was different. I didn't play it because I was always afraid of getting my clothes wet with colour. But, no, our Hindu neighbours didn't participate.

AB: That is interesting because in Rahi Masoom Raza's novel, *Aadha Gaon*, there are long descriptions of the Hindus helping the Muslim community with every aspect of Moharrum. Recently, Qurratulain Hyder told me that one of the chief singers in the Ram Lila performances in Lucknow was a Muslim. In fact, in her recent documentary on Lucknow, she has a brief conversation with him. He is now an old man, but he still sings in the Ram Lila. Was there a similar tradition of Muslim singers performing in the Ram Lila plays in your village?

IH: You know, the tradition of Awadh is different from the one in which I grew up. In Lucknow, I know that Hindus used to take part in celebrating Moharrum. In fact, some history books even suggest that a few of the marsias there were even written by Hindus, and that many Hindu households used to keep tazias. In Lucknow and in Gorakhpur district, where Rahi Masoom Raza grew up, there was a very close relationship between the Hindus and the Muslims. In Dibai and Hapur, where I grew up, Hindus and Muslims were not as intimate with each other. The Moharrum procession, however, used to go through Hindu bazaars. I don't remember a single instance of tension between the communities during those days. No one ever protested when the procession went past a temple. In fact, it was the Sunnis who used to protest when nauhas were read in front of their houses or mattam was performed in their neighbourhood. There was always some tension between the Shias and the Sunnis, not between the Hindus and the Muslims.

AB: How big was Dibai?

IH: It was originally a small village that had grown into a *kasba*. It retained, however, all the characteristics of a village. Hapur, too, was a kasba, but since it was closer to Meerut, it was more open to the influences of the outside world. It was one of the better-known *mandis* of the region.

AB: You have said that your father was an orthodox Shia. Did he have any Hindu friends?

IH: My father was a very orthodox man, a maulvi. He was, therefore, always at odds with the people of his own community. If he had good relations with anyone, they were with a man we used to call Bhagatji. He owned a shop in the market and we used to buy our groceries from him.

He was my father's real friend. Bhagatji, like my father, was an orthodox man. An orthodox Hindu, he used to keep a *choti*, go to the temple regularly etc. Strangely enough, my father and he became the best of friends. In fact, I still remember that when I went back to Dibai after my BA and met Bhagatji, he said to me, 'Maulvi Sahib borrowed hundred rupees from me when he moved to Hapur. When you get a job and start earning, you can pay me back.' It was then that I realized how deep a regard my father had for Bhagatji. He would never have borrowed money from any member of his own community. The thought of doing so would never have crossed his mind.

AB: It is important to keep a record of such relationships in the context of the history of the Partition. There is a large body of contemporary liberal intellectuals who think that unless we are completely secular and free from religious illusions, we will never be able to escape from the kind of communal fights we have witnessed since 1947 in India and Pakistan. From what you have said, it seems to me that in pre-Partition India one didn't have to be a secular atheist in order to establish peaceful and respectful relations with each other. Gandhi and Dr M. A. Ansari are good examples of religious men who were also respectful of other traditions. I have always felt (I say this even though I hardly have a grain of religiosity in me) that there is greater religious tolerance amongst the genuinely religious people than amongst those who flaunt their secular credentials. You would, I am sure, appreciate Gandhi's statement that he was a good Muslim because he was a good Hindu—there are some crass modern commentators who would dismiss such a statement as mere mumbo-jumbo. But, then, their understanding of the religious history of India is merely bigoted.

IH: I agree with you. I would like to add that my experiences in life have confirmed that genuinely religious Hindus and Muslims have had no difficulty in living with each other.

AB: Your father and Bhagatji were good friends not because they tolerated each other, but because, secure in their own religious convictions, they had an abiding respect for religious modes that were different from their own.

IH: My father always told me that Bhagatji was a very honest man because he was very religious. That's why we used to buy our groceries from him. He was the only honest shop-keeper in the kasba. We knew that Bhagatji never cheated on weights and never sold adulterated goods. He was an ideal businessman, and we had complete faith in him.

AB: Would you say, considering your experiences of growing up in pre-1947 India, that there was a functioning pluralistic society that had enough space for orthodox Muslims and orthodox Hindus to practice their own religions and yet be respectful towards each other? Or do you think that the relationship you have just described was unique to your father and his friend?

IH: I am not sure if I can answer the question unambiguously. What I can say, however, is that as far as Bhagatji was concerned, the entire Muslim community respected him. They all thought of him as an honest man.

There were other Hindu shopkeepers who were rather popular amongst the Muslim children. They were the *halwais*. We knew where we could get good sweets and never let religious sentiments get in the way (*laughs*). There was a Muslim halwai in Dibai, but we never patronized him because he was not very good.

AB: I remember a story of yours about a Muslim halwai in Delhi…

IH: I am sure it was about a halwai who used to adulterate his *mithai* (laughs). In fact, Muslim shopkeepers in our area had a bad reputation. We always assumed that if a Muslim owned a shop, it sold bad stuff. It wasn't only a question of good sweets.

AB: I sympathize. When it comes to sweets one must never make religious distinctions! Did you have many friends in your own age group even though you didn't go to school?

IH: No, as a child I didn't have many friends. I did, however, play with the children of my neighbourhood.

Even after we moved to Hapur, my father insisted that I continue to study at home till my matriculation and after that go to Lucknow to study Arabic. My elder sister, who used to live in Hapur with her husband, protested. She argued with my father about his plans to make me an Arabic scholar. 'He must go to a regular school, then go to a college and become an ICS officer,' she said. That was her dream. There were a few members of our family who were officers and lived in Hapur. She was impressed by their style and standard of living. She said, 'It's enough if my father is a maulvi. It's not necessary that my brother should be one too.'

My mother, on the other hand, said, 'No. What is all this about going to a school and then going to a college to get a BA? Let him find a job after he completes school.' In those days very few children from our community went to college. My mother didn't even know what a BA was!

Anyway, the government school in Hapur refused to admit me into the ninth standard because I had had no formal schooling. I was, therefore, sent to private school set up by Aggarwal Sahib. It was a high school. Someone in my family knew him and persuaded him to admit me. He gave me an entrance test, and agreed to admit me into the eighth standard. Now, one peculiarity of the school was that it had only Hindu teachers and didn't have many Muslim students. Anyway, since I was educated in a Hindu school, all my friends were Hindus.

There was one teacher whom I used to admire. He was our Hindi teacher. His Hindi was very sanskritized—he was educated, I think, in Mathura. He was a good debater. I was interested in public speaking in those days. He also taught History. My interest in debates brought me close to him. He was charmed by my Urdu because he didn't know any. I was fascinated by his Hindi. His name was Vijendraji. I met him recently in Delhi. He retired as the Head of the

Sanskrit Department of Delhi University. It was Reoti Saran who told me that Vijendraji was living in Delhi. I went to meet him. He remembered me. My experience has been that the teachers I have admired the most have been Hindus. My Hindu classmates used to come to school and repeat speeches of Congress leaders.

AB: You have been particularly interested in History. What kind of History did Vijendraji teach? Was it anti-Muslim?

IH: No, not at all. There was no bias. In fact, I can say that the texts were not influenced by any specific Hindu ideology. Nor did our teachers give it a Hindu slant. Our history teacher, as I have told you, was an orthodox man, but I can't remember any instance when he said something that could be construed as anti-Muslim. Not even when he spoke about Aurangzeb. In fact, I would say that he was a very good teacher.

AB: Did you talk about the Partition when you met Vijendraji recently?

IH: No, in fact, we talked more about the dialect spoken in our area, and he explained to me the dialect in Tulsidas. Those days the fight over the mosque in Ayodhya was in full swing. As I was leaving, he said, quite casually, 'I don't even know if Ramji was a historical figure who was born in Ayodhya.'

   After we took leave of him, I said to Reoti, 'It is surprising to hear him speak like a *nasik*.' Reoti, rather mischievously, replied, 'Just as there are Sunnis and Shias amongst the Muslims, we also have our sects. He has more faith in Krishanji than in Ram.'

AB: Could we now turn to the political environment in which you grew up? You grew up at a time when the national movement against the British was intensifying. You said that your Hindu classmates in Hapur used to repeat the speeches of the Congress leaders. You were in Dibai and Hapur in the 1930s. What were political discussions in your family like? What did your relatives say about their vision of India after the British left?

IH: As a child I used to watch a procession pass through the market in Dibai every morning shouting slogans like 'Mahatma Gandhi zindabad,' 'Pandit Nehru zindabad.' In fact, the protestors also used to shout, 'Dr Kitchlew zindabad.' I also remember that there were Muslims amongst the processionists. But, in my house, politics weren't discussed much. There was no talk about the Congress or the Muslim League. In fact, I don't remember if the Muslim League was ever mentioned in our home in Dibai. However, by the time we moved to Hapur, and I started going to college, there was some talk about the Muslim League and its demands for a separate Muslim state. In my own family, most people were supporters of the Muslim League. There were a few who were Nationalist Muslims—as they were called. There were intense debates about who was right and who was wrong.

AB: Do you remember the reasons they gave for supporting either the Muslim League or the Congress?

IH: Not really. My father used to talk about the fears of the zamindars. But he was not a committed supporter of either the Muslim League or the Congress. The one thing they all agreed upon was that the British should go. There were, however, differences over the kind of India that should come into existence once they left.

AB: Did those who supported the Muslim League offer seriously think out social, political or religious reasons for their support?

IH: No. It was more an emotional affair. No one had really thought about these matters with any degree of profundity. Jinnah Sahib had recently organized a huge meeting at Lucknow, and had appealed to the Muslims for support. Just as a film becomes a hit, he was a hit! (*laughs*) Soon there came a time when the personality of our Quaid-i-Azam, Muhammad Ali Jinnah, became a hit amongst the Muslims and began to appeal to them. Whatever he said became a part of their emotional make-up, and they took it to heart. I think his success played a part in the politics of the times.

That is why each time he made a statement, everyone got excited. His emotional appeal was strong and Muslims tended to side with him. He gained more and more popularity. But I don't think anyone made a serious critical analysis of what he was saying. This was so in every family. People were just swayed.

AB: Are you talking about the period prior to 1940?

IH: Yes, about 1937–8 when the call for a separate nation had not yet been made. At that time the concern was not with the formation of Pakistan. Slogans about Pakistan came later.

AB: What made Jinnah's appeal so strong from 1930s onward? There was a time when he wasn't only a leader of the Muslims.

IH: I can't remember if anything special happened in Hapur and its neighbourhood that made the Muslims of the region gravitate towards Jinnah. There was, rather, a more undefined sense of change in the country that caused this tilt towards Jinnah.

AB: In the histories of the Pakistan movement, it is repeated again and again, that there were no major riots between the Hindus and the Muslims prior to 1920. What made the Muslims feel, soon after the Khilafat movement, that the Hindus could not be trusted and that the two communities could not live together? Were there riots in your area? Did you feel threatened?

IH: No, there were no conflicts in our area prior to the 1940s. We did get news of riots in distant places like Bihar. That, however, didn't affect the political loyalties of the people immediately. Yes, once riots began in our region the attitudes of the ordinary people began to change. But that happened later.

AB: Prior to 1940, did the Muslims of your area feel that the situation in the country was such that the two communities should live separately?

IH: There was a feeling that the Muslims should support the Muslim League. Muslims began to worry about what would happen to them after the British left and they had to live in a country where the Hindus were in a majority. They wondered if they would be treated fairly. That is why the slogans of the Muslim League began to appeal to them.

AB: But, from all you have said thus far, there seems to have been no instance when the Muslims were treated unfairly.

IH: Yes, but the British were still present. The Muslims were afraid of what would happen to them after the British left.

AB: Did they feel that the Hindus would begin to oppress them, treat them with genocidal frenzy?

IH: No, there were still no riots in the area. But, there certainly was the feeling that since they were in a minority, they should find ways of protecting their interests.

AB: Earlier you said that in Dibai your father's best friend was a Hindu. How did these suspicions develop in people like your father?

IH: Let me, in fact, emphasize that even after we moved to Hapur, and even after the Muslim League began to gain popularity, the real friendships that members of our family established were with Hindus.

There were a few members of our family in Hapur who had a 'status' in society. In those days the British appointed 'honorary magistrates' in the districts. My Dada was an honorary magistrate. One of his sons, who had passed away by the time we moved to Hapur, was in the Intelligence Department and had reached the highest position possible for an Indian to attain at that time. He had been given a *khitab* for his services to the British and was called Khan Bahadur Tasadduq Hussain, OBE. Because of him the British respected our family. The result was that many poor and jobless people used to approach our Dada Mian for favours and request him to put in a word on their behalf with the British. Members of our family were often nominated as chairman of this or that committee of the municipality. Now, Tasadat Hussain's son was a great friend of Seth Tarachand, who was the richest Seth in Hapur. They used to spend all their time in each other's company. So, the social relations of our family with other Hindu families in the region were extremely good. But, at the same time, politically there was, in our family, a slight 'tilt' towards the Muslim League. Members of the family drifted towards the politics of the Muslim League. That didn't, however, make the slightest difference to their friendships with the Hindus.

AB: The 'tilt' didn't affect their friendships with the Hindus in any way?

IH: No. The only difference was in their political preferences. The *siyasi rai* (opinions about the state) of one was in favour of the Muslim League and the other in favour of the Congress.

AB: Up to now you have talked about your grandfather, father and uncles. What about your mother and sisters—how did they feel about the emerging politics?

IH: I had five sisters. Only one of them was younger than me. My eldest sister, as I have already mentioned, was deeply attached to me. She continued to live in Hapur. I fulfilled her desire for a younger brother and she spoilt me thoroughly. My mother was a quiet sort of person. She was quite the opposite of my father who was fond of giving lectures and sermons on religious and political issues at any majlis.

AB: Your stories are filled with characters who love to talk and argue.

IH: I am sure they are (*laughs*).

AB: Were the women in your family interested in or involved in the political affairs of the time.?

IH: No, no. They had no interest in the political affairs of the state.

AB: Even though there were debates in the family between the supporters of the Muslim League and the Congress?

IH: No, they were not interested in the debates. They dismissed them as part of the usual arguments that went on in the family. Remember that girls were rarely educated in those days. They spent most of their time in purdah and stayed indoors. At home, they did the routine tasks—stitch, cook, read a little etc.

AB: I asked you this question because I recently read Mumtaz Shah Nawaz's autobiographical novel, *A Heart Divided*. The novel is about a young girl's education and the ways in which the debates about the two-nation theory affect her.

IH: In Hapur, there were no schools for girls. That had its impact. Those members of our family who lived in Aligarh sent their daughters to the Muslim schools there. Some of them even went to the Aligarh Muslim University. As a result, that branch of the family was better educated. But that was not the case in Hapur.

AB: Would it be true to say that the educational level of the Muslims in India—of both boys and girls—was rather low? At least that is what many of the histories say.

IH: In those days, Muslim boys generally stopped studying after their Matriculation. Instead of studying further, they looked for a job. Things were slightly different in Dibai. It was close to Aligarh. Boys who did well in school did aspire to study at the Aligarh Muslim University. Often they got scholarships that helped them to carry on. One could, therefore, find more boys with degrees in Dibai. In Hapur it was rare to find boys with BA degrees. Meerut College, which was the closest place where a boy from Hapur could go to do his BA, was more expensive than Aligarh.

AB: Was the educational level in the Hindu households much higher?

IH: I did notice that even amongst the Hindus of Hapur there wasn't much emphasis on education. I don't think many of my classmates in school went on to a college. The case of Reoti is interesting. I knew him in school. His father was very rich, but he was not willing to send him to Meerut for his BA. I was, in comparison, from a poor family. My father was not keen that I study further, but my sister was insistent. Reoti was fond of reading. We became closer when he decided to do his Intermediate as a private candidate—our friendship continues to this day. Whenever possible, I used to pass on my notes and books to him, tell him what we had studied in college, and discuss the subjects with him during my vacations. He and I were interested in the same subjects. We did our Intermediate together. Only then did he succeed in persuading his father to let him go to Meerut College. Even in middle-class Hindu households in those days (especially in Hapur where the Hindus were quite well-off) there was not much interest in higher education. There wasn't that much difference in the educational levels of the Hindus and the Muslims. There were, of course, more Hindu students in Meerut College since it was in a Hindu-majority area, but there were many good Muslim students—even in the English classes.

AB: What subjects did you study in Meerut for your BA?

IH: I was more interested in the language and literature courses. So, I studied English Literature, Urdu and Persian. I also did courses in Civics, Political Science etc.

AB: Reoti was your neighbour in Hapur. Was Hapur divided into Hindu and Muslim mohallas?

IH: Yes, by and large. But the mohallas were close to each other. The Hindu mohalla began where the Muslim mohalla ended. They were really joined to one another. There wasn't any antagonism between them.

AB: Did Reoti come from an orthodox family?

IH: Yes, a very orthodox one.

AB: Did that create any problems for the two of you? Did anybody prevent you from meeting each other?

IH: No. Though there were the usual concerns with ritual pollution when I went to his house. That was, however, only in the beginning. After a while, I became so much a part of his family that they forgot to discriminate against me (*laughs*). They served me food in the same kind of plates that they ate off themselves. Maybe they washed them a little more thoroughly later, I don't know (*laughs*)!

AB: Was Reoti allowed to eat at your house?

IH: Yes. Reoti didn't have any reservations. Maybe his parents did; I don't know. But he didn't. In fact, his sisters also used to visit our house often. There was no problem.

AB: In your fine essay, 'Journey Across the Border,' you describe your friendship with Reoti in some detail. If in the novel, *Basti*, the village of your childhood is presented as an ideal village, in the essay your friendship with Reoti is presented as an ideal friendship.

IH: Yes. The funny thing is that when Reoti married Sarla, who was Krishan Chander's sister, she found it more comfortable to be at our house in Hapur than at her in-laws' place. She came from a Kayastha family, and like most Kayasthas, ate meat. Reoti's parents were orthodox Hindus and vegetarians. So, when she first came to Hapur to visit them—after they had accepted her—the poor thing was at first very nervous. So, Reoti told her, 'You can always go to Intizar's house.' The result was that she would spend most of the day with my nieces. At my sister's house, she would eat non-vegetarian food without any inhibitions.

AB: One of the most moving parts in your essay is the sense that the Partition not only cut you off from a place you thought of as an ideal home, it also made it difficult for you to continue with a friendship which was so deep. Given this, why did you decide to migrate?

IH: In fact, it was a decision made on the spur of the moment. My teacher and guru, Prof. Karar Husain, used to argue that the Muslims of Uttar Pradesh should not migrate. They should stay on in the places where they lived. That was also the opinion of Mohammad Hasan Askari, the distinguished critic, to whom I was specially attached. I agreed with them. But deteriorating conditions compelled both of them to migrate. Askari's radio message from Lahore was enough to persuade me to join him there.

I had the image of Lahore as a place of literary culture. I didn't want to be stuck in Meerut. I wrote a letter to Reoti informing him that I had decided to go. No one in my family was contemplating migration. I went to Hapur to tell my sister. She didn't raise any objections. No one urged me to go either. So, I left. At that time I had no idea that if I once went to Lahore, I would never be able to come back—that return would be impossible. Once I reached Lahore,

I realized that I had somehow 'arrived'—that I had done my *hijrat* (*laughs*); that I hadn't come on a visit; that my migration was what hijrat was all about.

AB: According to your essay, when you left for Lahore there were riots all around.

IH: Yes, there were riots. The railway stations were being attacked. But the months of the greatest massacres were over. I went in November. When I left, I had no idea that people who migrated could never go back to the place they had left behind. That their link with the past had snapped.

AB: Your family stayed back in Hapur. What did they feel about your decision?

IH: A few months later two of my nephews—my eldest sister's sons—joined me in Lahore. They decided to migrate after the riots. When I left, my sister had no idea that she would soon send her sons across. But the riots made everyone feel insecure. Other relatives also made their way across to Pakistan after some time. My elder sister stayed on in Hapur for about three more years. But eventually, she, too, decided to join us.

AB: What did you first notice about Lahore when you got there?

IH: That the days of the riots were over. There were mohajirs everywhere, in the streets, in the tents besides the railway station. The mohajirs had set up a bazaar in the street where I was staying. Walking around the city, I would often run into people I had known in Meerut. We would greet each other, 'So, you too are here?' There was a sense of having been uprooted. People wandered in the streets trying to figure out what to do next. A few decided to leave for Karachi having failed to make any arrangements for themselves in Lahore. Perhaps, they found places for themselves there.

AB: Were there any riots in Lahore after you got there?

IH: No. They were over. I was only told about the great fire in the Hindu mohalla near the Shahi Almi Gate. I went to see the ruins. There was no fire in the other big Hindu mohalla,

Krishan Nagar. There it seemed as if everyone had suddenly shifted out of the locality.

AB: The Lahore of your romantic dreams was obviously not the Lahore you found once you got there.

IH: No, it was certainly not that Lahore. My friends used to tell me that many of the streets I used to walk through were very beautiful once upon a time. For example, I was told that Nisbat Road, which I visited regularly because the office of *Mashriq* was there, was a Hindu mohalla where one could see pretty girls strolling up and down the street. It was a very posh area, but was no longer so when I saw it after the Partition. Its character had changed completely.

AB: The other day I was rereading a story by Manto called '*Dekh Kabira Roya*' (Kabir Wept When he Saw...). It is made up of a series of vignettes about Lahore after the Partition. As Kabir, the saint poet, walks down the streets of Lahore he notices the defilement of Lahore—not only of the Hindu Lahore, but also the Muslim Lahore. He weeps when he realizes that Lahore, which was once a symbol of India's composite culture, had become very crass. Not only had it lost its beauty, but it was also a city where there would never again be a sense of religiosity and ethicality. Like Faiz Ahmad Faiz, Manto suggests that at the very moment Pakistan was founded, the dream of a religious homeland for the Muslims had vanished. What did you feel about this seeming disjunction between your expectations and the reality? You do describe that feeling in 'An Unwritten Epic.'

IH: Those who had lived in Lahore or had seen it before the Partition certainly felt that the new Lahore was radically different. I had only heard that Lahore was a fashionable city, a city of elegance. That Mall Road was one of the finest anywhere.

AB: When Reoti came to visit you in Lahore, did he try to persuade you to return?

IH: (*Laughs*) No, he didn't argue with me about my decision. Perhaps he thought, 'He has made up his mind and he is here. There is no point in trying to persuade him.' He did, however, say to me, 'Had you talked to me before you migrated, I would have tried to stop you. Unfortunately, I got your letter after you had left.' He was in Delhi in those days and there was a lot of trouble there. Letters were delayed.

AB: I would like to read this story of your friendship with Reoti, which has lasted nearly 50 years after the formation of Pakistan, as emblematic of the Partition. Every time you have talked about him there is a note of sadness and loss— sadness that comes with the realization that the loss wasn't necessary.

IH: Well, I would interpret it like this. I migrated to Pakistan and became a citizen of a new country. Reoti continued to be an Indian. Perhaps, I should now defend Pakistan. The stories and essays I wrote soon after migrating to Pakistan were unacceptable to Reoti and he even wrote me a few angry letters. But our differences never threatened our friendship—our friendship never broke up. He understood that I had begun to think differently. But there was no change in our relationship (*laughs with delight*). I wonder why something similar didn't happen in the relations between India and Pakistan. If our friendship could survive political differences, it should have been possible for India and Pakistan also to live amicably. In fact, Reoti still quotes a sentence from one of my letters to him. Apparently, I had written, 'The friendship between you and me is not like the friendship between Abul Kalam Azad and Pandit Nehru. Their friendship was political, ours is not. I am not Abul Kalam Azad. Nor are you Pandit Nehru.'

AB: On what grounds did you defend the formation of Pakistan, particularly since you were not, according to what you have just said, too enamoured of the Muslim League?

IH: Actually, when Reoti came to see me in Lahore, we didn't argue about the issue. We didn't debate whether the establishment of Pakistan was right or wrong. He simply accepted the fact that I had migrated and that was that.

I should, however, tell you that when I was in Meerut,

and there were bitter arguments either in favour of the League or the Congress, I never got involved in the debates. In those days, I was not interested in politics. I used to live in a mohalla near the Town Hall. Every other day, there were political rallies in the open ground near the Town Hall. I used to pass by the place without paying too much attention to what was being said over the loudspeakers. One day, I heard that Pandit Nehru was to address the people gathered there. I thought that I too should go and listen to him. I stood with the others in the crowd and heard him. At one point, a member of the Muslim League asked him a very sharp question. There was a lot of protest over it. Pandit Nehru asked the crowd to calm down and told them that he wanted to reply to the question. The League group, however, left the ground shouting slogans against the Congress. Of course, Nehru spoke eloquently.

Some time later, I went there to listen to a speech by Hasrat Mohani of the Muslim League. I felt sad when I realized that he was not a very good speaker. Anyway, apart from these two, I didn't go to listen to any other leader.

AB: When you heard Pandit Nehru, did you think about the argument he was making—the argument that India was a composite nation?

IH: I was not sure till the very end that Pakistan would be formed. No one was. In fact, events after 1946 moved very fast. Even in my family, where there were serious debates about politics and the Muslim League, no one thought that India would be divided.

AB: What about those members of your family who were Muslim League supporters?

IH: They gave their votes to the Muslim League because they thought that by doing so they were actually supporting the cause of the Muslims. I don't think they realized that a new nation was about to be formed. It was only around 1946 that people began to seriously believe that Pakistan could become a reality. There was an incident in 1946 which actually changed the perception of Muslims in my area.

This was the riot in Garhmukhteshwar where there was a small settlement of Muslims. There used to be an annual fair at Garhmukhteshwar. It used to attract thousands of people. As a child, I remember watching caravans of carts passing through Hapur taking people to the fair. Anyway, in 1946, a group of Sikhs attacked a Muslim settlement and killed everyone living there. That massacre sent shock waves through the area and generated a lot of resentment against the Congress, the Hindus and the Sikhs. I remember that when I went back home during the vacations, there was so much tension in the air that I was convinced that something awful was about to happen, something explosive. And, sure enough, riots did break out in Meerut a few days later. There were even some minor incidents in Hapur. The violence was quickly brought under control. Those riots were, of course, nowhere close to the riots of 1947. A few people were killed and a curfew was imposed upon the city. But the riots changed people's attitudes radically. Earlier the debates were largely academic. They had no effect on the daily lives of people. We read newspapers and argued with each other. But after the Garhmukhteshwar incident, it seemed as if the Hindus and the Muslims could no longer live with each other.

AB: Even after that, did anyone suspect that the Partition would turn genocidal? Did anyone seriously believe that the Hindus and the Muslims hated each other so much that their relationship would end in massacre?

IH: No one anticipated riots of such ferocity. Nor did anyone imagine that the Muslims would have to go on a hijrat. Some people hoped that Pakistan would be formed, but no one thought that they would have to migrate.

AB: This is similar to what others too have said to me. Nearly everyone I have talked to has said that people felt that even if the nation was divided, communities would never be forced to move. After all the division of the nation was a matter of politics and had little to do with the division of old and settled communities.

IH: Yes. Nor did they feel that if Pakistan were formed, it would have no relationship with India. Instead, they thought that even if Pakistan were formed, most people would continue to live where they always had and establish relations with the new nation.

AB: Let me add to that. When I talked to Bhisham Sahni, he told me that he left Lahore to go and see the Independence Day celebrations in Delhi little knowing that he would never be able to return. He took, what turned out to be the last train to India. During the journey, one of the passengers wondered where Jinnah would live since his house was in Bombay. Another passenger replied that Jinnah would, of course, continue to live in Bombay and commute to Karachi which was nearby. This suggests that a majority of people thought that a society in which the relations between the Hindus and the Muslims were so deeply intertwined, the question of a division of the people did not arise. No one imagined that the Partition would lead to the largest migration in the history of the world and to a holocaust.

IH: No one ever imagined that a thing of that sort would happen. It never occurred to anyone. We were, of course, used to riots or fights, but they lasted for a day or two and then subsided. I don't know if the leaders of the Muslim League and the Congress foresaw such violence.

AB: I read a very interesting letter from Nehru to a friend about his perception of the Partition. In the letter, he said that the division was only a temporary one. It was the result of a momentary madness and things would soon return to normal because people didn't want to leave the places where they had lived for ages. In retrospect, historians suggest that the Partition demand was accepted because the leaders feared a civil war. Did you, during those days, feel that there would be a civil war if the Partition plan was not carried out?

IH: Not really. I didn't ever feel that there would be a civil war. It is true that the communal tensions were very high, especially after the Calcutta riots. By 1946, it was clear that the situation was rapidly deteriorating. But I still don't understand the reasons for such large-scale violence. Though now, given the present political relations between the two countries, I do find that the question you have asked has begun to trouble me. I had hoped that with time the tensions would begin to recede—which they had for a brief period. But given the direction of politics in Pakistan these days, these questions have become important again.

AB: Have people begun to wonder why Pakistan was formed?

IH: Yes, they did when East Pakistan seceded from West Pakistan. The argument then was that the Bengalis had a separate identity. People had, at that time, begun to wonder if Pakistan was a failed state, and if it was, then who was responsible for its failure. The same question was asked in Sindh because of tensions between the local Sindhis and the mohajirs. Did the political leadership cause the problem in Sindh? Or was it a result of martial law? Where did things go wrong?

AB: In 'Shahre-e-Afsos' (The City of Sorrows), you seem to suggest that the problems in East Pakistan were a direct consequence of the Partition and the very conception of Pakistan.

IH: A story is not history. I am never sure what meanings a reader may derive from a particular tale I write. I don't have the right to tell the critic how he should interpret a story. He has the freedom to understand it in his own way. Fiction and poetry invite different interpretations. The same was the case with my novel, Agey Samundar Hai. Critics in Pakistan have read different meanings and intentions into it. I refuse to enter into a discussion with any of my critics.

AB: I wasn't asking you to interpret the story. I was rather trying to say that stories like 'Hindustan Se Ek Khat' (A Letter from India) and 'Shahre-e-Afsos' are marked by a sense of despair about our societies as they emerged from the days of the Partition. 'Shahre-e-Afsos,' for example, is about a group of men who must carry the corpses of those whom they have murdered from one place to another trying to find a place where they can bury them. Only if they can bury them can they find redemption from a history of sorrow and pain which they have themselves brought into existence. Till they bury the corpses, they can only live in a condition of death-in-life. The story is horrifying. It suggests that from its very inception, Pakistan was marked by violence—that it came into being in the midst of the madness of communal riots. And since the story deals as much with the creation of Pakistan, as with the time when East Pakistan broke away from West Pakistan to create a new nation called Bangladesh, it also suggests that it has not been possible for Pakistan to exorcize the horrors associated with its very origins—overcome the history of violence that accompanied its formation—bury its dead and carry on with the process of finding new life-giving forms of being.

Indeed, it has not been possible for any of us to bury the past because we have failed to acknowledge our role in the massacres—each of us carries the corpses of those we have killed, and each one of us, in our self-righteousness, refuses to acknowledge our complicity in the murders. The story could, then, be read as an allegory of the two-nation theory and its consequences. It offers a very despairing vision of history of the Indian subcontinent. And what is worse, it refuses to hold out any hope. How can it? Its assumption is that we, as Hindus and Muslims, as Bengalis and Biharis, have been responsible for the horror that has haunted us since 1947, and yet refuse to acknowledge our complicity in it. As post-colonialists we blame the British, as Pakistanis we accuse the Indians, as Hindus we assert that it is the Muslims who started it all, etc. But we never look at our own selves and say that we—each of us—contributed to the nightmare that our lives have become since 1947. Till we can do that we shall never be able to bury the dead—or find ways of living within a peaceful civilization.

IH: Yes, perhaps there is a suggestion in the story that no single person or community was responsible for the horrors of the Partition and the subsequent violence in East Pakistan.

I did not, for instance, want to suggest that the Bengalis were responsible for what happened because they wanted to create a state which was independent of Pakistan. Nor did I want to say that it was the Punjabi bureaucracy which was responsible—that was, as you know, being said. I also did not want to blame the army alone. I feel that when there is a major event like the war in East Pakistan, it is useless to point a finger at any particular community or group.

I have written another story which is similar to '*Shahre-e-Afsos*'. It is entitled '*Andhi Gali*' (Blind Alley). It is about a Bihari Muslim who seeks refuge in his hometown. As he walks through familiar streets, he identifies the house he had lived in, the streets he had known. He hopes that the neighbours will recognize him, and yet is afraid that they will. He meets a baniya who fails to do so. He feels relieved and terrified at the same time. In that strange mental state, he turns into a lane only to discover that it is a dead-end.

AB: Other than stories which deal with the violence that accompanied the Partition, you have also written stories which describe nostalgically a world that you had obviously known prior to the Partition—a world rich in memories of families with long histories of pleasantly-lived lives in India, a world where friendships were formed, stories were exchanged, or love happened. In the story, '*Hindustan Se Ek Khat*' (A Letter from India), for example, or the novel, *Basti*, the old men who have left their bastis behind, mourn for lost genealogies, ancestral graveyards, crumbling homes and disappearing fortunes. The central concern in these tales seems to be with the important issue of identity, an issue which you have been grappling with since your earliest writings. Having migrated from India and settled in Pakistan, you seem to have been trying, in a variety of complex ways, to ask: What is the cultural, or rather, the civilizational identity of the nation called Pakistan? What is the relation of Pakistan with the larger entity called India of which it was once a constituent part? What is and can

be the historical relation between the two nations at the
political and cultural level?

In many of the stories, you suggest that the historical
relations between the Hindus and the Muslims, which have
been so violently ruptured, cannot be repaired. Yet, at the
same time, there is a lot of nostalgia for a world that seems
to have been so irrecoverably lost. These stories acknowledge that there is no way of judging the nature of this
relationship and its future possibilities without a thorough
knowledge of the history of Islam in the subcontinent—a
position which is consistently denied in the history taught
in Pakistani schools.

In this context, let me remind you of the extremely important statements you had made to me when I had met
you in Lahore a few years ago—statements which were
picked up by the Indian press when you came to Delhi to
receive the first Yatra Award for lifetime achievement as a
writer. You had said to me: '*I have always felt that there is
a Hindu sitting inside me,*' and '*I have one foot in Karbala and
the other foot in Ayodhya.*' Later on, as a gloss, you added
that the Hindu inside you was an interlocutor, who helped
you to sharpen your sense of your Shia identity, just as the
idea of Ayodhya helped you to think about your historical
and literary identities. You were speaking about your sense
of the self as a metaphysical and a historical entity.

IH: Yes. The entire question of personal, historical and metaphysical identity became urgently important for me only
after the Partition. Before Pakistan historically came into
being, one of the slogans of Mohammad Ali Jinnah was:
'*Hum das crore Musalman Hindustan ke ek kaum hain*' (We,
the ten crore Muslims, are one of the communities of
India). This slogan was an appeal to all Muslims from
Dhaka to Peshawar to keep in mind that they were a part
of the history of India. It was meant to invoke everything
from the Lal Quilla and the Taj Mahal to the names of the
cities which had come into existence after the arrival of
Islam, from the names of the Urdu poets to the festivals of

importance to the Muslims. The slogan suggested to all the Muslims of India that their cultural and historical existence was not separable from the geographical space called India. But the Partition changed all those perceptions about what constitutes the Muslim identity. Muslims suddenly found that they had to redefine who they were, and what their culture and their heritage was. It is possible that some could, in their imaginations, construct an identity for themselves which was satisfactory to them. But for many others the question of identity could not be so easily imagined. They wondered about their relation with the past that had once defined them—a past which they had left behind in India. They realized that all that they had taken for granted as being a part of their Islamic past—the Taj and Mughal architecture, Mir and Ghalib—were now a part of India. How could the Muslims of Pakistan relate to that past and use it to define their identity? It seemed to them that even history had been divided by the Partition. They wondered where and when the history of Pakistan began. They asked if Urdu was really the language of the Muslims. Urdu after all had its roots, its first flowering, in an India they had left behind. All these and other questions became painfully difficult for the Muslims to answer.

As a fiction writer, I have tried, to the best of my ability, to grapple with these questions. I am, of course, neither a philosopher nor a historian. Thus, the concern of many of my stories, as you know, is with aspects of my own life prior to 1947. All my thinking about these questions has been as a writer of stories, and I have tried to understand them through my stories. These problems have been, in some form or another, a central aspect of my fiction. Memories of my basti haunt me. I think of life back there as having been lived in, what may be called, a composite culture. Of course, as a Muslim, my relationship with my own community was deeper, but I have also tried to explore the relationship my community had with the Hindus.

As the question of identity became more insistent, more

urgent, I decided to move further back in time, further from the immediate concerns with life before and after 1947. I asked myself: Where and how did our journey as Muslims begin in the Indian subcontinent? If the Muslims had a long historical and cultural role to play in India, why do we want to disown it? If Amir Khusrau or Ghalib lived in Delhi, shouldn't I acknowledge Delhi and all its past as a part of my identity? Why should I try to forget it? I have, therefore, been asserting repeatedly, that we should not only acknowledge the historical and cultural past which we left behind in India, but that we should also make it an important aspect of our present concerns.

I should add that there is another aspect of my sense of self which has been a consistent part of my fictional work and which casts its shadow on all that I have written. I am a Shia Muslim. For me, as for all Shias, Karbala is a potent symbol. It is an aspect of my inner space, a part of the very geography of my inner being. It defines my cultural and moral identity. Karbala may not be in Pakistan, but it is certainly a part of me, just as Mecca and Medina are for all Muslims.

Having arrived thus far in my quest for an identity, I found that I had to go back to an even more distant past. I had placed a lot of emphasis on Islamic history, but I realized that my Islamic past in India did not exist in isolation from the history of the other communities that lived there, that it could not be separated from the history of the rest of the land. If that were the case then it would be more appropriate to speak not merely of an Islamic history, but of a Hind-Islamic history. I have often written about this. We have to, I think, consider the relation of Islam to the land called Hindustan. With these concerns began another phase of my intellectual journey. I began to look into the history of India before the arrival of Islam, a history which has, I think, given Islam here its unique character. The history of Islam in India is very distinct from that of Islam in the rest of the world.

My interest in exploring the relationship of Islam to India's past led me to read the Mahabharata, the Ramayana, the Vedas, and the entire tradition of storytelling in India. I read the *Panchtantara, Katha Sarit Sagar, Baital Pacchisee*. I read these not only as a writer of fiction interested in the craft of ancient storytellers, but also as a person interested in the Hind-Islamic culture. I wondered how I could own this tradition, how I could make it a part of my inner being. I was sure that owning a thousand years of Islamic history was not sufficient. I also had to find a way of acknowledging and appropriating the long history that lay prior to it. The more I studied that past the more involved I became in it, not only as an explorer of culture, but also as a storyteller.

The world of stories had a special attraction for me. When I read the *Jataka* tales, for example, I felt as if I was another Columbus who had seen a new continent. I was surprised and enchanted by the *Jataka* tales. I was already familiar with the tradition of fiction written in the west that I had learnt about from my teachers and my fellow writers. But, I was very unhappy when I realized that our major critics and writers like Firaq Gorakhpuri and Mohammad Hasan Askari had never talked about our own tradition of storytelling. Firaq used to tell us about Kalidas's *Shakuntala* and about Tulsidasji, but he never indicated, in any of his essays, that there was a vast and very rich tradition of story-telling in the Indian past. I discovered that tradition on my own. I may have read about the *Katha Sarit Sagar* in the work of some scholar or the other, but I realized much later that it was a part of my tradition which I ought to know as well as I know Kalidas. I discovered it on my own.

Readings into this tradition became a part of my new intellectual journey. I was already familiar with the European realist tradition, and I knew the Persian tradition of the *dastan* and *Alif Laila*. But the stories of the *Jatakas* and *Katha Sarit Sagar* opened up an utterly new world for me. I began to wonder how I could make it a part of my being and incorporate it into the Urdu tradition. I understood that the structuring of the stories in *Katha Sarit Sagar* was the result of a sensibility which was remarkably different from anything I had encountered earlier. I tried to understand it so that I could somehow evolve a new mode of storytelling. I thought that I could combine all that I had learnt from European fiction, the tradition of the *dastan*, and the Indian mode of fictional narratives. Of course, I knew that such an ambition could only be fulfilled by a great writer who could make better sense of the magnificent experience these texts had given me.

I should add that Urdu is a very fortunate language. It is so located that it can not only draw upon the vast and rich tradition of European literature, Persian poetry and the dastan narratives, but can also lay a claim to the entire literary tradition of India. The Urdu writer can use the dohas of Tulsidas, evoke the lyrics of Hafiz Shirazi, and make references to *Alif Laila*.

I know that I am not that great fictional writer who has the ability to create something uniquely his own out of these three traditions, but that is my dream, my ambition. I am disappointed that I haven't, thus far, written the kind of story I want to write.

AB: On the contrary, I think your achievement has been considerable. Some of your more recent stories are amongst the finest written in our times. They have had a considerable impact on Indian writers like Githa Hariharan or Rajee Seth who openly acknowledge your influence on them.

IH: In stories like '*Patey*' (Leaves) and '*Kachuwe*,' (Tortoise), I used the techniques I learnt from my reading of ancient Indian fictional narratives which I found very attractive. I was enchanted by the idea of a story emerging from another story like threads in a spider's web. That is not the case in the tradition reflected by *Alif Laila* where each story exists in its own watertight compartment. In *Alif Laila*, a new story begins only after the previous story is finished. The narrator merely strings them together. Sometimes, of course, a story intrudes into another one. The same is the case with

the stories in *Baital Pacchisee* (Twenty-Five Ghost Stories).
But in *Katha Sarit Sagar* there is a labyrinth of stories. A
story emerges from another in such a complex way that one
has to turn back often to recall who the original narrator
was. The structure is far more complex and enchanting
than the structure of *Alif Laila*. In western realistic fiction—
think of Maupassant or Chekhov—each new story is independent of the previous one. This is not always the case
with our traditional stories. The stories in *Baital Pacchisee*
are interlinked. It seems to me that according to the
philosophy of life which informs our traditional tales,
things of this world are not discrete, isolated and utterly
separate from each other, but are, somehow or the other,
related to each other—connected to one another. I sometimes feel that the earlier stories, which I had written under
the influence of western realism, are anti-eastern in their
form. I have now been trying to write stories that are
independent yet interlinked with other stories.

AB: What you have said thus far concerns the structural differences between eastern and western fiction. You have hinted
at some of the metaphysical suppositions that inform these
forms of fiction. Could you elaborate on the philosophy of
life that determines the form of the Indian or Persian
tradition of storytelling?

IH: I hesitate to comment on it in great detail because I do not
know Vedantic philosophy well enough. It is not my area.

AB: But you are fascinated by ancient Indian tales, not only
because you find their structures interesting, but also
because they help you to think about your civilizational
identity—your identity as an inheritor of the entire literary
tradition of the Indian subcontinent.

IH: Yes, when I speak about the form of the stories in the *Katha
Sarit Sagar* or in *Alif Laila*, I have in mind something that
Mohammad Askari said in one of his essays. He said that
the world-views that link the ancient Indian forms of
storytelling and *Alif Laila* to each other are different yet
related. We have inherited both these traditions.

.AB: Your own concerns with the Vedanta or with the Ramayana are a part of your own quest for who you are. It is this quest which makes you want to write stories like '*Kishti*' (The Boat) in which you draw upon a variety of mythic lore. Are you not also searching for a metaphysical position?

IH: I am a Muslim—a Muslim who was born within a geographical and a historical space. A Muslim is not a single entity. Some people think that a Muslim belongs to a unified community. But I think there is an Irani Muslim, an Arabi Muslim, a Sufi Muslim etc. In our tradition, there is a sharp distinction between an Arabic Muslim and an Iranian Muslim. There are differences between Iranian and Arabic cultures within the Islamic world. I, of course, have relations with that complex Islamic world, but I also have a bond with the culture of the subcontinent—one can call that culture Hindu or Aryan or whatever else one likes. As a writer of fiction, I carry *Alif Laila* in one hand and *Katha Sarit Sagar* in the other. They are the two 'mothers of fiction' (*laughs*). I want to use both, create something of my own out of them. That is my present concern.

AB: But connected with the search for a new fictional form is also your quest for an identity, is it not?

IH: Yes, that is the case.

AB: What is your understanding of a Hind-Islamic identity?

IH: As a storyteller I am not bothered about my identity as a member of a particular religious or political community. When I sit down to write a story, I only think as a writer of *afsanas* or stories. All other matters are left behind. The three traditions of storytelling that I have been talking about have become a part of me. If I can succeed in combining them to create a new fictional form, I shall make a distinctive space for myself in the history of Urdu literature. That is my ambition as a writer. In my fiction my concern is not with the making of any national or communal identity.

AB: It is precisely the position that you have outlined which distinguishes you from many other writers in Pakistan and

India who either write about local social issues or about alienated figures. What is distinctive about your work is not merely the fact that it has created a new form, but also the fact that you seem to be concerned with the difficult issue of what it means to be a member of a subcontinent whose history is sometimes nightmarish and sometimes glorious—along with what it means to be a Shia Muslim who grew up in India and who now lives in Pakistan—a writer in Pakistan who still longs for his friends in India and who is conscious of Hindu influence.

IH: Yes, absolutely.

AB: As a storyteller, therefore, your concerns are not only with the form of the story. The complexity of form that you are searching for has to do with the kinds of difficult and complex civilizational questions you seem to be trying to grapple with. That is why you say that you are a Muslim, but there is a Hindu sitting inside you.

IH: Yes, you are right.

AB: You have said again and again that you are a Shia Muslim from an orthodox family. This is an important consideration in a Sunni-dominated Pakistan. You have never shied away from acknowledging your Shia heritage. Nor have you ever denied that you have been influenced by the Hindu, the Sufi, the Bhakti, and the *Katha Sarit Sagar* traditions of India.

IH: I must be careful here. Our social and political conditions are such that all the things I have said can be interpreted in communal terms. If I say that I am a Shia or a Muslim there is every possibility that people will think that I am some kind of a sectarian thinker. But the thrust of all that I have been trying to say is very different. I believe that communalist parties are anti-religious. A fundamentalist, I think, is anti-Islam or anti-Hindu. According to my way of thinking, the purpose of religious thought is radically different. I can, therefore, say with some degree of confidence that I am a Shia Muslim who thinks that there is a Hindu sitting inside me, because I was born in this land.

AB: I find myself in agreement with you. I think that a religious
        person, a genuinely religious person, is also a very tolerant
        person. There are countless stories in India of genuinely
        religious men and women of different religions living in
        great friendship with each other.

IH: Sufis, for example, are very religious. It would, however, be
        difficult to find more tolerant people than Nizammudin
        Aulia or Moinuddin Chishti, Kabir or Mirabai. They were
        steeped in religious experience, yet were never confined by
        the boundaries of Islam or Hinduism.

AB: One of the myths we grew up with was that Mirabai and
        Kabir were great friends. The point of the story, I think, is
        that the good and the saintly learn from and support each
        other. The story also points to the fact that in the history
        of the subcontinent there was not only continuous inter-
        action between the Hindus and the Muslims, there was
        often a deep bonding between them.

IH: These myths suggest that the people thought these two
        saintly figures ought to be friends. Yet we must not forget
        that the Hindus and the Muslims also fought each other,
        and fought each other bitterly. When two communities
        meet, when two traditions interact—especially when one
        has come from outside—there are bound to be conflicts.
        These conflicts can be over beliefs and customs, but they
        can also be over land and power. Hindus and Muslims made
        friends with each other, understood each other, but also
        fought each other. At the cultural level they also exchanged
        experiences with each other and formed, what historians
        like Tara Chand have called, a composite culture. Muslim
        architecture, for example, borrowed the motif of the lotus
        from the Hindus. The story Tara Chand tells is very differ-
        ent from the history written by those who write about the
        battles of Rana Pratap and the Muslim kings. At the political
        level, kings and princes tended to make and break alliances.
        To be fixated by the political is, I think, a mistake.

AB: Over the years, you have been equating the migration of the
        Muslims from India to Pakistan with the hijrat of the early

Muslim followers of the Prophet. In doing so, you have been trying to give to Partition-related migration a spiritual meaning. I am disturbed by this move, because I am not sure if a politically created event of such brutality can be transformed into a religious experience. In addition, you have spoken in these terms only about the Muslims who fled from India without telling us how their migration was so different from that of the Hindus as to acquire religious sanctity. I say this because earlier you had talked about the fact that exile and migration have been a major part of almost all the foundational stories of the Indian subcontinent.

IH: Let me clarify. When I talked about hijrat, I did so soon after the experience of the Partition and migrations in the 1950s. It was, in the life of the Muslim community, a time of idealism. Pakistan had been newly created, and the people who came here wanted to do something for the community as a whole. I, too, thought in idealistic terms and wanted to give to the entire experience of migration and suffering a meaning, a purpose and a direction. I thought that I could do so by trying to understand the migration in terms of the hijrat which had a great significance for the Muslims. The Muslim calendar, as you know, begins with the hijrat. I thought that I could interpret the migration to Pakistan in idealistic terms. I wrote quite a bit about it. In Pakistan, many of my friends criticized me for the attempt and dismissed it. But I continued to be idealistic and felt that a migration of such magnitude ought to have a meaning. At that time, I had not yet made my intellectual journey toward the Ramayana and the Mahabharata. I did not know then that the experience of migration or of exile—the experience of being forced to leave one's basti, one's home— has been a part of the historical tradition of people of the Indian subcontinent too. Hijrat, of course, had its own meaning and place in the history of Islam, but it was only later that I realized that stories of migrations also possessed a unique meaning in the history of the subcontinent. I had, of course, limited my thinking only to the formation of a Muslim selfhood without realizing that the very idea of migration had been a part of the historical experiences of different peoples. My recognition of other exiles, as I have said, was a result of my later intellectual journey. I did write, in my later stories, about the wanderings of Rama and the Pandavas. I did try to make use of the dastans about caravans leaving a basti and travelling all across the continent in search of a home. I wanted to know if they had any meaning for our historical times. So my attempt to use the hijrat as a reference so as to give my experiences of migration a meaning and a purpose was a phase in my intellectual journey.

AB: You have spoken about it in your recent essays also. What disturbs me, as it has disturbed your critics, is the fact that the notion of hijrat tends to cast the violence of the migrations during the Partition into a religious haze. It diverts attention away from the fact that the migrations were brutal and completely unexpected.

IH: Let me interrupt you. I have suddenly remembered what I wrote in an article recently. In the article, I said that the Partition was not a phenomenon of our times alone, but a part of the very civilization of India. The entire history of exile and migration during the Partition is a repetition of what people have experienced since the days of the Ramayana and the Mahabharata. Even in those days, the Partition of land and of the kingdom between members of the same family was a violent event. It resulted in the writing of wonderful epic poetry. The frustration felt by the Pakistanis seemed to be like the frustration of the Pandavas. Indians should understand that what happened in 1947 was akin to what was often described in their traditions.

AB: What you are now saying is that the violence during the Partition was in many ways similar to what had happened often in the subcontinent.

IH: Yes, I think violence of that kind had happened often in India and has been described in its literature.

AB: According to you, the migrations and the violence of 1947 can acquire a meaning of some sort if it is placed within the framework of the foundational stories of the Hindus and the Muslims?

IH: Yes.

AB: My understanding of the violence of the Partition days is different. I think what happened in 1947 was both unexpected, unprecedented and utterly meaningless. I suspect that for those who got caught in the carnage, your analysis, that the holocaust and the migrations were a familiar part of the archetypal history of the Indian subcontinent, would not offer any consolation. They would not understand, if you told them that the loss of their homes or the massacre of their families was a necessary sacrifice in any hijrat.

IH: Perhaps, but in order to make any sense of the Partition and its violence, one may have to say that there was, even in the foundational stories of Islam and Hinduism, destruction on a similar epical scale. The entire Kaurava clan was annihilated. And even after their victory, the Pandavas were so scarred by their memories of the war that they ultimately decided to abandon their reign and seek refuge in the mountains far from the city they had fought for.

AB: One reading of the Mahabharata could be that at the end of the war there was no moral meaning available. The fact that the Gita was preached on the battlefield does not really amount to a plea for a different, a less egotistical mode of living. But this, surely, is not a possible interpretation one can give to the Karbala story. According to any orthodox Islamic reading of that history, there is at the end of all the suffering and pain, a sense of being one with the Holy. Those who suffer do arrive at an understanding of what ethical existence means—or at least what ethicality ought to be. Migration, exile, sorrow appear to be a part of some divine plan and make suffering endurable.

IH: Similarly, one should try to find, in our time and our history, a meaning and a purpose in the violence inflicted upon and the pain endured by our contemporaries. I think that as a writer it is my duty to find that meaning. Some may believe that the massive migrations that took place in 1947 were utterly absurd, but even then I must insist that it is my duty to find in them a purpose, a plan. If I didn't make the effort, the history of the Partition will always appear absurd. You have said that in the past there had never been a migration on such a massive scale. As a writer of stories, I must confront an experience of such epic proportions. Poor Tolstoy had to go back to historical accounts to find a similar experience when he wrote *War and Peace*. I have, in my lifetime, undergone an experience of epic proportions. I must deal with it if I have to say something worthwhile about the history of the subcontinent. When my critics object and tell me that I am obsessed by the experience of the Partition, trapped in it, my response is that what happened in 1947 was so complex, so utterly devastating, that I have yet to understand it fully. How can I get away from it? Had I managed to write a novel on the scale of *War and Peace*, or written an epic, I could have freed myself from the history of those days. I could then have told myself that I had confronted a great human event where complex issues of politics, ethics and religion were at stake, and that I had treated them with some degree of satisfaction. Unfortunately, I haven't yet done so. No writer has. That is why I continue to believe that if I can place the events of the Partition within the framework of some experience from our past, I may be able to make sense of them—even if some aspects of those days continue to seem absurd.

AB: In *War and Peace*, Tolstoy does arrive at an understanding of the absurdity of war. There is a glorious scene in which Pierre has a vision of the holiness of the small things of life, of the divinity that is interfused in the daily rhythms of any ordinary day.

IH: It is not necessary that every writer must interpret historical experiences in the same way. I can look at the history of violence in the subcontinent from a different perspective.

Events that happen in human history cannot be fitted into prefabricated categories. We tend to do that. We often see what happens in history in black and white terms. But reality is more complex and ambiguous. There are some meaningful acts which contain in them degrees of absurdity—a sense of the absurd exists alongside acts which are purposeful. Human experiences are so entangled that we must describe them with care. We could, of course, declare that they are absurd, that they have no meaning and stop grappling with them any further.

I feel, however, that after the formation of Pakistan we did try to establish a new relation with a new land. We wondered about the values our new country ought to have, we asked ourselves about the experiences and the values that the people who had migrated to the new country had brought with them, and we struggled to understand how they could be fitted meaningfully in the history of the subcontinent we had inherited. It was like the experience of the Pandavas, not that of the Kauravas. It is the Pandavas who had to leave their homeland, wander from place to place and lay the foundation of a new city. Think of the Muslims who had to leave the one piece of land, the one place, and the one basti they had loved. They were well settled in their homes. Each had a place in his community. They were confident of who they were. Consider the Muslims of Uttar Pradesh. One was a zamindar, another was a talukdar, another a nawab. In their arrogance, they used to look down upon the Hindus. After they came to Pakistan, they had to run from pillar to post to find a job, to get a house allotted, to claim compensation for the properties left behind. They were confronted with the fact that in order to survive they had to make a new nation; they had to make new bastis or face the taunts of those who had lived for generations in the cities they had migrated to. And they were taunted. They were told that they had to stop feeling nostalgic for the ancestral lands they had left behind; face the new reality; accept the place they had migrated to as their own. I believe that the struggle of the mohajir, the exile or the migrant was the most unique and difficult one of our times. My friend, Reoti Saran—well settled as he is in his home—doesn't know, and cannot know, how an exile feels or what it is to find oneself in a new country and try to make it one's own. To survive as a migrant requires great courage and great strength. Reoti doesn't understand that. He cannot. I do.

AB: That statement is heart-felt. I hope, however, that our future will be more tolerant and compassionate; that friends will not migrate across hostile borders and ask each other for a greater understanding of their political plight. Judging from all that you have said and written there is a rich tradition which we ought to share between us with gratitude instead of tearing it to shreds.

Glossary

abba	father
abbay	hey you
abbajan	father
afsana	story; romance
agarbatti	incense
alam	a standard carried in procession during Moharrum
Ambale-wali	a woman from Ambala, a town in Haryana
amma	mother
ameen	amen
ammi	mother
annas	Indian coins, no longer in use
apsara	celestial, dancing nymph
arrey	an exclamation
ashram	hermitage
ashoora	tenth day of Moharrum; day the Imam Hussain was martyred
azan	call for prayers
aziz	friend
bade abba	grandfather
badi Amma	grandmother
bahen	sister

bahu	daughter-in-law; wife
bandhu	brother, kinsman
basant panchami	spring festival
bashao	colloquial use—O kings
basti	village; small town
batasha	sweet made of sugar
battair	quail
bawa jaan	father
betey	son
bhagyawan	lucky one, blessed
bhagyavati	lucky woman, blessed
bhai	brother
Bhanumati	a woman in folklore who has a strange assortment of members in her family
bhikshu	mendicant, monk
bibi	polite form of addressing a woman
bigha	five-eighth of an acre of land
Bodhisattva	the Buddha in his previous incarnations
brahmastra	a divine weapon which can destroy the world; according to Indian mythology it is a missile made out of a blade of grass
bua	father's sister; a suffix meaning aunt
burqa	veil
chacha	father's brother
chachi	father's brother's wife
chakva, chakvi	duck
channa	chickpea
chillum	earthen pot of a hookah in which tobacco is burnt
Chote Hazrat	Imam Hussain. The Prophet's grandson who was martyred at Karbala
choti	tuft of hair
dadima	grandmother
Dajjal	a popular figure in the Muslim folklore tradition who has only eye and who, it is said, will appear on earth on Doomsday
dastan	fable; story

dargah	shrine; a saint's mausoleum
dharna	strike, picketing
dhobi	washerman
Dilli-wali	a woman from Delhi
doab	land between two rivers
dugdugi	small drum
dupatta	a long scarf worn by Indian women
Durga	the Goddess of destruction in Hindu mythology
durbar	king's court
dur-i-najaf	a pearl from Najaf, the city in Iraq where Imam Ali, the Prophet's son-in-law, and the father of Hassan and Hussain, is buried.
Enlil	a character in *The Epic of Gilgamesh*
fanoos	a paper lantern
Gaya	the place where the Buddha achieved enlightenment
ghee	clarified butter
ghee-wala	a man who sells ghee
gyani	a learned man
gulal	red-coloured powder
gulgulay	fried sweet
haazri	the sacred funeral dinner offered in commemoration of the martyrdom of Imam Hussain
halwa	sweet dish
halwai	a sweet-meat seller
haramzada	bastard
Hatamtai	hero of a popular Urdu romance
haveli	mansion
hazrat	a title of veneration, especially for a religious person
Hazarat-I-Jibreel	Archangel Gabriel
Hazarat Issa	Jesus
hijrat	exile; migration
hisaar	a ritual prayer in Arabic which fortifies one against evil spirits

huzoor	the Prophet Mohammad
idgah	a spacious building where Muslims offer prayers especially on the two festivals of Id
imambara	a religious building of the Muslims where religious discourses are delivered; the house of the Imam where tazias are kept
inshallah	god willing
ittar	perfume
jalebi	a sweet
janab	Mr
janamashtami	Lord Krishna's birthday
ji	a respectful suffix added to proper names
jhatka meat	non-kosher meat
kafir	infidel
kaga	crow
kalaam	religious verse
kasba	a small town
kattha	catechu; *terra japonica*; made into a red paste smeared on betel leaves
keema	a dish made of minced meat
khalifa	prince; leader
khichdi	a dish made of rice and lentils
khidkion-wali gali	lane of windows
khitab	an honour given by the British government
lathi	stick
majlis	a gathering where religious discourses are given; gathering to commemorate Imam Hussain's martyrdom
mandi	market
Mara	Lord of death
mashak	water bag made of leather
marsia	an elegy commemorating Imam Hussain's martyrdom
mattam	mourning during Moharrum for Imam Hussain's martyrdom

maulana	a respectful term for a man of religious learning
maulvi	Muslim priest
maya	illusion
mazar	the grave of an Islamic saint
mehndi	henna
merey	my
mewa	the Prophet Mohammad's accession
mithai	sweets
mian	a respectful way of addressing a Muslim man
mohajir	migrant
mohalla	neighbourhood; a small locality
Moharrum	the first month of the Muslim calendar. The month when Imam Hussain was martyred. A month of mourning, especially for the Shias
motrima	respectful address to a woman
muni	hermit, wise man
mussalmani	identity as a Muslim
naan	unleavened bread
nastik	atheist
nauha	an elegiac verse or lamentation sung to commemorate Imam Hussain's martyrdom to the accompaniment breast-beating
nekbakht	one who is virtuous
niaz	an offering
nikah	Muslim marriage ceremony
paan	betel leaf
paandan	box for keeping betel leaves
panja	a cloth standard in the form of an open palm carried during the Moharrum procession
peda	a sweet made of milk
pehalwan	wrestler
phupha	father's sister's husband

poodna, poodni	warbler
prabhu	lord, master
pulao	a rice dish
qazionwali gali	court lane
qibla	Mr
quissa	popular tale; anecdote
rasoolallah	god
rishi	hermit, wise man, ascetic
roti	unleavened bread
saab-i-barat	ninth month in the Islamic calendar; A holy night when prayers are offered for salvation
sadhu	mendicant, hermit, ascetic
sahibzade	a respectful way of addressing a young man
Sakyamuni	the Buddha
salay	bastard
samadhi	meditation
sant	saint, priest, ascetic
shahadat	martyrdom
shanti	peace
sheer-maal	unleavened bread
Sheikh Chilli	a braggart; name of a popular character in folklore
sherwani	a long coat
Shikwa	complaint, lament; title of a famous book by Muhammad Iqbal
shishya	student; disciple
sindhoor	vermillion
sirtaj	crown
Subhan Allah	praise be the Lord
surahi	an earthenware pot for cooling water
swamy	master
taya	father's elder brother
talaq	divorce
talukdar	a village officer
Tathagata	the Buddha

tazia	replica of the tomb of Imam Hussain at Karbala
teetar	partridge
tehmad	lungi
tezi	third month of the Islamic calendar
tonga	a horse-driven carriage
tunta	a man with a deformed hand
ustad	boss; guru
Utnapishtim	a character in *The Epic of Gilgamesh*
vaid	ayurvedic doctor
yaar	friend
zamindar	landlord
zindabad	long live